Public Speaking
A Transactional Approach

DAVID M. JABUSCH
University of Utah

ALLYN AND BACON, INC.

Boston   London   Sydney   Toronto

Copyright © 1985 by Allyn and Bacon, Inc., 7 Wells Avenue, Newton, Massachusetts 02159. All rights reserved. No part of the material protected by this copyright notice may be reproduced or utilized in any form or by any means, electronic or mechanical, including photocopying, recording, or by any information storage and retrieval system, without written permission from the copyright owner.

Library of Congress Cataloging in Publication Data
Jabusch, David M.
   Public speaking.

   Bibliography: p.
   Includes index.
   1. Public speaking.   2. Transactional analysis.
I. Title.
PN4121.J2   1985   808.5′1   84-9339
ISBN 0-205-08193-2

Production Services: *Helyn Pultz*
Cover Designer: *Lynne Beighley Abell*

All photographs are courtesy of the Public Relations Office, University of Utah, except page 146, which is courtesy of the University of Utah Medical Center.

Printed in the United States of America

10 9 8 7 6 5 4 3 2 1   89 88 87 86 85 84

To my parents, **FRED AND THEO JABUSCH,**
who first encouraged me to enter the public forum

Contents

Preface ix

1 Introduction 1

Why Study Public Speaking? 2
How to Study Public Speaking 5
What Is Public Speaking? 6
Summary 10
Barbara Jordan, Democratic Convention
Keynote Address (1976) 11
Endnotes 14

2 Analyzing the Transactional Situation 15

Analyze Your Audience 16
Analyze Yourself 24
Analyze the Social Situation 26

        Analyze the Topic   *29*
   Culmination of Transactional Analysis   *35*
            Summary   *36*
Abraham Lincoln, First Inaugural Address   *37*
           Endnotes   *44*

3   Developing Content   45

    Communicative Transactions   *46*
     Data-Claim Relationship   *48*
Developing Ideas with Supporting Ideas   *49*
  Generating Supporting Material   *53*
 Audio-Visual Aids to Developing Ideas   *57*
          Summary   *62*
Martin Luther King, Jr., "I Have a Dream..."   *63*
          Endnotes   *67*

4   Organization Using the   69
      Transactional Focus

       General Approaches   *70*
        General Principles   *71*
Introductions: Transactional Functions   *75*
 Conclusions: Transactional Functions   *78*
   Techniques of Organization   *80*
         Summary   *86*
Barbara Ward, "Only One Earth"   *88*
        Endnotes   *93*

5   Transactional Style and Language   95

The Transactional Nature of Language   *96*
  Transactional Language Variables   *98*

Characteristics of Style *102*
Developing Oral Style *108*
Summary *110*
Henry W. Grady, "The New South" *111*
Endnotes *118*

6   Delivery: 121
Transactional Synthesis

Transactional Functions of Delivery *122*
Traditional Characteristics *124*
Transactional Characteristics *131*
Preparing for Delivery *134*
Summary *137*
William Jennings Bryan, "Cross of Gold" *138*
Endnotes *144*

7   Informative Transactions   145

Analyzing Informative Transactions *147*
The Content of Informative Transactions *151*
Organizing Informative Transactions *153*
Language in Informative Transactions *155*
Summary *156*
Chase Peterson, Post-Operation News Conferences *157*
Endnote *162*

8   Persuasive Transactions   163

Defining Persuasion *164*
Sharing Rationality *165*
Sharing Motivation *174*

Sharing Trust *182*
Building Resistance to Change *186*
Organizing Persuasive Speeches *188*
Summary *189*
Ronald Reagan, "Stay the Course" *190*
Endnotes *199*

9 Specialized Transactions 201

Speeches That Entertain *202*
Speeches That Pay Tribute *207*
Transactions of Courtesy *210*
Combative Transactions *212*
Summary *217*
Abraham Lincoln, Gettysburg Address *218*
Endnotes *219*

Index 221

Preface

In cultures where freedom of expression has been protected, public speaking has been highly valued. It stands to reason, since public dialogue constitutes such an important component in the decision-making process in a democratic society.

For centuries, the study of public communication focused primarily on the speaker and "message preparation." In recent years, communication scholars have begun to look at communication in general as more of a transaction, with greater focus on the listeners and the *simultaneous* transmission and reception of messages by both speakers and listeners.

In the public speaking context, however, one person does more of the speaking and the audience appears to be "just listening." It looks like a transmission, or "I speak, you listen."

It is my intent in this book to apply the transactional perspective to the public communication context; you will find no chapter on listening here. Every chapter is addressed to both speakers and listeners as they attempt to understand the process of, and develop competence in, sharing meanings in public communication transactions.

Achieving competence in public speaking is the major focus of this text. Competence is based not only on practice, but also on insight into the process of preparation and delivery as well as the ability to analyze experiences in public speaking. This ability to analyze will go far beyond any single class your students may be taking.

Any project of this nature depends on the support and cooperation of many individuals. I wish to thank Paul Berkhardt, Carl Kell, and Ron Manuto for reviewing the manuscript and offering many helpful suggestions for improvement. I am grateful to Jackie Byrd and Loa Nebeker for typing the manuscript, and to Bill Barke and Helyn Pultz for skillful editorial and production leadership. I am particularly indebted to my mentors at Penn State University, who introduced me to a transactional approach to public communication long before the perspective became popular; as well as to my students and colleagues at the University of Utah who have helped me focus that perspective. Finally, I am grateful to my family for their support and understanding.

D.M.J.

1

Introduction

In this chapter:
Why study public speaking?
How to study public speaking
Public speaking perspectives
Summary
Barbara Jordan, Democratic Convention Keynote Address (1976)

Summer of 1976 was unique in the history of American politics. The country had recently—and somewhat ignominiously—concluded the first nonvictorious war in our history. Three years earlier the first boycott of Arab oil supplies had dramatically demonstrated that the U.S. was not only no longer energy independent, but drastically overextended in our consumption of energy. In the aftermath of the Watergate scandal our first nonelected president, Gerald Ford, was standing for election. Opposing Ford was a relatively unknown Georgia governor, James Earl Carter, who had virtually clinched the Democratic nomination by winning a majority of Democratic primaries on a populist platform that was antigovernment in general and anti-Washington in particular. In the midst of the malaise and disillusionment that followed Viet Nam and Watergate, the country was attempting to celebrate its Bicentennial anniversary with activities ranging from vigorous and meaningful town meetings to the banality of painting fire hydrants red, white, and blue. People were clearly disillusioned, disappointed, and cynical about our government and not optimistic that life in the United States would be better in 2076, if our system existed at all by that time. In response to this atmosphere of political cynicism, and great partisan opportunity, the delegates to

INTRODUCTION

the Democratic National Convention met in New York to draft a platform, nominate a president, and rally support for their candidates and causes. And the speaker they chose to keynote that rally was a dynamic Congresswoman from Texas, Barbara Jordan.

WHY STUDY PUBLIC SPEAKING?

The formal study of public speaking dates to the fifth century B.C. in ancient Greece and perhaps beyond. It has been important ever since, especially in those societies that value freedom of expression and making decisions democratically. In such societies the ability to clearly express one's own ideas and those of others has been highly valued. As you continue in the educational process, the study of public communication can contribute to your general education, your professional competence, and your leadership ability.

General Education[1]

Although colleges and universities do not provide the cure-all for personal and social problems once expected of them, they can provide an important liberalizing and liberating experience for those who choose to participate. What can you expect to get from your college experience? In addition to the specific job skills you may acquire, your education should provide important career and life orientations.

There has been an unfortunate and false distinction between *liberal education* and *career education*. People tend to consider career education as that which prepares the individual for specific job tasks. Since job entry is so important for making a living, students and parents have come to value career education above all. Liberal education, on the other hand, has been identified with the arts, humanities, and sciences, which are thought to be less relevant to job placement. But real career education is much more than job training. Career education, aimed at preparing people for life and living, must include the goals of liberal education.

To make it in any profession, you must have certain human sensitivities. To participate with others responsibly on the job, in the family, and in the community, you should be an open and thinking person. What, then, are the goals of liberal, career education?

A liberally educated person communicates well. Communication is the first goal of liberal education because it is the foundation of all the others. A good communicator has an analytical attitude, attempting to discover how and why we are affected by messages. A good communicator is an articulate speaker and a clear writer, and a good communicator listens and reads with sensitivity. Finally, a good

2

communicator is aware of the importance of the media in our social environment, is sensitive to its effects, and receives media messages with an analytical and critical stance.

The liberally educated person thinks critically. Critical thinking involves the ability to see relationships between things, to understand how concepts are made of parts, and to evaluate the validity of statements based on certain assumptions and values. The critical thinker is able to ferret out the assumptions, observations, and values behind a claim, and to make assertions with full understanding of the observations and inferences behind the assertions. Competent communication and critical thinking are closely related: good communicators are critically involved in the production and reception of messages, and good critical thinking involves careful, sensitive understanding of messages from others.

The liberally educated person is able to solve problems. No profession can be approached with a recipe box; we cannot proceed through life as we might prepare a meal. As we all know, there are no easy formulas for living. The liberally educated person attempts to understand problems and to create appropriate solutions. Most problem solving involves more than one person, and communication is an important part of the process.

The liberally educated person adapts to change. We live in an era of rapid change. There is increasing need for people to understand and adapt to this flux. Adaptability requires relating to others in various ways and understanding new kinds of messages. In other words, we cannot adjust to the onslaught of change without being competent in communication.

The liberally educated person is open to new ideas. Open-mindedness is essential for problem solving and adaptation to change. One of the most important insights to come from a liberal education is that events, ideas, and things can be legitimately expressed in many different forms. The open-minded person knows there is no "absolutely right" way to conceptualize the world. The open-minded person is sensitive to the rich variation in human lifestyles, and attempts to understand a variety of perspectives. Open-minded communicators treasure their own values but respect and attempt to understand different perspectives reflected in the messages of others.

The liberally educated person is interculturally aware. We live in a multi-cultural society. The vast majority of people on this small earth represent cultures different from middle-class America. The liberally educated person understands this fact. In our communication with others, we must recognize that all messages are filtered through the communicator's cultural screen. And in a shrinking, changing world, we encounter screens of many different colors and shapes.

The liberally educated person is environmentally sensitive. More than ever before, it is important for us to understand that we exist in a social and natural environment. We are dependent on these environments. Each person's relationship to the niche involves a delicate balance of forces, which must be understood and respected. How we communicate with others is very much a function of the social, natural, and created environment.

The liberally educated person is personally integrated. Above all, the educated person knows and respects him- or herself. She or he is a healthy, happily functioning adult, behaving congruently and creatively. We have long known that how we feel about ourselves affects and is affected by how we relate to others. A competent communicator is a well-adjusted, mature human being.

These eight aims of liberal education are *goals* (ideals) toward which healthy people strive. Nobody is perfectly liberal in all these ways, but college education should provide a good beginning. And public communication education is an integral part of this process.

I hope that three important points are obvious from the discussion so far. First, society depends on communication. Second, the success of social participation in our society demands competent public communication. Third, a liberal education must deal with public communication.

Professional Competence

The study of public communication is important not only for your general education but also, in more specific ways, for the enhancement of your professional competence. Many professions such as law, teaching, and the ministry obviously involve extensive public speaking. In the business world, too, public presentations are continually made in order to acquire contracts, to interpret company policy to service clubs and other large groups, or to inform the public of a new development in the industry. In fact, few occupations today have no need for exposure to communicating in public—as exemplified by the public speaking workshops I have recently conducted for labor unions, traffic officers, pipeline corporation executives, hairdressers, and a state department of social services, to mention only a few.

Leadership

Finally, competency in public communication is an important component in leadership in any field. People who can stand up in a meeting and skillfully say what others may be thinking, or persuade the group to undertake a productive new course of action, will soon find themselves in leadership positions. Conversely, some people are elevated to leadership positions because of their expertise in other areas but find they spend substantial amounts of time in public speaking situations. Later in this book we will discuss the "super-representative." This is a person who is a member of a group and shares its beliefs, values, and behaviors, but transcends the group in important ways. One of the skills that contributes to the rise of the super-representative is competence in public speaking.

Finally, I feel that experience in public speaking has a positive effect on self-concept generally. Like most experienced public speaking teachers, I have observed many students develop a greater self-esteem and assertiveness resulting in their feeling better about themselves.

HOW TO STUDY PUBLIC SPEAKING

The focus of this book is clearly on the development of competency or skill in public speaking. However, I do not believe the age-old myth that practice makes perfect. Psychology has demonstrated conclusively that practice only makes permanent. As we shall see throughout this book, practicing what feels natural can often result in the development of counterproductive habits.

Furthermore, the study of public speaking can be terribly deceptive. The principles in this book look to be so easily understood as to be obvious. My experience has been, however, that while the recommended approaches may *seem* easy, inexperienced speakers frequently disregard them to opt for counterproductive approaches to the various stages of preparation, again because they want to be "natural."

A sound approach to achieving competence in public speaking involves three interrelated processes: principles, practice, and critical analysis.

Principles

Principles are generalizations about effective public speaking which have been learned from research or from many years of experience. Principles are not invariant laws or rules. Rather, they are concepts that give insight into how the process of public communication works. By better knowing how the process works we can focus our practice on the most productive activities.

In this book we will discuss two basic kinds of principles. First, we will reduce the process to its many component parts so that you can see and understand each step or function in preparing to communicate in public. At the same time, we will provide general principles that allow you to look at the process in complete or global ways and from new perspectives or points of view.

Practice

A large part of your development as a public communicator comes from experience. In addition to the principles underlying the process of public communication, there are techniques that must be practiced to be mastered. It is all well and good for a golfer to know he or she must keep the left arm straight, watch the ball, shift weight to the right leg, slow the backswing, shift the weight back to the left leg, follow through high, and a myriad of other principles of swinging a club. But without practice—lots of it— the golfer will never become skillful. Neither will a public speaker.

Critical Evaluation

Finally, your development as a competent public communicator is enhanced by critical evaluation of your practice, so that you can become aware of the areas in which you need to improve. During the early stages of development it is common to make some mistakes and have many successes. Learning from your mistakes and successes involves identifying exactly what happened, determining what caused it, and formulating recommendations for improvement; just as a doctor must first determine "where it hurts" (symptoms), diagnose the cause, and prescribe a cure.

You and your classmates (the listeners) can be very helpful in determining the symptoms. "I didn't get the central idea," or "The story of the accident made the third idea very compelling for me," can provide the necessary raw data for critical evaluation.

Early on, your instructor will probably do most of the diagnosis and prescription, but as the term progresses and you master more and more of the principles, you should be able to diagnose and prescribe for yourself and your classmates.

By learning the principles that give insight into the process, mastering the correct techniques through practice, and critically evaluating your competence, you will have the best chance of developing into the most competent public speaker you can be.

WHAT IS PUBLIC SPEAKING?

Like most definitions, a definition of public speaking can be pretty arbitrary. However, in this book public speaking is defined as *a communication transaction in a public context*. Let's look at three major aspects of this definition.

Communication

First and foremost, public speaking is a form of communication. Some inexperienced public speakers think more about themselves (i.e., how they look and sound and think) than about the listener, and then public speaking comes across as display, self-expression, or self-centered performance.

Scheidel has defined communication as

> ...that process which occurs when speaking/listening agents interact by transmitting and receiving verbal and nonverbal messages in communication contexts.[2]

Note that this definition has several implications. First, communication focuses on a response or end result. This response usually takes the form of meanings, feelings, or behaviors, which are *shared* by participants in the communication event. This awareness makes the public speaker more oriented to the audience and their response than to him- or herself. Being guided by the needs of listeners will be a major focus of this book.

Second, Scheidel's concept of communication includes both verbal and nonverbal messages. Chapters 2, 3, and 4 discuss the thought processes you can use to determine these messages. Chapter 5 deals directly with the use of words, or the verbal dimension of your message, while Chapter 6 discusses delivery, or the nonverbal dimension of the message.

Third, Scheidel's definition of communication states that there is an interaction among the participants. In a moment we will pursue this idea and argue that the relationship between the speakers and listeners is a *transaction*. Suffice it to say here that listeners are active, not passive. While speakers are transmitting messages, both verbally and nonverbally, listeners too are providing *feedback*, nonverbally and sometimes even verbally. The skillful speaker, then, is also simultaneously a receiver or listener. The speaker constantly monitors feedback and adjusts to it. Hence there is an ongoing *interaction* between the speaker-listener and listener-speakers.

What Is Public?

The distinction between a "group" and a "public meeting" is not altogether clear. Imagine yourself in your "speech" classroom. You have arrived early and are explaining to a friend an abstract concept such as "symbolic interaction." Two or three more classmates arrive. You continue your explanation as the class grows to ten or twelve. Before you have finished, the entire public speaking class of twenty-five people is listening. When did that conversation become a "group" and when did the group become a "public"? I think it is helpful to look at public speaking as an elevated conversation—just as personal, just as animated, and natural.

There are some differences, however. The most obvious is the number of other participants or listeners. Two people make a dyad. Three or more make a group. With somewhere between a dozen and twenty or more, a group becomes a "public."

In order to adapt to speaking to a "public" you need to make adjustments. It is usually necessary to stand up to be seen and to speak up to be heard. It is necessary to adapt to a wider range of understandings, beliefs, values, and behaviors. These adjustments are, of course, the subject matter of the remainder of this book.

INTRODUCTION

Transacting in the public speaking context

The Transactional Perspective

One of the most important aspects of learning any subject, public speaking included, is the general attitude with which you approach it. Just as a piece of wood or a rock looks different depending on the angle at which you cut it, so public speaking will be different for you depending on how you approach it. This is called your *perspective*.

The early study of public speaking viewed it as something a person transmitted to an audience. It was epitomized by the familiar phrase "I speak—you listen." This of course implies that if a speaker prepares and presents a good speech and the listener pays attention, everything will work out. This is not only a very naive and oversimplified view of the situation, but it focuses your attention on yourself as the speaker and the message. It tends to ignore the audience, as if speeches could be prepared for any old audience. This approach can be represented

$$\text{Speaker} \rightarrow \text{Message} \rightarrow \text{Listener.}$$

With the movement to a more psychological approach to communication in the 1950s and '60s, the emphasis in the study of public speaking shifted to the audience. The *response* of the listeners was the primary focus of public speaking. This added an important dimension to the study of public speaking, but attention to the quality of messages was lost.

Recall that Scheidel's definition of communication described *interaction* between speakers and listeners; that is to say, the speaker says something, the listener responds, communicates feedback, to which the speaker adjusts, and so forth. This approach is illustrated in Figure 1–1.

Although this perspective is useful and subsumes the previous two approaches, in this book we take a slightly different tack. We are going to look at public speaking as a *transaction*. Just as two business people reach out and shake hands on a business transaction, so speakers and listeners reach out to each other in order to complete a communication transaction.

**FIGURE 1–1
Interactional communication**

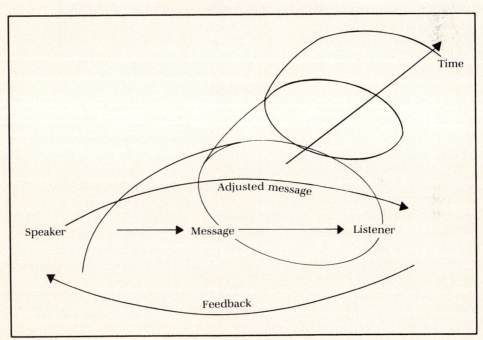

This perspective has some important implications. First, it implies that both speakers and listeners transmit and receive messages simultaneously. Speakers talk but also monitor the nonverbal (and sometimes verbal) transmissions of listeners. Listeners, on the other hand, receive the message but simultaneously nod, laugh, sleep, or transmit in a variety of other ways.

Furthermore, skillful listeners may supply part of the speaker's message. I know students who organize a professor's lectures better than the professor does, thereby supplying a missing dimension of the message. It is not uncommon for a listener in a speech class to state the central idea of a classroom speech more cogently than the speaker. Why do some students get better grades than others? Not always because they are smarter. Frequently it is because they bring more alertness and effort to the transaction and therefore are able to reach out further in order to transact with the teacher. I know listeners who relate an idea in a speech to some experience they have had and thereby remember it longer than other, less active listeners.

Note that there is no chapter on listening in this book. Every chapter is about both speaking and listening simultaneously. That is to say, rationality, motivation, trust, and the other concepts discussed in the book are simultaneously shared by speakers *and* listeners. Organization, supporting materials, or the meaning of words can be supplied by speakers, or listeners, or both (or neither).

Public communication is deceptive—on the surface it *looks* more like a transmission. Usually only one person is talking and a lot of people are sitting there, presumably receiving. But as we have just seen, in reality all are actively thinking, transmitting, and receiving to a greater or lesser degree. Looking at public communication as a dynamic transactional process, I think, can enhance your study and development as a public speaker.

SUMMARY

In this chapter we have introduced public speaking as a communication transaction in a public context.

We have seen how important it is in contributing to our general education, augmenting professional competence, and developing leadership capabilities.

Competence in public speaking is developed by understanding its basic principles, practicing its techniques, and critically analyzing the results.

Looking at public speaking as a communication transaction emphasizes the response of the audience, the interaction between speaker and listeners, both verbal and nonverbal messages, and the process nature of interaction, as well as the variety of ways in which speakers share meaning and identify with listeners.

Democratic Convention Keynote Address

Barbara Jordan

One hundred and forty-four years ago, members of the Democratic Party first met in convention to select a Presidential candidate. Since that time, Democrats have continued to convene once every four years and draft a party platform and nominate a Presidential candidate. And our meeting this week is a continuation of that tradition.

But there is something different about tonight. There is something special about tonight. What is different? What is special? I, Barbara Jordan, am a keynote speaker.

A lot of years passed since 1832, and during that time it would have been most unusual for any national political party to ask that a Barbara Jordan deliver a keynote address . . . but tonight here I am. And I feel that, notwithstanding the past, that my presence here is one additional bit of evidence that the American Dream need not forever be deferred.

Now that I have this grand distinction, what in the world am I supposed to say?

I could easily spend this time praising the accomplishments of this party and attacking the Republicans, but I don't choose to do that.

I could list the many problems which Americans have. I could list the problems which cause people to feel cynical, angry, frustrated: problems which include lack of integrity in government; the feeling that the individual no longer counts; the reality of material and spiritual poverty; the feeling that the grand American experiment is failing or has failed. I could recite these problems and then I could sit down and offer no solutions. But I don't choose to do that either.

The citizens of America expect more. They deserve and they want more than a recital of problems.

We are a people in a quandary about the present. We are a people in search of our future. We are a people in search of a national community.

We are a people trying not only to solve the problems of the present—unemployment, inflation—but we are attempting on a larger scale to fulfill the promise of America. We are attempting to fulfill our national purpose; to create and sustain a society in which all of us are equal.

Reprinted by permission of *Vital Speeches of the Day* 43 (August 15, 1976), pp. 645–646.

INTRODUCTION

Throughout our history, when people have looked for new ways to solve their problems, and to uphold the principles of this nation, many times they have turned to political parties. They have often turned to the Democratic Party.

What is it, what is it about the Democratic Party that makes it the instrument that people use when they search for ways to shape their future? Well, I believe the answer to that question lies in our concept of governing. Our concept of governing is derived from our view of people. It is a concept deeply rooted in a set of beliefs firmly etched in the national conscience, of all of us.

Now what are these beliefs?

First, we believe in equality for all and privileges for none. This is a belief that each American regardless of background has equal standing in the public forum, all of us. Because we believe this so firmly, we are an inclusive rather than an exclusive party. Let everybody come.

I think it no accident that most of those emigrating to America in the 19th century identified with the Democratic Party. We are a heterogeneous party, made up of Americans of diverse backgrounds.

We believe that the people are the source of all governmental power; that the authority of the people is to be extended, not restricted. This can be accomplished only by providing each citizen with every opportunity to participate in the management of the government. They must have that.

We believe that the government which represents the authority of all the people—not just one interest group, but all the people—has an obligation to actively underscore, actively seek to remove those obstacles which would block individual achievement . . . obstacles emanating from race, sex, economic condition. The government must seek to remove them.

We are a party of innovation. We do not reject our traditions, but we are willing to adapt to changing circumstances, when change we must. We are willing to suffer the discomfort of change in order to achieve a better future.

We have a positive vision of the future founded on the belief that the gap between the promise and reality of America can one day be finally closed. We believe that.

This, my friends, is the bedrock of our concept of governing. This is a part of the reason why Americans have turned to the Democratic Party. These are the foundations upon which a national community can be built.

Let's all understand that these guiding principles cannot be discarded for short-term political gains. They represent what this country is all about. They are indigenous to the American idea. And these are principles which are not negotiable.

In other times, I could stand here and give this kind of exposition on the beliefs of the Democratic Party and that would be enough. But today that is not enough. People want more. That is not sufficient reason for the majority of the people of this country to vote Democratic. We have made mistakes. In our haste to do all things for all people, we did not foresee the full consequences of our actions. And when the people raised their voices, we didn't hear. But our deafness was only a temporary condition, and not an irreversible condition.

Even as I stand here and admit that we have made mistakes I still believe that as the people of America sit in judgment on each party, they will recognize that our mistakes were mistakes of the heart. They'll recognize that.

And now we must look forward to the future. Let us heed the voice of the people and recognize their common sense. If we do not, we not only blaspheme our political heritage, we ignore the common ties that bind all Americans.

Many fear the future. Many are distrustful of their leaders, and believe that their voices are never heard. Many seek only to satisfy their private work wants, to satisfy private interests.

But this is the great danger America faces: That we will cease to be one nation and become, instead, a collection of interest groups, city against suburb, region against region, individual against individual. Each seeking to satisfy private wants.

If that happens, who then will speak for America?

Who then will speak for the common good?

This is the question which must be answered in 1976: Are we to be one people bound together by common spirit, sharing in a common endeavor, or will we become a divided nation?

For all of its uncertainty, we cannot flee the future. We must not become the new puritans and reject our society. We must address and master the future together. It can be done if we restore the belief that we share a sense of national community, that we share a common national endeavor. It can be done.

There is no executive order, there is no law, that can require the American people to form a national community. This we must do as individuals and if we do it as individuals, there is no President of the United States who can veto that decision.

As a first step, we must restore our belief in ourselves. We are a generous people, so why can't we be generous with each other? We need to take to heart the words spoken by Thomas Jefferson:

Let us restore to social intercourse that harmony and that affection without which liberty and even life are but dreary things.

A nation is formed by the willingness of each of us to share in the responsibility for upholding the common good.

A government is invigorated when each of us is willing to participate in shaping the future of this nation.

In this election year we must define the common good and begin again to shape a common good and begin again to shape a common future. Let each person do his or her part. If one citizen is unwilling to participate, all of us are going to suffer. For the American idea, though it is shared by all of us, is realized in each one of us.

And now, what are those of us who are elected public officials supposed to do?

INTRODUCTION

We call ourselves public servants but I'll tell you this: we as public servants must set an example for the rest of the nation. It is hypocritical for the public official to admonish and exhort the people to uphold the common good if we are derelict in upholding the common good. More is required of public officials than slogans and handshakes and press releases. More is required. We must hold ourselves strictly accountable. We must provide the people with a vision of the future.

If we promise as public officials, we must deliver. If we as public officials propose, we must produce. If we say to the American people "It is time for you to be sacrificial," sacrifice. If the public official says that we (public officials) must be the first to give, we must be. And again, if we make mistakes, we must be willing to admit them. We have to do that. What we have to do is strike a balance between the idea that government should do everything and the idea, the belief, that government ought to do nothing. Strike a balance.

Let there be no illusions about the difficulty of forming this kind of a national community. It's tough, difficult, not easy. But a spirit of harmony will survive in America only if each of us remembers that we share a common destiny. If each of us remembers when self-interest and bitterness seem to prevail, that we share a common destiny.

I have confidence that we can form this kind of national community.

I have confidence that the Democratic Party can lead the way. I have that confidence. We cannot improve on the system of government handed down to us by the founders of the Republic, there is no way to improve upon that. But what we can do is to find new ways to implement that system and realize our destiny.

Now, I began this speech by commenting to you on the uniqueness of a Barbara Jordan making the keynote address. Well, I am going to close my speech by quoting a Republican President and I ask you that, as you listen to these words of Abraham Lincoln, relate them to the concept of a national community in which every last one of us participates: "As I would not be a slave, so I would not be a master." This expresses my idea of Democracy. Whatever differs from this, to the extent of the difference, is no Democracy.

ENDNOTES

1. I am indebted to Stephen Littlejohn for writing this section.
2. Thomas Scheidel, *Speech Communication and Human Interaction* (Glenview, Ill.: Scott, Foresman, 1976), p. 5

2
Analyzing the Transactional Situation

In this chapter:
Analyze your audience
Analyze yourself
Analyze the social situation
Analyze the topic
Culmination of transactional analysis
Summary
Abraham Lincoln, First Inaugural Address

During the early decades of our nation's history, the union of the formerly independent states was tenuous, at best. Debates over economic policy, tariffs, and especially the right of slave owners to move west with their slaves, and thereby spread the institution of slavery into the far reaching western territories, were hotly contested by Senators Clay, Calhoun, Webster, and Hayne. Compromise legislation helped postpone the inevitable conflict, but in 1860 the young Republican party nominated and elected as president an obscure Western lawyer named Abraham Lincoln. Although he had considerable identification with the voting public, Lincoln had been ridiculed as crude and unlettered by elements of the Northeastern establishment and he had been vilified as an "enemy of the human race" by angry slave owners in the South. He had been inaccurately labeled as a bloody abolitionist by his opponents, and his election had fanned the fires of secession throughout the South. As his inauguration approached, Lincoln wanted, above all, to stem the tide of secession and hold the Union together. What could he say in his inaugural address to meet this critical situation? The conclusion of his first inaugural gives us a sample of his eloquent but unsuccessful attempt to save the Union by public persuasion:

> I am loath to close. We are not enemies, but friends. We must not be enemies. Though passion may have strained, it must not break our bonds of affection. The mystic chords of memory, stretching from every battlefield, and patriot grave, to every living heart and hearthstone, all over this broad land, will yet swell the chorus of the Union, when again touched, as surely they will be, by the better angels of our nature.[1]

Most public speakers do not face the critical situation confronted by Lincoln, but every person who has been called upon to speak in public faces essentially the same basic problem or question: What will I say to this audience, at this particular time with this particular purpose? The answer to this somewhat broad question lies in a process here called *analyzing the transactional* (or public speaking) *situation*.

Lloyd Bitzer[2] claims that rhetorical or transactional speaking situations grow out of an exigency, or demand, placed upon an individual to speak. The demand can come from group expectations: Presidents are expected to deliver inaugural and State of the Union addresses; clergy are expected to preach at worship; and students in public speaking classes are expected to speak on the day assigned by the instructor.

In most cases, however, the exigency is less predictable: if you are an expert in some field you may be asked by a group to share your knowledge with them for a particular reason. Or you may be sitting in a meeting and someone might ask to hear your opinion of the issue at hand. Frequently the exigency comes from within yourself: something said in a meeting, or an action by an individual or group, simply cries out for your response. The passage of the Kansas-Nebraska Bill in 1854 is credited, by some historians, for motivating Lincoln to turn from his private law practice to the public, and ultimately the national, forum.

Once you have accepted the exigency to speak, you can begin to answer the rhetorical question asked above by analyzing or breaking down the transactional situation into its component parts. They are (1) the audience, (2) yourself, (3) the social situation, and (4) the topic, all of which culminate in your formulation of (5) a specific purpose, and (6) a central idea.

ANALYZE YOUR AUDIENCE

The entire reason for speaking in public is to share some type of response with your listeners. It stands to reason, then, that the better you know your listeners, the more effective this communicative transaction will be. A few years ago, a student was speaking to a group of classmates about the considerable advantages of living in a rural environment. Not having analyzed the audience before speaking, the student was surprised to find at the conclusion of the speech that a majority of the listeners had been raised in a large metropolitan area, and could offer counterarguments for every advantage of a rural upbringing the speaker had presented. Furthermore, several of the classmates were antagonized by the speech and believed even more strongly than before that the city was a great place to live! If this type of resistance is encountered on a relatively benign topic, how many more difficulties could you have on a highly controversial topic? Does this mean that you need to choose topics that will never be controversial? On the contrary; that would ensure either dullness, or irrelevance, or both. The solution is simply to find out as much as you can about your listeners before, during, and after you speak.

People in an audience often respond differently to the same message

Analyze Fundamental Variables

The two most fundamental things you must learn about your listeners are what they *know* about your topic and what they *believe* about your topic. If you were concerned about the plight of the farmers in our country and wanted your audience to agree with you that the farmers should be supported at a particular percentage of parity, it would be important to know at what level of parity your listeners presently believe farmers should be supported. Even more specifically, you would need the answers to questions like the following:

1. What do you think of government supports for specific segments of our society?
2. Do you think farmers need any help from the government?
3. If so, what form should that help take?

Indeed, you might find out that many in your audience don't even know the meaning of the word *parity*. The answers to these questions would, of course, vary considerably depending on whether your audience was composed predominantly of college undergraduates, farmers, government employees, or the "silent majority." Only by determining the knowledge and beliefs of your listeners could your message be adapted appropriately to transact with your specific audience.

Analyze Demographic Variables

The quickest and easiest way of analyzing your audience is to look at demographic characteristics. *Demographic variables* are easily observable audience characteristics which can suggest similarities or differences in knowledge and belief. Some of the most important variables are (1) age, (2) sex, (3) education, (4) occupation, (5) religion, (6) geographic location, (7) marital status, and (8) life style.

Age. Combined with other variables, age can be a predictor of what people know, believe, and are concerned about. Young adults are usually concerned with finding and adjusting to a new spouse, perhaps beginning a family, or launching a career.

People in their thirties who have focused on their family may begin to look for a career, while those who have postponed a family in order to pursue a career may want to begin a family. People in the more publicized "midlife passage" of the late thirties and early forties may be looking to change almost everything—jobs, homes, spouses, and so forth. The elderly are predominantly concerned with health, as well as continuing to be self-sufficient and needed by society.

Not only do individuals' concerns change with age but beliefs differ among generations. There are wide disparities about life styles today between people over fifty and people under fifty; presumably people under fifty will carry the same attitudes into later life. In any case, the age(s) of the listeners can help speakers decide how to tailor ideas to each unique audience or segment of an audience.

Sex. Differences of knowledge, interest, and beliefs related to sex seem to be diminishing in recent years. Nevertheless, certain topics and beliefs continue to correlate with sexual differences. Women seem to find issues related to child rearing, family planning, social service, and religion more salient than do men. On the other hand, men continue to be more concerned with contact sports, the draft, and occupation. In the 1980 election, men and women voters seemed to favor different candidates based on their stand on issues related to war such as military expenditures and specific weapons systems.

Education. People can vary in their beliefs and knowledge about certain subjects depending upon their educational level and the kind of education they have received. More highly educated people tend to be somewhat more liberal on social issues than are their less educated counterparts. Furthermore, there is some evidence to suggest that the greater the education, the more likely one is to recognize a whole spectrum of possibilities on a given issue, instead of having an either-or orientation. Liberally educated people tend to approach issues with a broader geographical, cultural, and historical perspective.

Occupation. Perhaps the most important audience variable for the public speaker to analyze is the chosen or current occupation of listeners. One of the first questions any new acquaintance asks is, "What is your job?", or for a student, "What is your major?" In many cases, if people are asked "Who are you?" they will define themselves by their occupation—"I'm an attorney." And no wonder, since most of us spend at least half our waking hours at work. It should come as no surprise, then, that business people, teachers, federal bureaucrats, engineers, and doctors may view federal aid to education (or most other issues) somewhat differently from one another. Business people I know seem preoccupied with interest rates, inflation, government regulations, profit margins, and more recently, foreign imports. Social workers, on the other hand, seem to talk more about poverty, juvenile crime, divorce, social service programs, and the like.

Not only do people in different occupations find different issues salient, but they may approach the same issue from different perspectives. I never cease to be impressed in our University Senate how engineers, mathematicians, physical scientists, artists, social scientists, and humanists approach the same question so differently. There seem to be very different sets of assumptions, priorities, and methodologies involved. Occupation is indeed one of the most useful demographic variables in analyzing an audience.

Religion. Religion is another important variable to examine. Public opinion polls invariably analyze results according to religious preference, and on some topics there are wide variations in attitude among various religious traditions. Several Protestant denominations have published fairly liberal positions on a variety of social issues related to war, social inequality, and sexual behavior. More traditional denominations such as Roman Catholics and Mormons have taken somewhat different stances on abortion, families, and the Equal Rights Amendment.

Some caution is in order, however. Churches vary considerably in the degree to which they expect their members to follow the pronouncements of the leadership. Catholics and Mormons tend to expect more compliance than Quakers, Congregationalists, and other Protestant churches. Furthermore, people vary in the degree to which they follow their church's official position, regardless of what the hierarchy expects. Many Catholics practice birth control and perhaps even abortion, and Mormons who were for passage of E.R.A. publicly and bitterly opposed their church leadership.

Geographic location. Public opinion polls tell us that people's opinions also vary according to the geographic location in which they live.

Variations can also occur on a much smaller geographic scale. Northern and Southern Californians are bitterly divided on water issues simply because there is so much water in the north and so little in the south. Likewise, debates over the deployment of the MX missile system have been heated in Nevada, Utah, and Wyoming when my friends and relatives in California had hardly heard about it. Questions of energy, defense, emigration, and many others are highly geographical in nature and the speaker is well advised to consider this variable.

Marital status. Marital status is yet another demographic variable the prospective speaker should consider. Time was when the typical American family was composed of a mother and father, and two to four children. No longer is this the case. Recent studies indicate that this "typical" family constitutes only 20 to 25 percent of U.S. families today. Many couples, both young and old, have no children. An increase in the divorce rate has resulted in numerous single-parent families, as well as many people living alone or with roommates of the same or opposite sex. Homosexual marriages are becoming more common, or at least more visible.[3] Thus, with the increasing heterogeneity of family styles in America, it seems apparent that people living in different family arrangements will have different knowledge and beliefs about related topics.

Life style. Marital status is, of course, only part of a more comprehensive demographic variable which I will call life style. In addition to marital status, people vary in their eating and drinking habits, dress, grooming, and a variety of other characteristics which serve to define their *life style*. It is usually not too difficult to spot a "superstraight" person or a "counterculture" individual. Furthermore, predictions can be made about their shared experiences, knowledge, and opinions, especially on specific subjects such as divorce, food stamps, or the draft.

Life style may be a better predictor of current beliefs than of knowledge, since many people undergo radical changes in life style. It is not uncommon for middle-aged people to adopt more relaxed life styles (and presumably changed attitudes). Former counterculture people and political activists may turn to the "straight" life. While all these people may have a much wider set of experiences and understandings than their current life style indicates, *current* life style is the better predictor of *current* beliefs, attitudes, and values than is life style any time in the past.

Analyze Group Characteristics of Audiences

The discussion above focuses on ways individuals within audiences are likely to vary in their knowledge of and beliefs about a topic. However, audiences vary also according to group characteristics, which can significantly affect the way you should approach the public speaking transaction.

Self-selection. First, you need to be aware that audiences are *self-selecting*; that is, they assemble in ways that make them far from random or typical of the general population. It is not uncommon for people to be required, or at least feel obligated, to be in attendance. Some time ago I was asked to consult with a group of reading specialists who conducted in-service workshops for reading teachers. Contracts were signed with entire school districts and teachers were required to attend. Under these circumstances even dedicated professionals felt resistance, and some even read novels during the presentations! Every teacher knows teaching required courses is different from teaching electives.

Even when attendance is voluntary, audiences self-select in interesting ways. People often attend meetings when they expect to hear what they *want* to hear. On the other hand, highly controversial speakers, or speakers on highly controversial issues, can attract very bimodal audiences. At a speech by Sonia Johnson, president of the Mormons for E.R.A., at Idaho State University (strong Mormon country), nearly half of the audience were there because they expected to hear what they already believed, almost half were strong pro-Mormons and anti-E.R.A., and a small but significant number were there out of curiosity. In any event, as a speaker you need to ask yourself (1) how this particular speaking situation has resulted in audience self-selection and (2) what kind of audience the self-selection has produced.

Homogeneity. The second group characteristic to assess is its *homogeneity* or *heterogeneity*; that is, how similar or dissimilar the audience members are from each other and from you. For instance, public speaking classes are usually pretty homogeneous in age, education, socioeconomic status, and sometimes race. They are usually fairly evenly divided on sex and marital status, with a wider variety of occupational interests and religions.

According to DeVito—

1. The greater the homogeneity of the audience, the easier will be the analysis and subsequent adaptation, and less chance of making serious mistakes as a speaker.
2. When the audience is too heterogeneous, it is sometimes helpful to subdivide it and appeal to each section separately.
3. Homogeneity does not equal attitudinal sameness.[4]

Involvement. The involvement of the audience in the topic is another group characteristic requiring analysis. Audiences for whom attendance is expected or required may be completely uninvolved, while voluntary audiences may vary widely in their involvement. During Martin Luther King's "I Have a Dream" speech (see Chapter 3) there was significant audience involvement, as evidenced by the tremendous overt feedback. This is not surprising, inasmuch as most of the audience were highly involved in the civil rights movement and had traveled great distances at their own expense to be there.

Position. Finally, you need to assess the general favorable or unfavorable position of the audience toward you or toward your topic. We saw in the case of Sonia Johnson, for example, that the audience was both divided and extreme in their positions toward her and her ideas. Sometimes audiences will be almost completely favorable or unfavorable, but usually there will be a *distribution* of positions.

Since the 1960s and '70s it has become fairly common for significant minorities unfavorable to a speaker to vocalize their opposition in the form of heckling and other overt demonstrations. If a disruptive group is small and does not create too much noise, it is best ignored. If it is loud or constitutes a significant proportion of the audience, it must be dealt with.

On the other hand listeners' opposition is not always overt; sometimes it is manifested by sullen disregard or apathy. In other instances listeners who strongly disagree will even nod in compliance! This type of unfavorable response is extremely difficult to detect and deal with.

These group characteristics—self-selection, homogeneity, involvement, and especially favorableness—should have a significant influence on your choice of a specific purpose, the focus of your organization, and even the delivery, and hence they will be referred to again as we discuss other aspects of preparation for the public communication transaction.

Topic-Specific Analysis

While demographic variables and group characteristics are useful in audience analysis, they provide, after all, only approximations of what the audience knows or believes about your specific topic. In the final analysis, there is no substitute for analyzing your particular audience in relationship to your particular topic. For instance, although most women find issues related to family planning salient, there are wide variations among women's groups as well as individual women as to how best to practice family planning; different groups and individuals can be equally adamant in their support or opposition to birth control or abortion. Thus, if you were addressing either men or women on the question of family planning, you would need to find out not only what they already know about birth control, but also where they stand on questions such as the following:

1. When do you think human life begins?
2. Should teenagers be provided with birth control information without the consent of their parents?
3. Does the right of choice of a prospective mother supersede the right to life of a fetus?
4. Have you ever known anyone who had an abortion?

Most people would agree that topic-specific analysis is necessary, but how does one accomplish it? The most important step is simply for you to *care* about what your listeners think about your topic. If you have a genuine concern about what they know and believe about your topic, several methods of finding that information will suggest themselves. In a public speaking class, you can decide on a topic a week or more before you are scheduled to speak and then ask your classmates specific questions like the ones above on family planning. If you are speaking to any group to which you belong or that you know well, this procedure will work well.

If the group is a new one or not easily accessible to you, however, you would do better to ask a member of the group to estimate the knowledge and beliefs of the audience for you.

As a last resort, some speakers even ask questions of the audience in the introduction of the speech itself. This technique is *not* appropriate in a speech class or in other groups with which you are familiar, since it is considered a clear sign of procrastination and inadequate preparation.

Continuing Analysis

From our transactional perspective, it is important to analyze your audience not only before the speaking event, but during and after it as well. In these cases, you can focus on the same variables and issues that you would in analyzing your audience prior to the event.

The composition of an audience is not always predictable, and there may be people present who do not belong to an identifiable group and who hold beliefs quite different from those you expected. You should be sensitive to changes of this kind, and be prepared to adjust your message immediately before and during the time you are speaking.

Speakers often address the same audience on a number of occasions; teachers, business people, legislators, religious leaders and sales people frequently do this. In this case you should analyze your audience after each occasion that you speak to them. Finding out how people responded to previous messages makes your objectives and strategies clearer for subsequent occasions. If public speaking were merely a transmission, audience analysis generally, and continuing analysis in particular, would not be important. But in order to *transact* with listeners, both initial and continuing analysis are crucial.

ANALYZE YOURSELF

Although the audience in the public communication transaction deserves a great deal of emphasis, you, as a public speaker, are also an integral part of that transaction, and hence you need to analyze yourself. Characteristics important to examine are your desire to communicate, feelings of anxiety, knowledge, and attitudes.

Desire to Communicate

Anyone who has been misunderstood has experienced not only the desire but the urge to communicate. He or she cannot wait to set the other person straight, or to explain what seems to have been misunderstood. Most people who accept public speaking engagements feel either an obligation or a desire to communicate, with that particular group, on a particular subject. Outside of the public speaking class, you should not agree to speak in public unless you genuinely have something to say—something you consider to be of value to that particular group. If you have this desire to communicate, your preparation and speaking experience will be both more pleasurable and more effective.

Speaker Apprehension

In all the time I have been working with people who are inexperienced in public speaking the one thing I have found that causes the most concern is speaker apprehension. Research has indicated that speaker apprehension takes two general forms. The first is called *trait apprehension* and refers to a general fear of communicating, regardless of the context. This type of apprehension may cause a person to fear and avoid an important interview or even a date as well as a public speaking event.

The other type of apprehension is called *state apprehension*, and refers to a fear of speaking in a particular context such as an interview, intimate self-disclosure, or speaking in public, but not necessarily all of them. In this instance, a person might be very verbal in one context but not another. It is this type of apprehension, applied to public speaking, that some people refer to as *stage fright*. It is this type we are concerned with here, for it has been cited in a national survey as the number one fear of adult men and women, and it constitutes one of the major reasons why people elect to take public speaking classes.[5]

Some years ago I taught a public speaking class to a group of convicts at a Utah state prison. The inmates could surely be considered the most fearless group I ever saw and yet when each of them rose to speak to his peers in that class there was not an individual who did not admit to anxiety, if not downright fear, in that situation. I have often asked myself why speaker apprehension is so pervasive. I believe it is related to three variables.

First is the significance of the situation. I still become extremely anxious while delivering a paper before professional colleagues, but considerably less anxious before a citizens' group. The second variable is anxiety over the unknown. Relatively inexperienced speakers are not sure they know what they are doing, and hence are anxious about the results. Third is lack of experience itself. People who perform potentially dangerous tasks, from astronauts to movie-stunt performers, train and practice the task over and over in order to be sure it will work. Without that kind of positive experience, potentially threatening situations seem even more so.

There are several principles for dealing with speaker apprehension. The first thing to realize is that *speaker apprehension is not only normal but almost universal*. Virtually everyone experiences it to one degree or another. If you are one of the 10 to 20 percent for whom it is a serious barrier to public speaking, consult with your instructor early. For the majority of people a public speaking class itself suffices to help not only control anxiety but use it to advantage.

The second principle of dealing with anxiety is *thorough preparation*. The remainder of this book deals with this process, so I need only emphasize here that the better prepared you are, the more certain you will be that your speaking experiences will be successful. This knowledge will in turn give you greater confidence and less apprehension.

Third, *practice several times* before you speak. With each practice (not for the purpose of memorization) you become more confident that you will have the words to effectively share the ideas and supports you have so carefully planned. Also know that experience helps immeasurably: by the time you complete this class you will have considerable confidence in yourself, and every successful subsequent speaking experience will add to your confidence.

During the actual speaking event, physical activity also helps you deal with apprehension; any purposeful bodily activity allows you to burn off some of that excess energy generated by anxiety. Some instructors also suggest a few deep breaths just before you speak.

Finally, it helps to keep the entire matter in perspective. Of course we always want to do our best, and some speaking situations are more intimidating than others, but how serious are a few bobbles anyway? From our transactional perspective, the most important thing is for the audience to share our meaning, and most superior speakers make minor errors, which the audience seldom notices, or accepts as normal in oral communication and quickly forgets. It is only when the speaker attracts attention to the error or overreacts that it becomes an issue. I recall walking out of a class one day musing to myself how well my lecture had gone only to discover the zipper to my fly was open! A disaster? Hardly. Life (and the class) went on as if nothing had happened, although I now check my zipper before public appearances....

Speaker Mind-Set

You must analyze not only your apprehension and desire to communicate, but also your own *knowledge*, *attitudes*, and *values*. Earlier we discussed your analysis of these factors in your audience. It is equally important that you be in tune with your own cognitive system, especially as it relates to your potential subject.

Much of what we discussed under audience analysis is applicable here. You should be particularly aware of what you know (and don't know) about your potential topics. You should survey your relevant attitudes and be sure that any particularly strong biases are not clouding your judgment and, later, the objectivity of your research. You should clarify the underlying values that bear on this communication transaction.

You are also well advised to examine your knowledge and attitudes toward the audience itself. We are not always privileged to speak to groups we respect or those who respect us. There may be factions within the audience toward which you have attitudes different from the majority of the audience, and which would cause trouble. In any case, you must become aware of your knowledge and attitudes about the audience so these variables can be addressed.

ANALYZE THE SOCIAL SITUATION

After you have analyzed the major participants, yourself, and the audience, you are ready to analyze the context or *social situation* in which the transaction is to occur. There are two factors to consider: physical setting and psychological climate.

Physical Setting

There are several aspects of the physical setting that may or may not be under your control, and they can work to your advantage or disadvantage.

Location. The first thing to consider is the location of the meeting. Most people imagine speeches given in an auditorium, and many are. However, I've also seen them in school cafeterias, ski lodges, chapels, street corners and the steps of the U.S. Capitol Building. Not only are the possible locations endless, but the size and configuration of these locations vary widely. Auditoriums and other facilities can be too large or too small, opulent or austere, rigid or flexible, too hot or too cold, spotless or filthy, easily accessible or virtually inaccessible. If you have control over the selection of a location, choose one that will contribute to the meaning of the transaction. It was no accident that Ted Kennedy announced his candidacy for the 1980 presidential campaign from Faneuil Hall, Boston's historic town meeting hall and the scene of several of the most memorable public speeches in United States history.

If you do not have control of the selection, at least analyze the location ahead of time and make whatever adjustments you can to enhance the interaction. Buildings can be cleaned, temperature regulated, extra seating made available, or seating roped off to consolidate the audience. I know one teacher who does not begin a class before the blackboard has been erased from the previous class, in order to eliminate any possible distractions.

ANALYZE THE SOCIAL SITUATION

Former senator George McGovern talks with a political caucus. How would you analyze this social situation?

Arrangement. Adjustments can also be made in the arrangement of the facilities. Movable chairs or banquet tables can be placed in straight lines to increase formality, or in concentric semicircles to enhance informality. You can place the head table or the podium strategically on or off a stage (if there is one), depending on the effect you want. These are not rules, but I have seen many public communication events destroyed because people did not plan ahead and apply common sense to these variables. On the other hand, I have seen a touch of class added to an artists' and speakers' series by having the lectures scheduled at a nearby ski resort, which was not only cooler during the hot summer evenings, but featured a magnificent panoramic view of surrounding mountains as well.

Equipment. Another aspect of the physical setting to analyze is the equipment you will need. If the audience is estimated to be over fifty people and/or the acoustics are poor, you should have a public address system available. You may not need it but it is nice, just in case. We have all observed public meetings that became almost a joke because of a faulty P.A. system. Get there early, check it out, and do without it if you can, especially if it is not completely reliable. Check to see if you have a fixed or movable microphone, or both.

Although the public address system can be your most important piece of equipment, you should also check on the availability of blackboards, flip charts, slide projectors and screens, or any other piece of special equipment you may need. Interestingly, the use of equipment may be part of the communicative expectations of an audience: I recently presented a paper at a convention of medical specialists where I was advised to have some graphs on slides because everyone else would have them!

Decor. The last aspect of the physical setting that requires your analysis is the decor. Consider not only the permanent decor such as carpeting, draperies, fixtures, and the like, but the temporary things you can do as well. Flowers, posters, logos, and the like can be used to create an atmosphere that is festive or somber, formal or informal, opulent or austere, depending on what is appropriate for the occasion.

I know a group that conducted "town meeting" celebrations during the country's Bicentennial, and decorated a school cafeteria with preprepared posters with quotations of famous Americans, flags, and bunting—all in about thirty minutes. In any case, the decor of the event can not only enhance the context in which the speech is given, but actually augment the transaction itself.

The Psychological Climate

A second aspect of the social situation that requires your analysis is the psychological climate in which the speech is to occur. I have already touched on your analysis of the audience's beliefs, attitudes, and values, but here I would like to discuss audience variables that are more rooted in the psychological context in which the speaking event occurs: traditions, current events, and images.

Traditions. I was once told, by a debate coach yet, when questioning the somewhat cumbersome procedure used in a public speaking contest, "Well, we've *always* done it that way!" Every group has its time-honored "way of doing things," its celebrations and rituals, and woe be to the person who ignores or challenges these traditions. Communities and organizations have periodic art festivals, rodeos, Shakespearian festivals, religious observances, athletic events, and holidays which may have begun for some now-obscure reason but which have become highly valued ends in themselves.

In some cases these traditions have become highly visible preoccupations of the entire group and are easily detectable. Others are much less obvious but are nonetheless important. One of the most subtle and difficult for the outsider to analyze is the traditional way certain groups talk about aspects of their lives. The Communist party has been said to have a "party line" or rigid traditional ways of talking about almost every issue, but *every* group has its "party line" on certain issues, if you can but detect it. Although you need not adopt the linguistic traditions of the group, by being aware of them you can not only avoid the pitfalls they represent, but perhaps use them to enhance the public speaking transaction with your audience.

Current events. Current events can also radically affect the psychological climate. How do you recall feeling (if you can remember) the assassinations of John Kennedy or Martin Luther King, or the more recent shootings of Ronald Reagan and Pope John Paul II? These events were so dramatic that some meetings were canceled, and others convened because the events either made them impossible communication situations or particularly timely ones. But consider less dramatic events—the impact of a well-publicized execution on a scheduled speech about capital punishment; or the TV series "Roots" on a speech about human rights, or genealogy. Politicians worry about a dramatic event, beyond their control, that might change the psychological climate of a campaign and cost them the election. Because of the profound effect of these current events on the psychological climate within which you will speak, you must not only consider them as part of your analysis during preparation, but also be ready to adjust your remarks to them immediately prior to or during your speech.

Images. All of the variables we have discussed thus far are part of your listeners' general images of themselves and their environment. However, people and groups also have specific images that profoundly affect the way they think and behave. These images are pictures people have of themselves or stories they tell about themselves that help to determine who they consider themselves to be. Individuals and groups of individuals can have images of themselves as winners or losers, beautiful or ugly, playboys or producers, and so forth. Athletic teams seem to win or lose the close ones depending on whether they image themselves winners or losers; school children are known to achieve pretty much what they and their teachers *think* they can achieve. People in communities, religious organizations, and service clubs tend to live up to, or down to, the image of the group. These images are not always easy to find, and in some cases the individuals or groups are unaware of their existence. If you can discover these images, however, you can use them in your speech, and even attempt to change the image as the purpose of your speech. Such was the case of a student speaker who detected the negative image of mathematics in her audience and spoke to the central idea that "math can be fun."

ANALYZE THE TOPIC

Having analyzed the various aspects of your speaking situation—the audience, yourself, and the physical and psychological context—you are now ready to proceed to more specific preparation by analyzing the topic on which you wish to speak. I will discuss choosing, focusing, and researching the topic; and formulating a general purpose.

Choosing Your Topic

Second only to speaker apprehension, choosing a topic is the chief bugaboo of inexperienced speakers. It is also a stage where you can go very wrong, and yet the correct procedure is not all that difficult. Most beginning speakers are looking for a topic that will be a "natural," so they go looking for one in all sorts of places—the fraternity files, *The Readers Digest*; and even the best students may go to *The New York Times Index* or other worthwhile sources in the library. They inevitably end up with a topic that interests neither themselves nor their audience.

The first place to look to is *yourself*. What do you know about? What excites you? How do you spend your spare time? Go back to the questions you asked when you analyzed yourself. What are you the most qualified to talk about? Outside of the public speaking classroom you will probably not be asked to speak on a subject you don't know about, but if you are and you don't have huge amounts of time for research, you should refuse. Within the classroom you are first assigned to speak and then you choose a topic, so be sure you choose one that you *know* and *care* about.

The second criterion for selecting a topic is its *significance* to the audience. Of all of the things you could talk about, which one will be significant to the people you are addressing? It is difficult to have a meaningful public communication transaction on "Mickey Mouse" topics. Superior speeches cannot happen with topics that are insignificant to the audience. This does not mean that any topic is inherently "bad," but that it must be weighed against its relevance to the audience. I once had a student athlete who explained the "fast break" to his classmates, since most of them attended the basketball games and that play was used extensively. I'm sure their enjoyment of the game was enhanced, but the student who speaks on the diplomatic recognition of the People's Republic of China has a much greater potential for significance. One word of caution is in order: For your very first speeches don't pick a topic that is too difficult, but do try to challenge yourself. When in doubt, ask your instructor.

Finally, the *occasion* will frequently dictate the topic. Speeches of acceptance, dedication, remembrances at memorial services, and the like leave little leeway in the choice of topic, but they can be approached in different ways.[6]

Focus the Topic

Once they begin addressing the issues listed above, most people have little difficulty choosing an appropriate topic. Focusing or limiting that topic is quite another matter. It is the first step in the continuing struggle toward what students of composition call *unity*. When you are first assigned to speak, your initial reaction is "How will I ever be able to talk *that* long?" But in fact, most people's problem is quite the opposite: most speakers, beginners and "pros" alike, usually try to do or cover too much. This leads to overgeneralization, dullness, and confusion. If you have chosen your topic well, you will have much more to say than can possibly be covered in a three- to ten-minute classroom speech.

I would suggest two criteria for limiting your topic. From our transactional perspective, the most important one is the *needs* of your audience—not interests nor wants, since we frequently need what we neither want nor are interested in. I once had a student who wanted to talk about woodworking. Think of the myriad possibilities for limiting that topic. You could speak on how to operate any one of several tools, or on how to build any one of dozens of kinds of furniture. When I asked him, however, how most people would come in contact with furniture, he correctly responded, "When they buy it." He limited his topic to what they most *needed* to know: what to look for when buying furniture. Incidentally, notice how he started with a topic he knew and cared about, and although not a highly intellectual topic, he made it highly significant to the audience.

The second criterion for limiting your topic is the *time available*. Although your first, and transmissionally self-centered, reaction is usually "How can I fill the time?", you will find that "time flies when you're having fun." Furthermore, it takes more time than you suspect to properly develop an idea so that your audience will transact in the desired way. I once heard a doctor address a group of ushers for a large public meeting on the subject of first aid. He could have touched on many aspects of the topic in the hour he had. He chose, rather, to deal with only three major things to do in order to keep the patient alive until help arrived. His was a superb solution to the focus problem of *"What can I say to this particular audience, in this amount of time, that they most need to know about my topic?"*

Research the Topic

Even though you would know a great deal about your topic at this point, you still need to do considerable research in order to have the necessary detailed information to support your ideas. In some circles, we worry about the problem of plagiarism. In a public speaking class plagiarism is unthinkable, not only because it is unethical and defeats the purpose of the assignment, but also because it leads to poor public communication. It is axiomatic that any public speech drawn from a single source is likely to be inadequately adapted to the immediate audience, to be either too subjective or not personal enough, and to violate a plethora of other principles of sound public communication.

Furthermore, although we may agree that everyone is entitled to his or her own opinion, or misinformation as the case may be, you must assume a significant measure of responsibility for the accuracy of your message when you elect to share it with the public.

There are four major places to look for materials for your speech: (1) yourself, (2) the library, (3) government and private agencies, and (4) interviews.

If you chose a topic you know and care about, you are well on your way to having substantial information for your speech. Every speech should contain something of yourself—personal involvement. Reexamine the questions you asked earlier when you analyzed yourself. What experiences or specific data do you already have at your disposal? What ideas or arguments can you list on the topic? Only when you have made a thorough inventory of what you already know about the topic are you ready to look elsewhere for new data and ideas.

Library research. Most people who are qualified enough to speak in public are also somewhat familiar with library research. However, there are some resources in the library that are of particular value to a speaker who wishes to obtain added information on a contemporary topic. Perhaps the first place to look in the library is in the *general* indexes under your specific topic. The *card catalogue* indexes books by title, author, and subject. *The New York Times Index* is an excellent reference on any current event that has been published in the *Times*, and is also an excellent source of documentary data such as Congressional voting records, original texts of major speeches, and the like. *Psychological Abstracts* is an index of published psychological studies, and of course the *Readers' Guide to Periodical Literature* is a most comprehensive index of articles in current magazines.

There are also some excellent sources of specific data. If you wish to find a quotation of a famous person on a particular topic, the *Oxford Dictionary of Quotations* or *Bartlett's Familiar Quotations* provide numerous apt quotations which are indexed by both subject and author. If you are looking for specific statistical data on a particular point, you can consult *Statistical Abstracts*. I once wanted to make the point in a speech that a particular state had the resources to give more support to public education. It took me some time in *Statistical Abstracts* to discover that the particular state was well down the list of states in the amount it spent on public education per thousand dollars of income. Many other statistics related to education were readily available, but the statistic relating support of public education with income was the only one that would adequately support the point I wanted to make.

It is usually helpful to read the most recent source first. The author usually footnotes significant older sources, saving you considerable time winnowing out the less helpful sources.

Remember also that modern libraries are actually multimedia resource centers. You should be able to find various pictures, slides, and perhaps even charts and graphs to augment your ideas. When in doubt, the reference librarian can be of substantial help in finding the great variety of materials available on your topic.

Government and private agencies. Frequently the most overlooked sources of information are your government, private agencies, and even corporations. There is hardly a topic of contemporary interest that has not been extensively researched by several of these agencies. If you are speaking on gun-control legislation, contact not only the National Rifle Association, but several agencies that support gun control. I once had a student who received hours of help from an oil company executive on a question related to the impact of oil exploration on the local environment.

At this point you must be cautious about bias; both your own and the agency's. You have not yet formed your purpose, so ideally you have not even taken a side (if there is a side to be taken) on your topic. Carefully weigh the bias of the material provided by an agency and be sure to obtain several different points of view before you finally make up your mind.

Interviews. Like government and private agencies, individual experts can help you make your research more efficient. Qualified experts can quickly point you toward key readings, and can also offer direct evidence from their own experience. Interviews are last in our discussion of research because you should do enough research in order to ask informed questions, and not waste the time of the person you are interviewing. Even a short interview with the right person, however, can save you hours of research time.

Finally, as you research you should take careful notes. It is extremely frustrating to have an apt quotation or powerful statistic in your memory and not be able to use it because you are not sure of its accuracy or source. If you find truly superior and obviously usable information, write it on a file card with precise accuracy as well as the specific source. This way you can not only use it with confidence but quickly verify it, if necessary. Most academic debaters know the value of accurate file cards, but I also know a well-paid after-dinner speaker who has thousands of quotes, stories, and statistics carefully filed in his study for future use.

Formulate the General Transactional Purpose

Speeches in a public speaking classroom are typically assigned by their general transactional purhose, i.e., to inform, to persuade, or to entertain. Outside the classroom, however, you are most likely the one who must decide what the general thrust of your message will be.

As traditionally treated, general purposes had a decidedly speaker-centered, transmissional focus. In actuality, however, each has a clear audience response implicit in it and this should be recognized. Speeches to inform are designed to get listeners to understand a concept or process, or to correct a misunderstanding. Speeches to entertain are designed for listeners to enjoy themselves.

Speeches to persuade have presented special problems for those attempting to distinguish among the several types. Traditionally we have labeled them speeches to convince, to stimulate, or to actuate. Speeches to convince are designed to get listeners to change, to strengthen and weaken attitudes or beliefs toward an object. Speeches to stimulate are designed to heighten feelings about an object. Speeches to actuate are designed to get listeners to change their behaviors. Fotheringham[7] has suggested that a speech to actuate can involve four types of shared behavior: adoption, continuation, discontinuation, and deterrence. The relationship between the speaker's general purpose and these audience-oriented transactional responses can be represented as follows[8]:

Speaker's purpose   *Transactional response*
  to inform   shared understanding
  to entertain   shared enjoyment
  to persuade
    to convince   shared, strengthened, or attenuated
                                   attitude
    to stimulate   shared feeling
    to activate   shared overt behavior
                                   adoption
                                   continuation
                                   discontinuation
                                   deterrence

These persuasive purposes actually represent only general points on a spectrum of stances your listeners can take, from violent disbelief to shared action. This spectrum can be represented thus:

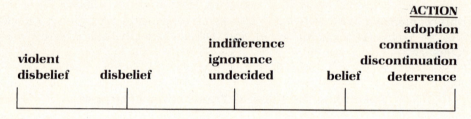

If your listeners move or change on this spectrum in the desired direction, persuasion will have occurred. Furthermore, an audience of more than one person will not occupy a single point on this spectrum, but a distribution of points:

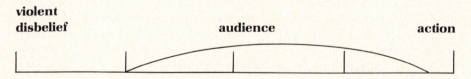

It is your job to discover the location and shape of this distribution and then decide how to address the range of viewpoints you find. Usually you will find it advantageous to address the middle cluster within your audience, assuming that those who are more favorably disposed will go along and those on the negative extreme are hopeless cases anyway. This generalization will not always hold true, and you must decide who to address on the basis of your analysis of this issue.

You will also find that these general purposes are related in rather complex ways. Some persuasive speeches can be both informative and entertaining and vice versa. And certainly, a speech can have more than one purpose. Your primary purpose may be to win an election, but even if you lose you may want to educate the public on issues you consider important. Such may have been the purposes of John Anderson in the election of 1980. It will be helpful, in any case, for you to be aware of the possibilities and decide on a major goal or primary purpose for your speech. Failure to do so can lead to difficulties, as in the case of a teacher who attempts to sell biases to the students, or the salesperson who explains too many details and loses the sale.

CULMINATION OF TRANSACTIONAL ANALYSIS

This entire analytic process has been leading up to the formulation of the two major cornerstones of your message: (1) the specific purpose and (2) the central idea.

Specific Purpose

The specific purpose of your speech, much like behavioral objectives in teaching, is the specific response you desire from your listeners when you have completed your speech. It contains a statement or implication of your general purpose applied to your topic in terms of an audience response. To do so, you should begin your specific purpose "I want my audience to (general purpose) + (desired response)." Consider the following examples of transactional specific purposes:

1. I want my listeners to *understand*—
    a. basic elements of first aid.
    b. the meaning of parity.
2. I want my listeners to *believe*—
    a. the MX missile should not be deployed.
    b. human life begins at conception.
3. I want my listeners to *enjoy*—
    a. highlights of my trip to Japan.
    b. the unusual foibles of college professors.
4. I want my listeners to—
    a. *vote* for candidate X.
    b. *give* to the American Cancer Society.

Central Idea

Where the specific purpose is the desired response or goal of the speech, the central idea is the theme or means of reaching that goal. It is the *single, simple, complete, declarative sentence* which, if the audience accepts it, will share the desired meaning and hence the response you are after.

Although a good central idea is difficult to devise, it is the next step toward the unity of your message. There are several pitfalls in conceptualizing your central idea. First, don't phrase it as a question. "What is life?" is not nearly as clear as "Life begins when an egg is fertilized." Second, don't make it too complex: "Although candidate X appears cold and aloof, he is really very bright, and furthermore is a competent administrator." Just focus on "Candidate X is the best person for the job." Third, don't summarize or number your major arguments in the central idea, as in "There are three things to remember in first aid." But what *distinguishes* first aid? What is the one thought that includes all the rest? In this case, "Keep the patient alive." While this may seem very obvious, it does eliminate a great deal of irrelevant material (setting broken bones, etc.) and focuses attention on the crux of the matter. Finally, you cannot express a complete idea in less than a complete sentence. "The MX Missile" leaves great doubt, perhaps even in your own mind, as to where you are going. Are you for it or against it? Why? A central idea like "The MX Missile will do more harm than good" leaves no doubt about the focus of your speech.

SUMMARY

In this chapter we discuss analysis of the public speaking transaction.

We found that you must analyze your audience's knowledge and beliefs about your topic. Demographic variables such as age, sex, occupation, religion, education, geographic location, and life style can provide helpful clues about what your audience knows and believes. However, you must also analyze their knowledge and beliefs, specifically with respect to your particular topic, and not only before but also during and after the speaking event.

You must also analyze your own feelings of desire to communicate, anxiety, knowledge, beliefs, attitudes, and values.

You will want, also, to analyze the physical and psychological aspects of the social situation. Important aspects of the physical setting include location, arrangement, and decor of the setting, as well as any special equipment required. The psychological climate includes traditions, current events, and images that members of the audience share.

As you analyze the topic you should select a topic you know and care about, and one that is significant to your listeners as well. You can limit or focus the topic to fit the needs of listeners and the time available. Sources of research for your topic can include the library, yourself, government and private agencies, and interviews. The general purpose of your speech can be to share understanding, enjoyment, beliefs, attitudes, feelings, or action.

Finally, you should focus your preparation on a specific response you desire from the audience in order to formulate a clear, simple, declarative central idea.

First Inaugural Address

Abraham Lincoln

Fellow citizens of the United States:

In compliance with a custom as old as the government itself, I appear before you to address you briefly, and to take, in your presence, the oath prescribed by the Constitution of the United States, to be taken by the President "before he enters on the execution of his office."

I do not consider it necessary, at present, for me to discuss those matters of administration about which there is no special anxiety, or excitement.

Apprehension seems to exist among the people of the Southern states, that by the accession of a Republican administration, their property, and their peace, and personal security are to be endangered. There has never been any reasonable cause for such apprehension. Indeed, the most ample evidence to the contrary has all the while existed, and been open to their inspection. It is found in nearly all the published speeches of him who now addresses you. I do but quote from one of those speeches when I declare that "I have no purpose, directly or indirectly, to interfere with the institution of slavery in the states where it exists. I believe I have no lawful right to do so, and I have no inclination to do so." Those who nominated and elected me did so with full knowledge that I had made this and many similar declarations, and had never recanted them. And more than this, they placed in the platform, for my acceptance, and as a law to themselves, and to me, the clear and emphatic resolution which I now read:

"RESOLVED, that the maintenance inviolate of the rights of the states, and especially the right of each state to order and control its own domestic institutions according to its own judgment exclusively, is essential to that balance of power on which the perfection and endurance of our political fabric depend; and we denounce the lawless invasion by armed force of the soil of any state or territory, no matter under what pretext, as among the gravest of crimes."

I now reiterate these sentiments: and in doing so, I only press upon the public attention the most conclusive evidence of which the case is susceptible, that the property, peace and security of no section are to be in anywise endangered by the now incoming administration. I add, too, that all the protection which, consistently with the Constitution and the laws, can be given, will be cheerfully given

Source: From John G. Nicolay and John Hay, eds., *Complete Works of Abraham Lincoln* (New York: Francis D. Tandy Co., 1905), pp. 169–185.

to all the states when lawfully demanded, for whatever cause—as cheerfully to one section as to another.

There is much controversy about the delivering up of fugitives from service or labor. The clause I now read is as plainly written in the Constitution as any other of its provisions:

> No person held to service or labor in one state, under the law thereof, escaping into another, shall, in consequence of any law or regulation therein, be discharged from such service or labor, but shall be delivered up on claim of the party to whom such service or labor may be due.

It is scarcely questioned that this provision was intended by those who made it, for the reclaiming of what we call fugitive slaves; and the intention of the lawgiver is the law. All members of Congress swear their support to the whole Constitution—to this provision as much as to any other. To the proposition, then, that slaves whose cases come within the terms of this clause, "shall be delivered up," their oaths are unanimous. Now, if they would make the effort in good temper, could they not, with nearly equal unanimity, frame and pass a law, by means of which to keep good that unanimous oath?

There is some difference of opinion whether this clause should be enforced by national or by state authority; but surely that difference is not a very material one. If the slave is to be surrendered, it can be of but little consequence to him, or to others, by which authority it is done. And should anyone, in any case, be content that his oath shall go unkept, on a merely unsubstantial controversy as to how it shall be kept?

Again, in any law upon this subject, ought not all the safeguards of liberty known in civilized and humane jurisprudence to be introduced, so that a free man be not, in any case, surrendered as a slave? And might it not be well, at the same time, to provide by law for the enforcement of that clause in the Constitution which guaranties that "the citizen of each state shall be entitled to all privileges and immunities of citizens in the several states"?

I take the official oath today, with no mental reservations, and with no purpose to construe the Constitution or laws, by any hypercritical rules. And while I do not choose now to specify particular acts of Congress as proper to be enforced, I do suggest that it will be much safer for all, both in official and private stations, to conform to, and abide by, all those acts which stand unrepealed, than to violate any of them, trusting to find immunity in having them held to be unconstitutional.

It is seventy-two years since the first inauguration of a President under our national Constitution. During that period, fifteen different and greatly distinguished citizens have, in succession, administered the executive branch of the government. They have conducted it through many perils; and, generally, with great success. Yet, with all this scope for precedent, I now enter upon the same task for the brief constitutional term of four years, under great and peculiar difficulty. A disruption of the federal Union, heretofore only menaced, is now formidably attempted.

I hold that in contemplation of universal law, and of the Constitution, the Union of these states is perpetual. Perpetuity is implied, if not expressed, in the fundamental law of all national governments. It is safe to assert that no government proper ever had a provision in its organic law for its own termination. Continue to execute all the express provisions of our national Constitution, and the Union will endure forever—it being impossible to destroy it, except by some action not provided for in the instrument itself.

Again, if the United States be not a government proper, but an association of states in the nature of contract merely, can it, as a contract, be peaceably unmade, by less than all the parties who made it? One party to a contract may violate it—break it, so to speak; but does it not require all to lawfully rescind it?

Descending from these general principles, we find the proposition that, in legal contemplation, the Union is perpetual, confirmed by the history of the Union itself. The Union is much older than the Constitution. It was formed in fact, by the Articles of Association in 1774. It was matured and continued by the Declaration of Independence in 1776. It was further matured and the faith of all the then thirteen states expressedly plighted and engaged that it should be perpetual, by the Articles of Confederation in 1778. And finally, in 1787, one of the declared objects for ordaining and establishing the Constitution, was "to form a more perfect union."

But if destruction of the Union, by one, or by a part only, of the states, be lawfully possible, the Union is less perfect than before the Constitution, having lost the vital element of perpetuity.

It follows from these views that no state, upon its own mere motion, can lawfully get out of the Union—that resolves and ordinances to that effect are legally void; and that acts of violence, within any state or states, against the authority of the United States, are insurrectionary or revolutionary, according to circumstances.

I therefore consider that, in view of the Constitution and the laws, the Union is unbroken; and, to the extent of my ability, I shall take care, as the Constitution itself expressly enjoins upon me, that the laws of the Union be faithfully executed in all the states. Doing this I deem to be only a simple duty on my part; and I shall perform it, so far as practicable, unless my rightful masters, the American people, shall withhold the requisite means, or, in some authoritative manner, direct the contrary. I trust this will not be regarded as a menace, but only as the declared purpose of the Union that it will constitutionally defend, and maintain itself.

In doing this, there needs to be no bloodshed or violence; and there shall be none, unless it be forced upon the national authority. The power confided to me will be used to hold, occupy, and possess the property and places belonging to the government, and to collect the duties and imposts; but beyond what may be necessary for these objects, there will be no invasion—no using of force against or among the people anywhere. Where hostility to the United States, in any interior locality, shall be so great and so universal, as to prevent competent resident citizens from holding the federal offices, there will be no attempt to force obnoxious strangers among the people for that object. While the strict legal right may exist in the government to enforce the exercise of these offices, the attempt to do so would be so irritating, and so nearly impracticable with all, that I deem it better to forego, for the time, the uses of such offices.

The mails, unless repelled, will continue to be furnished in all parts of the Union. So far as possible, the people everywhere shall have that sense of perfect security which is most favorable to calm thought and reflection. The course here indicated will be followed, unless current events, and experience, shall show a modification, or change, to be proper; and in every case and exigency, my best discretion will be exercised, according to circumstances actually existing, and with a view and a hope of a peaceful solution of the national troubles, and the restoration of fraternal sympathies and affections.

That there are persons in one section or another who seek to destroy the Union at all events, and are glad of any pretext to do it, I will neither affirm or deny; but if there be such, I need address no word to them. To those, however, who really love the Union, may I not speak?

Before entering upon so grave a matter as the destruction of our national fabric, with all its benefits, its memories, and its hopes, would it not be wise to ascertain precisely why we do it? Will you hazard so desperate a step, while there is any possibility that any portion of the ills you fly from, have no real existence? Will you, while the certain ills you fly to, are greater than all the real ones you fly from? Will you risk the commission of so fearful a mistake?

All profess to be content in the Union, if all constitutional rights can be maintained. Is it true, then, that any right, plainly written in the Constitution, has been denied? I think not. Happily, the human mind is so constituted, that no party can reach to the audacity of doing this. Think, if you can, of a single instance in which a plainly written provision of the Constitution has ever been denied. If, by the mere force of numbers, a majority should deprive a minority of any clearly written constitutional right, it might, in a moral point of view, justify revolution—certainly would, if such right were a vital one. But such is not our case. All the vital rights of minorities, and of individuals, are so plainly assured to them, by affirmations and negations, guaranties and prohibitions, in the Constitution, that controversies never arise concerning them. But no organic law can ever be framed with a provision specifically applicable to every question which may occur in practical administration. No foresight can anticipate, nor any document of reasonable length contain express provisions for all possible questions. Shall fugitives from labor be surrendered by national or by state authority? The Constitution does not expressly say. May Congress prohibit slavery in the territories? The Constitution does not expressly say. Must Congress protect slavery in the territories? The Constitution does not expressly say.

From questions of this class spring all our constitutional controversies, and we divide upon them into majorities and minorities. If the minority will not acquiesce, the majority must, or the government must cease. There is no other alternative; for continuing the government, is acquiescence on one side or the other. If a minority, in such case, will secede rather than acquiesce, they make a precedent which in turn, will divide and ruin them; for a minority of their own will secede from them, whenever a majority refuses to be controlled by such minority. For instance, why may not any portion of a new confederacy, a year or two hence, arbitrarily secede again, precisely as portions of the present Union now claim to secede from it? All who cherish disunion sentiments are now being educated to the exact temper of doing this. Is there such perfect identity of interests among the states to compose a new Union, as to produce harmony only, and prevent renewed secession?

Plainly, the central idea of secession is the essence of anarchy. A majority, held in restraint by constitutional checks, and limitations, and always changing easily, with deliberate changes of popular opinions and sentiments, is the only true sovereign of a free people. Whoever rejects it, does, of necessity, fly to anarchy or to despotism. Unanimity is impossible; the rule of a minority, as a permanent arrangement, is wholly inadmissible; so that, rejecting the majority principle, anarchy, or despotism, in some form, is all that is left.

I do not forget the position assumed by some, that constitutional questions are to be decided by the Supreme Court; nor do I deny that such decisions must be binding in any case, upon the parties to a suit, as to the object of that suit, while they are also entitled to very high respect and consideration, in all parallel cases, by all other departments of the government. And while it is obviously possible that such decision may be erroneous in any given case, still the evil effect following it, being limited to that particular case, with the chance that it may be overruled, and never become a precedent for other cases, can better be borne than could the evils of a different practice. At the same time the candid citizen must confess that if the policy of the government, upon vital questions, affecting the whole people, is to be irrevocably fixed by decisions of the Supreme Court, the instant they are made, in ordinary litigation between parties, in personal actions, the people will have ceased, to be their own rulers, having, to that extent, practically resigned their government, into the hands of that eminent tribunal. Nor is there, in this view, any assault upon the court, or the judges. It is a duty, from which they may not shrink, to decide cases properly brought before them; and it is no fault of theirs, if others seek to turn their decisions to political purposes.

One section of our country believes slavery is right, and ought to be extended, while the other believes it is wrong, and ought not to be extended. This is the only substantial dispute. The fugitive slave clause of the Constitution, and the law for the suppression of the foreign slave trade, are each as well enforced, perhaps, as any law can ever be in a community where the moral sense of the people imperfectly supports the law itself. The great body of the people abide by the dry legal obligation in both cases, and a few break it in each. This, I think, cannot be perfectly cured; and it would be worse in both cases after the separation of the sections, than before. The foreign slave trade, now imperfectly suppressed, would be ultimately revived without restriction, in one section; while fugitive slaves, now only partially surrendered, would not be surrendered at all, by the other.

Physically speaking, we cannot separate. We cannot remove our respective sections from each other, nor build an impassable wall between them. A husband and wife may be divorced, and go out of the presence, and beyond the reach, of each other; but the different parts of our country cannot do this. They cannot but remain face to face; and intercourse, either amicable or hostile, must continue between them. Is it possible then to make that intercourse more advantageous, or more satisfactory, after separation than before? Can aliens make treaties easier than friends can make laws? Can treaties be more faithfully enforced between aliens, than laws can among friends? Suppose you go to war, you cannot fight always; and when, after much loss on both sides, and no gain on either, you cease fighting, the identical old questions, as to terms of intercourse, are again upon you.

This country, with its institutions, belongs to the people who inhabit it. Whenever they shall grow weary of the existing government, they can exercise their constitutional right of amending it, or their revolutionary right to dismember, or overthrow it. I cannot be ignorant of the fact that many worthy and patriotic citizens are desirous of having the national Constitution amended. While I make no recommendation of amendments, I fully recognize the rightful authority of the people over the whole subject, to be exercised in either of the modes prescribed in the instrument itself; and I should, under existing circumstances, favor, rather than oppose, a fair opportunity being afforded the people to act upon it.

I will venture to add that, to me, the convention mode seems preferable, in that it allows amendments to originate with the people themselves, instead of only permitting them to take, or reject, propositions originated by others, both especially chosen for the purpose, and which might not be precisely such as they would wish to either accept or refuse. I understand a proposed amendment to the Constitution—which amendment, however, I have not seen—has passed Congress, to the effect that the federal government shall never interfere with the domestic institutions of the states, including that of persons held to service. To avoid misconstruction of what I have said, I depart from my purpose not to speak of particular amendments, so far as to say that, holding such a provision to now be implied constitutional law, I have no objection to its being made express, and irrevocable.

The chief magistrate derives all his authority from the people, and they have conferred none upon him to fix terms for the separation of the states. The people themselves can do this also if they choose; but the executive, as such, has nothing to do with it. His duty is to administer the present government, as it came to his hands, and to transmit it, unimpaired by him, to his successor.

Why should there not be a patient confidence in the ultimate justice of the people? Is there any better, or equal hope, in the world? In our present differences, is either party without faith of being in the right? If the Almighty Ruler of nations, with His eternal truth and justice, be on your side of the North, or on yours of the South, that truth, and that justice, will surely prevail, by the judgment of this great tribunal, the American people.

By the frame of the government under which we live, this same people have wisely given their public servants but little power for mischief; and have, with equal wisdom, provided for the return of that little to their own hands at very short intervals.

While the people retain their virtue, and vigilance, no administration, by any extreme of wickedness or folly, can very seriously injure the government, in the short space of four years.

My countrymen, one and all, think calmly and well, upon this whole subject. Nothing valuable can be lost by taking time. If there be an object to hurry any of you, in hot haste, to a step which you would never take deliberately, that object will be frustrated by taking time; but no good object can be frustrated by it. Such of you as are now dissatisfied, still have the old Constitution unimpaired, and, on the sensitive point, the laws of your own framing under it; while the new administration will have no immediate power, if it would, to change either. If it were admitted that you who are dissatisfied, hold the right side in the dispute, there still is no single good reason for precipitate action. Intelligence, patriotism, Christianity, and a firm reliance on Him, who has never yet forsaken this favored land, are still competent to adjust, in the best way, all our present difficulty.

In your hands, my dissatisfied fellow-countrymen, and not in mine, is the momentous issue of civil war. The government will not assail you. You can have no conflict, without being yourselves the aggressors. You have no oath registered in Heaven to destroy the government, while I shall have the most solemn one to "preserve, protect and defend" it.

I am loath to close. We are not enemies, but friends. We must not be enemies. Though passion may have strained, it must not break our bonds of affection. The mystic chords of memory, stretching from every battlefield, and patriot grave, to every living heart and hearthstone, all over this broad land, will yet swell the chorus of the Union, when again touched, as surely they will be, by the better angels of our nature.

ENDNOTES

1. T. Larry Williams, ed., *Selected Speeches, Messages and Letters* (New York: Holt, Rinehart and Winston, 1957), p. 148.

2. Lloyd F. Bitzer, "The Rhetorical Situation," *Philosophy and Rhetoric* 1 (1968): 1.

3. See Roger W. Libby and Robert N. Whitehurst, eds., *Marriage and Alternatives: Exploring Intimate Relationships* (Glenview, Ill.: Scott Foresman, 1977).

4. Joseph A. DeVito, *The Elements of Public Speaking* (New York: Harper & Row, 1981), pp. 84–85.

5. DeVito, p. 57.

6. For further discussion, see John K. Brilhart, "What Will I Talk About," *Todays Speech* 4 (November, 1957): 19–20.

7. Wallace C. Fotheringham, *Perspectives on Persuasion* (Boston: Allyn and Bacon, 1966).

8. From David Jabusch and Stephen Littlejohn, *Elements of Speech Communication* (Boston: Houghton Mifflin, 1981), p. 246.

3
Developing Transactional Content

In this chapter:
Communicative transactions
Data-claim relationship
Developing ideas with supporting ideas
Generating supporting materials
Audio-visual aids to developing ideas
Summary
Martin Luther King, Jr., "I Have a Dream..."

During approximately sixty years following Booker T. Washington's "Atlanta Compromise" and the United States Supreme Court's "separate but equal" decision in the case of *Plessy* v. *Ferguson*, few inroads had been made in diminishing discriminatory behavior against blacks in the United States. Then, in 1954, in the case of *Brown* v. *The Board of Education*, the Supreme Court reversed the *Plessy* decision and mandated integration of the public schools in all of the United States. With this ray of hope, there followed a series of demonstrations, sit-ins, bus boycotts, and marches, aimed at integrating not only the schools but lunch counters, motels, and public transportation as well. In 1957 the United States Congress passed the first Civil Rights Act in eighty-two years, but a "jury trial amendment" reduced its effectiveness to almost nil. In 1963, fully nine years after the *Brown* decision, a stronger civil rights bill was introduced into Congress, but it met with stiff opposition. In order to impress on Congress the importance of this bill, it was decided by various civil rights groups to stage a "March on Washington." From every corner of the nation, traveling for the most part at their own expense, "black men and white men, Catholics and protestants, Christians and Jews" descended on Washington, D.C.

On August 28, over 250,000 demonstrators from all over the country assembled in front of the Lincoln Memorial to hear from the leaders of the march. The scene was impressive. The speaker's podium was erected on the steps of the Memorial, and the crowd stretched across the street and up both sides of the beautiful mirror pool toward the Washington Monument.

The keynote speaker was a young Baptist minister who had risen to fame by leading the Birmingham bus boycott, Martin Luther King, Jr. Beautifully articulate, the Harvard Ph.D. was an ideal choice to address the huge crowd. With a bigger than lifesize statue of Lincoln looking down over his shoulder, King dramatized the existing situation, underlined the "fierce urgency of *now*," and visualized his dream of a country where little black boys and girls would not be judged by the color of their skin but by the content of their character. The audience and the country were electrified, and the following year Congress passed the Civil Rights Bill of 1964.

King used a wide variety of ideas, appeals, illustrations, familiar quotations, and other content to establish transactional identification with his listeners. Once you have analyzed your rhetorical situation and distilled your topic into a clear central idea, you are ready to consider the ideas and material you will use to help your listeners accept or identify with that central idea. When we looked at public speaking as a transmission, we thought about developing arguments and evidence that would "prove" or "sell" our central idea to our audience. From our transactional perspective, we think about discovering, selecting, and developing ideas and concrete material with which listeners can identify, relate, and share. This content forms a bridge between our concepts and those of our listeners, which we can use to meet and thereby complete our communication transaction. Hence, our ideas and their supporting materials must be related to both our topic and the mind-set of our audience. Figure 3–1 illustrates this transactional bridge.

COMMUNICATIVE TRANSACTIONS

Shared Understanding

The first transaction we desire to have with listeners is shared understanding. Even with a persuasive purpose there may be concepts that the audience must understand before they can be persuaded to believe or act in a given way. To reiterate an example used earlier, if you wish them to believe that farm prices should be supported at 90 percent of parity, do they understand the meaning of *parity?* More important, the specific purpose of your entire speech may be to gain understanding. The communication gap of misunderstanding can be bridged by concrete data.

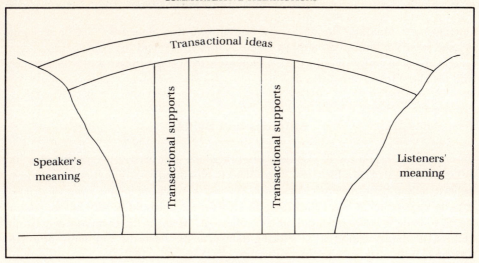

FIGURE 3-1
The transactional bridge

Clarity

The second communication transaction or function is shared clarity with your audience. While people may have a general understanding of your idea, added data may make it increasingly clear in the minds of listeners. Abstract ideas can be vague, but details make them specific and clear. People may have understood Ronald Reagan's political philosophy on the basis of his campaign statements, but his position on issues became increasingly clear with each new decision and event in his administration.

Interest and Attention

Listener interest and attention are another communicative transaction served by concrete data. Ideas, especially abstract ones, can be not only vague but dull; vivid detail makes them come alive. "Government ripoffs" or "con-games" have little impact until we experience a real one ourselves (or vicariously, on a TV news program). A generalization can leave us cold, but a story of a real person's tragedy can demand our attention and interest.

Memory

Memory is one of the chief transactions accomplished by supporting ideas and materials. How often have you thoroughly understood an idea in class, only to forget it during an examination? But have you forgotten your first plane ride? Traffic accident? A good joke? We tend to remember specifics, and then recall the point behind them. Interesting data which develop the idea you are attempting to share with your listeners will also help them remember it.

Attitudes and Beliefs

Specific ideas and data will also help you bridge the gulf between your attitudes and beliefs and those of your listeners. If you believe something you think they need badly to believe, telling them accomplishes little. Having them visualize and even vicariously experience your belief or attitude helps them accept it. It would be difficult for a labor union to believe that a corporation can offer high wages if the company reveals the statistics demonstrating that it is losing money, as has been the case with some U.S. automobile manufacturers in recent years.

Overt Behavior

Finally, specific forms of support can help you share overt behavior with your listeners. Some years ago, I listened to a physician attempting to get a large group of people to quit smoking. He gave impressive statistics and quoted the Surgeon General on the link between smoking and lung cancer. He told heart-rending stories of patients' suffering, and even showed pictures of blackened lungs removed from emphysema patients. Virtually every smoker in the audience was convinced he or she should quit, and several did. Certainly he got better results than if he had simply *told* them, "You should quit smoking. It's not good for you, you know." Now let us look at how we can combine ideas and concrete supports to accomplish these transactions or bridge these gaps.

DATA-CLAIM RELATIONSHIP

The crux of all composition, both written and oral, is the relationship between ideas and the concrete materials that support them, or what Stephen Toulmin called the *data* and the *claim*.[1]

Toulmin asserts that when people make claims they are implicitly or explicitly grounded in specific data or evidence. This relationship could be represented

$$data \rightarrow claim.$$

I will discuss Toulmin's more elaborate development of this relationship later. Suffice it to say here that this relationship between ideas or concepts and the concrete data that support them is the basic atom or building block of every speaking transaction. In outline form it would look like this:

I. Idea (claim)
   A. data
   B. data

Let us therefore look at how ideas can be supported or developed with other ideas and with data.

DEVELOPING IDEAS WITH SUPPORTING IDEAS

There are several different kinds of ideas, which can be analyzed and developed in several different ways. I will discuss developing ideas that share understanding, problem-oriented ideas, as well as questions of fact, policy, and value.

Information-oriented Ideas

As we saw in Chapter 2 and will discuss in more detail in Chapter 7, some speeches are devoted entirely to sharing information. However, regardless of the general purpose of a speech, there are individual ideas for which you and your listeners must share a common bond of understanding. Of the aforementioned transactions, sharing information-oriented ideas involves shared understanding, clarity, attention and interest, and memory. There is a wide variety of information-oriented ideas, which are in turn supported with other ideas, which serve to accomplish these communicative transactions. These ideas include abstract concepts, processes, history, distinguishing characteristics, space relations, misconceptions, functions, perspectives, and just plain categories. We will discuss the analysis of these types of information-oriented ideas in more detail in Chapter 7.

Suffice it to say here that information-oriented ideas can be better understood if we develop them with subordinate ideas that are simpler, more specific, and closer to our and our listeners' experience. Notice that this book contains essentially information-oriented ideas. If you follow the headings and read the paragraphs, you will see that it progresses from broader and perhaps less understandable ideas, to increasingly specific (and hopefully clearer) ideas, and finally to specific illustrations.

Problem-oriented Ideas

Many persuasive central ideas relate to personal, historical, or contemporary social problems. The process of problem solving has been widely studied in group, dyadic, and other contexts. It is not our purpose here to discuss problem solving as a process, but we will discuss an effective way, developed by the philosopher John Dewey, of analyzing and developing problem-oriented ideas. He suggested that a problem could be analyzed and more insightful solutions found if you address the issues represented by the following questions:

    I. What is the immediate cause for concern?
        A. What attracted our attention to the problem?
        B. How can we define the problem?
   II. What is the nature of the problem?
        A. What is the history of the problem?
        B. What is the scope of the problem?
        C. What are the effects of the problem?
            1. Immediate effects?
            2. Long-range effects?
        D. What are the causes of the problem?
            1. Primary causes?
            2. Secondary causes?
  III. What are possible solutions to the problem?
        A. How can this problem be viewed in new and different ways?
        B. By what criteria should a good solution be evaluated?
  IV. What is the best solution?
   V. What plan of action does this solution demand?

Another method of looking at problems has been devised by a community research and development organization named the Institute for Cultural Affairs. The method is designed to help people, organizations, and communities who are in a depressed or apathetic state recover their sense of identity and become more productive and actualizing; it is a combination of psychology and rational problem solving. Classic depression (either individual or corporate) results from being directed toward a goal and being blocked from achieving that goal, which results in frustration, then anger, and finally depression or giving up. Notice how the following questions are designed to reverse that process:

    I. What vision do you have for your life (community)?
        A. How do you wish it could be in one, five, or ten years?
        B. What dreams do you have for a better life (community)?
   II. What is preventing this ideal from being realized?
        A. What blocks stand in the way?
        B. What underlying attitudes or contradictions are causing these blocks?
  III. What specific proposals would remove these blocks or change the contradictions?
  IV. Which of these proposals take highest priority?
   V. What specific steps or actions are necessary to implement these proposals?

When a problem is analyzed and researched in this depth, you may have more ideas and material than a brief speech or even an hour's speech can adequately cover. In order to transact meaningfully, you must then focus on the aspect of the problem or solution that the audience most needs to hear about.

Questions of Policy

Ideas or proposals that advocate or suggest a plan for changing the status quo are called *propositions of policy*. They can usually be detected by the word *should*, as in "Pornographic literature *should* be prohibited in our community," or "You *should* get more exercise."

As suggested by these examples, questions of policy can be addressed to either public policy or personal behavior. A useful way of analyzing and developing questions of policy is by looking at supporting questions, called *stock issues*.

1. Is there a *need* for a change from the status quo?
2. Is there a practical *plan*?
3. Will the plan *meet* the need?
4. Is this the *best* plan for meeting the need?
5. Will the advantages of this plan outweigh the disadvantages?

For example, a person who supports the idea that the MX missile system should not be deployed on the Utah-Nevada border might support it with the following arguments. First, since the U.S. already has enough nuclear weapons on submarines and aircraft to destroy any possible enemy many times over, there is no need for the MX. Second, the "racetrack" basing mode is too complex and expensive, and hence is impractical. Third, the racetrack basing mode will be obsolete by the time it is completed, and hence won't meet the imagined need. Fourth, basing the MX in existing Minuteman silos or on shallow-water submarines is less expensive and more effective. Fifth, the expense of the racetrack basing mode would have disastrous economic side effects, which would be worse than any possible imagined advantage.

Note that similar ideas on the opposite side of the issue could also be stated. Furthermore, it is not enough just to assert these ideas, but they in turn must be supported by other ideas and considerable data.

Questions of Fact

A question of fact centers on a datum about the universe. It can be identified by the word *is* or some conjugation of the verb *to be*. For instance, you might ask, "Does capital punishment deter crime?" Or, "Is there a God?" Or, "Does physical exercise improve your general state of health?" Note that a person could take a position on either side of these questions and might transactionally be required by a skeptical listener to support that position. "Factual" ideas are considerably more difficult to develop because they have less in common than questions of policy. It is interesting to note that each of the stock issues above is itself a question of fact.

With questions or propositions of fact your supporting ideas will be more dependent on the topic. For instance, in developing the need for the MX missile you would have to ask what weapons we have now. How effective are they? What would the Soviet Union consider a deterrent to war? Will our present weapons systems provide that deterrent for the foreseeable future? For the question of the need to give to the American Cancer Society, however, you would ask an entirely different set of questions. Is cancer a serious disease? Is it being adequately treated now? If not, why not?

Although there are no stock issues for looking at all propositions of fact, there are some guides. If the proposition deals with a problem or solution, you can look at the questions suggested by Dewey's problem-solving sequence discussed above. In developing the practicality of a plan, whether it be MX or a new automobile for the family, you usually consider cost, how well it is built, how long it will last, the record and cost of repair or upkeep, and availability of materials.

Furthermore, certain kinds of questions of fact have recurring subordinate questions. For instance, a "plan meets need" issue which invariably arises on the question of giving to a charity is how much actually gets to the people who need it.

From our transactional perspective, as you begin to develop a proposition of fact you will want to look for the subordinate ideas that are not only crucial to that specific idea but are also uppermost in the minds of your listeners.

Questions of Value

Questions of value are questions of fact with a vector or direction. They deal with questions of more or less, better or worse—in short, evaluation. Even children argue, "My Dad's stronger than your Dad." Later they may say "The Soviet Union has surpassed the U.S. as the most powerful nation on earth." Questions of value also deal with standards of behavior, or life's goals. I will discuss values per se more fully in our discussion of persuasive speaking.

As you analyze a question of value, look for *standards of judgment* or *criteria* by which to make your evaluation. If you were developing the idea that one gem was more valuable than another, you would probably consider the clarity, cut, and karat (size). Criteria are highly individualized by topic, but they provide objective and rational ways of deciding relative value.

During a recent women's gymnastics meet, I was struck by the consistency in the judgments made by the judges on the relatively complex exercises. The gymnasts all looked equally outstanding to me, but the judges were able to make consistently fine discriminations in evaluation by using clear, uniform criteria or standards of judgment of which I was unaware. Most competent scholars are able to do the same in evaluating your speeches or other forms of oral discourse.

Thus far we have looked at developing ideas pretty much from the viewpoint of ideas that reasonably support the idea we want to share with the audience. However, because public communication is a transaction, you need to consider the listeners in your selection of these ideas. Once you have analyzed the ideas inherent in the idea you wish to develop, you should try to discover which ones the audience may already understand or believe, which ones may be too obvious or irrelevant and most important, and which ones most require their attention. From a variety of possible supporting ideas you will find different audiences require a different combination of supporting ideas for the same central idea.

GENERATING SUPPORTING MATERIAL

Not only can ideas be shared with listeners by developing them with other ideas, but specific data can also be used to develop an idea. Indeed, I have argued elsewhere that the primary job of getting listeners to identify and transact with your ideas is through the use of concrete data, or what we will call *forms of support*.[2] We will discuss examples, statistics, quotations, comparisons, stories, reiteration, and explanation.

Examples

Many claims, both informative and persuasive, are grounded in examples. Examples are instances of the idea you wish to share. The ideas "Beware of pickpockets when traveling," or "The Supreme Court has made some bad decisions" could be supported by specific examples of robberies or Court decisions. You have at your disposal general, hypothetical, and specific examples. "It would be scary to live in a country where the government was unstable—just look at Iran" is a statement supported by a general example. The use of general examples presupposes the audience's familiarity with the details; if this is not so, they are more effectively used in combination with specific examples or other forms of support.

Hypothetical examples are unreal (though perhaps typical) descriptions of a particular class of instances. You might say, "Let's look at a typical heart-attack victim—(description)." Hypothetical examples also presuppose some shared experience on the part of listeners. If not, then specific examples should be researched and used.

Specific examples are concrete, detailed descriptions of real instances. You have probably had teachers who used vivid specific instances to illustrate a difficult point; Ronald Reagan is also noted for using at least one detailed example or story in each of his major speeches.

From our transactional perspective, your selection and use of examples depends on your listeners. You might select different (adaptive) examples for the same idea in order to transact with audiences of different backgrounds, interests, attitudes, and so forth.

Statistics

Statistics are the expression of data in numerical form. They constitute essentially the same kind of data as examples, except that statistics serve to summarize large numbers of specific instances. For example, if a physician says, "There is a strong, positive relationship between smoking and lung cancer," he or she is relying on statistical studies of thousands of individual patients, all of whom have their specific, detailed, and perhaps tragic story.

Professional statisticians and scientists use statistics in very sophisticated ways to make dependable statements based on probabilities. In public speaking we are concerned with the accuracy of our statements, but we use simpler statistics, such as averages, ranges, totals, and perhaps correlations, for the purpose of relating our ideas to the immediate audience. Only if we were to address a group of scientists on a highly complex subject would sophisticated statistics be necessary or appropriate. If asked how your class did on the midterm exam, how would you respond? If you responded with every grade of every student, the listeners would probably become confused with information overload. You could give them a clearer idea by saying, "The top grade was 97 percent, the lowest 65 percent, and the average 80 percent. We did pretty well." Contrast this with the answer I heard recently: "The average was 41 percent and every last student failed it!"

Many people consider statistics dull. This need not be so if statistics relate information that is significant to listeners and are given in an interesting manner. Consider the impact of a speaker who was raising money for a mission hospital, who pointed out that in the U.S. more money is spent on pet food than on all of the mission work of all of the churches in the country!

Audience analysis sometimes reveals statistics you must have in order to get your listeners to identify or transact with your idea. How many times have you heard a person say, "I won't give a dime to that charity until I know what percentage actually gets to the needy"? For those people, the statistic is the key to the success of your entire speech.

Quotations

What we know or believe is developed from either direct experience or the authority of someone whose word we trust. Examples, statistics, and other forms of support are ways of sharing direct experiences or data about these experiences with your listeners. The less of an authority you are on your topic with the immediate audience, the greater your need to use other people's credibility by employing quotations. *Quotations* are simply the use of someone else's words to express your idea. Here we will use the term *testimony* to refer to quotations that are perceived as *authoritative* by you and, hopefully, by your listeners. Quoting the Secretary of Defense or a member of the Senate Armed Services Committee, for example, can lend authority to a claim about the deployment of a weapons system.

There are other kinds of quotations that are also helpful in developing ideas. Although not particularly authoritative (and not classified as testimony), historical and literary quotations can add interest, clarity, memorability, and perhaps credibility to your claim. But remember that if you use someone else's words you must of course give the author credit.

Comparisons

Analogies, similes, and metaphors are comparisons that enable you to share meaning with listeners by relating what they do not know and have not experienced with what they do know or have experienced. A *metaphor* is a comparison that assumes but does not state the comparison. "This schoolyard is a sea of mud" is a metaphorical way of expressing the idea that the schoolyard is very muddy.

A *simile* is a brief comparison that explicitly states the relationship by using the word *like*. A simile would be "He walks like a duck." An *analogy* is an extended explicit comparison using the word *like*. "State-controlled medicine in the U.S. would be a disaster. Look what has happened in England," and a detailed comparison of the two systems is an analogy.

Comparisons are superb ways of sharing clarity, interest, and memorability with an audience. Some writers have maintained that analogies are a weak form of support when attempting to change beliefs, attitudes, or behavior, because even a very literal analogy usually breaks down and figurative analogies are illogical by definition.

Although comparisons may not meet all the tests of formal logic, they can provide a very sound basis for reasonably sharing conclusions with your listeners. For instance, in the first year of the Reagan administration I was told that more money was allocated for military bands than for the entire National Endowment for the Arts! Or consider the figurative analogy given by a speaker who was criticizing the number of government appointments from a single corporation even though the appointees had divested themselves of their corporate holdings. The speaker compared the situation to a card player who innocently and accidentally sees the cards in an opponent's hand. "Now," he said, "how can the player complete the hand as if he had not seen the cards in the opponent's hand?" A very compelling argument based on a *figurative* analogy.

Stories

In addition to the supports discussed above, which are often communicated in the form of stories, there are also (1) parables, (2) anecdotes, and (3) fables.

Parables. The parables attributed to Jesus of Nazareth by writers of the Holy Bible have been used for centuries to clarify abstract concepts for listeners. The stories of the Good Samaritan, the Talents, and the Pearl of Great Price share understanding of neighborliness, utilizing one's gifts, and the proper order of priorities. The Parable of the Prodigal Son clarifies several concepts related to interpersonal family relationships, as well as responsibilities.

Fables. Aesop's fables have long been a favorite of small children and have taught profound concepts not easily explained to inexperienced listeners. Stories of "crying wolf" or "sour grapes" are legendary to the point of being overused. Other, more obscure fables can be equally effective with adults as well as children, and even the old familiar ones can be used in new ways. I recently heard the carelessness (after repeated false alarms) at Pearl Harbor in 1941 referred to as a case of crying wolf too often. Fables have been used most often to transact understanding, clarity, and memory, but advertisers also use them to share attitudes and behaviors.

Anecdotes. Anecdotes are humorous or entertaining stories. You should not use so much humor that you reduce a speech to persuade or inform into one merely to entertain, but a well-placed joke or two can be useful. Anecdotes can be used to establish attention, interest, and common ground in the introduction of a speech, as well as to maintain interest and enhance memory throughout the speech.

Scholars have studied humor for its effect on listeners and to date have found no relationship between humor and attitude change. However, a researcher named Gibb[3] discovered that listeners who heard a humorous lecture on biology scored better on a standardized biology test than listeners who had heard an identical, though non-humorous lecture.

Reiteration

Repetition and restatement are both forms of reiteration which can be used to transact an idea. *Repetition* simply means repeating the word or phrase over and over again. *Restatement* is stating an idea in several different ways. As a form of oral communication, public speaking requires instant intelligibility. As a listener you cannot go back and reread the message if your mind wanders as you can when reading. Nor do listeners usually interrupt a speaker and ask to have the message repeated, as they might in a conversation.

All oral communication is therefore redundant to a considerable extent. Supporting ideas are refinements of the central idea and the forms of support we are now discussing are merely interesting ways of restating the ideas they are designed to develop.

Reiteration is usually used for the transactions of understanding, clarity, and memory, but advertisers have amply demonstrated that even straight repetition can change attitudes toward their products as well as consumers' buying behavior. "Where's the beef?" is likely to sell lots of hamburgers.

Franklin D. Roosevelt used reiteration not only to clarify and to enhance memory but also to reinforce attitudes and motivate behavior when he described the events of December 7, 1941, with these words:

> Yesterday the Japanese government also launched an attack against Malaya.
> Last night Japanese forces attacked Hong Kong.
> Last night Japanese forces attacked Guam.
> Last night Japanese forces attacked the Philippine Islands.
> Last night the Japanese attacked Wake Island.
> This morning the Japanese attacked Midway Island.
> Japan has, therefore, undertaken a surprise offensive extending throughout the Pacific area.[4]

Explanation

Explanation is defined as the process of unfolding, making plain or intelligible, or interpreting.[5] It is an abstract verbal elaboration of an idea. Frequently overused, explanation is employed by speakers who have not adequately researched the other types of data described above.

Used in combination with other forms of support, however, explanation can be effective, if not indispensable. Statistics frequently need explaining, and the significance of examples, comparisons, and stories needs to be pointed out. Use explanation, but use it sparingly and in combination with other forms of support.

AUDIO-VISUAL AIDS TO DEVELOPING IDEAS

Over the years the United States Supreme Court has struggled with the problem of defining the word *pornography*. Even the brilliant legal minds have not been able to define the difficult concept to most people's satisfaction, but Associate Justice Potter Stewart once quipped, "I may not be able to define it, but I know it when I see it."

Communication research supports the notion that ideas generally are shared more effectively by appealing to more than one sensory mode than by appealing to any one alone. Furthermore, some people are more "literate" in one sense than another. It stands to reason, then, that the use of audio-visual aids can enhance the communication transaction with your audience.

Here we will look at audio-visual aids, not as distinct forms of support, but as ways of presenting supports using different sensory modalities. We will discuss (1) types of sensory aids and (2) principles for preparing and using them.

Types of Aids

There are of course many different types of highly sophisticated audio-visual materials. Most libraries today have audio-visual departments, and you should consult your library to ascertain what materials they may have on your topic. You will also come upon audio-visual materials in your own research, especially from government agencies and private corporations, that have produced visuals for their own public presentations. The types we will discuss here are (1) pictures, (2) graphics, (3) specimens, (4) models, (5) recordings, (6) demonstrations, and (7) chalk boards.

FIGURE 3–2
Some examples of graphic representations of statistics

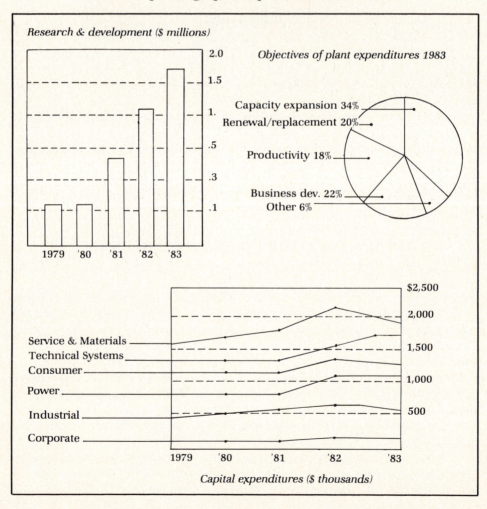

AUDIO-VISUAL AIDS TO DEVELOPING IDEAS

A speaker transacts using a model of the human brain

Flat or projected *pictures* are effective for communicating examples, statistics, and even comparisons. You may recall the communicative power of a picture of the war dead in Lebanon or El Salvador, a pastoral scene, or the wrenching picture of starving children.

Projected (slide) *pictures* can be used to present not only examples but also statistical data in graphic form. I once delivered a paper to a convention of anesthesiologists on doctor-patient communication where three slides of graphic data made it possible for a large audience to see statistical comparisons that would have been very difficult to explain without the slides.

Nonprojected *graphics* can also be used to present statistics to smaller audiences. Pie graphs and bar graphs can be used to show not only amounts, but trends and comparisons as well. (See Figure 3–2.)

In some cases an actual *specimen* of your subject can be used. A speaker on quality furniture could demonstrate how quality shows by comparing the design, material, and workmanship of a superior to an inferior piece of furniture. I have seen teachers use specimens of animals, rocks, foods, and stained glass to augment their explanations. As we will see in a moment, you must be careful that the specimen is large enough for the audience to see.

Models are sometimes used in place of specimens when the real thing is inaccessible, too small, or you want to be able to dissassemble it in order to see the component parts. You may have seen physicians use models of parts of the human body to explain how an operation works or how a system of the body functions. Although complex models are difficult to construct and expensive to buy, you can construct simple models, and sometimes the sources you go to in your research will have them already made.

Depending on your subject, *recordings* can be useful to amplify a specific point. Excerpts of musical compositions can be used to demonstrate any number of principles on a musical question, and how else would you learn animal or bird calls? Professors who teach the history of public communication frequently augment their lectures with records of excerpts or re-creations of famous speeches.

An often overlooked form of visual aid is the *demonstration.* In a "how to" speech, an actual demonstration is indispensable. Speakers sometimes forget that they are themselves a visual aid (or distraction) to their own message. We will pursue this issue more fully in Chapter 6.

Demonstrations can also be done using other people. I once had a student speaking on a central idea related to ballet, and three dancers demonstrated the ideas the speaker was making.

A final form of visual aid is the *chalk board.* It is perhaps the most overused visual of all. When speakers walk into the room and begin to draw or write on the board before they speak, it is a sign of inadequate preparation. Anything that can be prepared ahead of time should be, when greater care can be put into its preparation.

The chalk board is an effective device for evolving a concept before the eyes of the listeners or adapting to unexpected questions or changes during the speaking event. Information can be added as you speak and relationships demonstrated. Use the chalk board for flexibility, not as a substitute for the visual you could have prepared more carefully ahead of time.

Principles of Sensory Aids

Let us look at the principles governing the preparation and use of audio-visual aids: (1) intelligibility, (2) simplicity, and (3) coordination.[6] Please beware: These principles seem obvious at first glance, but recall how many times you have seen speakers who have ruined their communication transaction by violating them.

Intelligibility. This is the first principle. Visuals must be large enough to be seen. Appearances are deceptive. Printing or pictures which appear very large while you are

AUDIO-VISUAL AIDS TO DEVELOPING IDEAS

A speaker using the chalk board for developing a concept as he talks

preparing them at your desk may be difficult to see at the back of a moderate-sized classroom, to say nothing of a large auditorium. Furthermore, visuals need to be displayed so that they can be seen, not behind you, the podium, or some other obstruction. Audio materials must be loud enough for all to hear. The best way to test this is to try out the material: go to the location (or one like it) and check to see if the visual is large enough or at what setting a recording can be heard at the back of the room. As you use the aid in your speech, be cognizant of the listeners' vision and hearing. Don't be afraid to ask if they can see and hear.

Simplicity. Not only must sensory aids be intelligible but they should also be simple; it is easier for people to process simpler messages than complex ones. It is easier to process a little information at a time than a lot. When preparing your sensory aid, reduce the information on the aid to only that which is necessary to support your point. Elaborate art work is not necessary and can be distracting. I once had a student who presented a beautifully elaborate visual. After the speech classmates praised him on the impressive artistry of his visual but could not remember the point he was trying to make. If possible, have only one point per visual. A poster divided into four parts with four distinct ideas is better divided into four separate posters that can be presented one at a time. Information on your visual which does not relate directly to your point may be impressive, but transactionally it can also be distracting.

This does not mean that all visuals should be simply constructed. Models or mockups with compartments that open or pieces that can be removed can contribute to the principle of simplicity by allowing you to focus on one idea at a time. The point is that, regardless how physically complex a visual is, it should result in conceptual clarity and simplicity. It should not be complex for its own sake or just to impress people.

Coordination. Coordination is a principle with two implications. In the preparation of your aid, coordination implies *relevance;* that is, the information on the aid must be coordinated with the idea it is designed to support. How often have you seen a speaker display a picture roughly related to the topic and then never refer to it as a support for an idea? In this case it is nothing but a distraction.

As you deliver the speech, you should also bear in mind the principle of coordination. Practice introducing the visual smoothly at the time it will best reinforce your idea, and *remove* it when you have finished, unless you must relate it to a later point. Chalk boards and flannel boards are excellent devices for developing an idea before the eyes of the listeners. But when you have finished with a visual get rid of it or it will distract the listeners from a subsequent point. I am frequently asked if speakers should use handouts. My answer is, only if you have one for everyone and you intend to refer to it immediately. Remember that if you pass a single object around an audience of twenty people, only one person will have it when you want to refer to it; the other nineteen will be distracted from some other idea or concept you are discussing at the time.

Some final words of advice about the use of media aids: Don't let the aids become the object or focus of the message. Transactionally they are means of accomplishing your communicative purpose—not ends in themselves. You can avoid this pitfall by not considering sensory aids until after you have determined your specific purpose, central idea, main and subordinate ideas, and forms of support. *Then* ask yourself how those ideas and supports can be better communicated or shared with listeners through mediated materials. What ideas cry out for a picture, specimen, or chart? In the speech on yellow journalism referred to in Chapter 4, two characteristics discussed are the tabloid format and sensational photography. This speech was certainly enhanced when the speaker showed actual examples of the format and the pictures. Verbal explanation alone would have been inadequate; but the visuals were not the purpose of the speech, only a means of achieving that purpose.

SUMMARY

In this chapter we have examined the development of speech content that will help you get listeners to transact with you on your central idea.

We discussed the basic relationship between claims and the data from which they are drawn. We saw how ideas can be supported with other ideas. We discussed developing informative ideas in the form of abstract concepts, processes, history, space relations, common misconceptions, functions, perspectives, and categories. We discussed ways of developing problem-oriented ideas, as well as questions of policy, fact, and value.

Ideas can also be developed through supporting materials that establish communicative transactions of understanding, clarity, interest, memory, attitude, and behavior. Types of supporting materials included examples, statistics, comparisons, quotations, stories, reiteration, and explanation.

Finally, we discussed the use of audio-visual or multisensory material as aids in communicating ideas and forms of support. The types of materials included pictures, graphics, specimens, models, recordings, demonstrations, and chalk boards. Finally, we discussed the preparation and use of mediated materials, in terms of the principles of intelligibility, simplicity, and coordination.

"I Have a Dream..."

Martin Luther King, Jr.

I am happy to join with you today in what will go down in history as the greatest demonstration for freedom in the history of our nation.

Five score years ago, a great Amercian, in whose symbolic shadow we stand today, signed the Emancipation Proclamation. This momentous decree came as a great beacon light of hope to millions of Negro slaves who had been seared in the flames of withering injustice. It came as a joyous daybreak to end the long night of their captivity.

But one hundred years later, the Negro is still not free. One hundred years later, the life of the Negro is still sadly crippled by the manacles of segregation and the chains of discrimination. One hundred years later, the Negro lives on a lonely island of poverty in the midst of a vast ocean of material prosperity. One

Source: Robert T. Oliver and Eugene E. White, eds., *Selected Speeches from American History* (Boston: Allyn and Bacon, 1966), pp. 291–294. Reprinted by permission of Joan Daves. © 1963 by Martin Luther King, Jr.

hundred years later, the Negro is still languished in the corners of American society and finds himself an exile in his own land. So we have come here today to dramatize a shameful condition.

In a sense, we have come to our nation's Capitol to cash a check. When the architects of our republic wrote the magnificent words of the Constitution and the Declaration of Independence, they were signing a promissory note to which every American was to fall heir. This note was a promise that all men would be guaranteed the unalienable rights of life, liberty, and the pursuit of happiness.

It is obvious today that America has defaulted on this promissory note insofar as her citizens of color are concerned. Instead of honoring this sacred obligation, America has given the Negro people a bad check; a check which has come back marked "insufficient funds." But we refuse to believe that the bank of justice is bankrupt. We refuse to believe that there are insufficient funds in the great vaults of opportunity of this nation. So we have come to cash this check—a check that will give us upon demand the riches of freedom and the security of justice. We have also come to this hallowed spot to remind America of the fierce urgency of now. This is no time to engage in the luxury of cooling off or to take the tranquilizing drug of gradualism. Now is the time to make real the promises of Democracy. Now is the time to rise from the dark and desolate valley of segregation to the sunlit path of racial justice. Now is the time to open the doors of opportunity to all of God's children. Now is the time to lift our nation from the quicksands of racial injustice to the solid rock of brotherhood. Now is the time to make justice a reality for all of God's children.

It would be fatal for the nation to overlook the urgency of the moment. This sweltering summer of the Negro's legitimate discontent will not pass until there is an invigorating autumn of freedom and equality. 1963 is not an end, but a beginning. Those who hope that the Negro needed to blow off steam and will now be content will have a rude awakening if the nation returns to business as usual. There will be neither rest nor tranquility in America until the Negro is granted his citizenship rights. The whirlwinds of revolt will continue to shake the foundations of our nation until the bright day of justice emerges.

But there is something that I must say to my people who stand on the warm threshold which leads into the palace of justice. In the process of gaining our rightful place we must not be guilty of wrongful deeds. Let us not seek to satisfy our thirst for freedom by drinking from the cup of bitterness and hatred. We must forever conduct our struggle on the high plane of dignity and discipline. We must not allow our creative protest to degenerate into physical violence. Again and again we must rise to the majestic heights of meeting physical force with soul force. The marvelous new militancy which has engulfed the Negro community must not lead us to a distrust of all white people, for many of our white brothers, as evidenced by their presence here today, have come to realize that their destiny is tied up with our destiny. And they have come to realize that their freedom is inextricably bound to our freedom. We cannot walk alone.

And as we walk, we must make the pledge that we shall always march ahead. We cannot turn back. There are those who ask the devotees of civil rights, "When will you be satisfied?" We can never be satisfied as long as the Negro is the victim of the unspeakable horrors of police brutality. We can never be satisfied as long as our bodies, heavy with the fatigue of travel, cannot gain lodging in the motels of the highways and the hotels of the cities. We cannot be satisfied as long as the Negro's basic mobility is from a smaller ghetto to a larger one. We can never be satisfied as long as our children are stripped of their selfhood and robbed of their dignity by signs stating "For Whites Only." We cannot be satisfied as long as a Negro in Mississippi cannot vote and a Negro in New York believes he has nothing for which to vote. No, no, we are not satisfied, and we will not be satisfied until justice rolls down like waters and righteousness like a mighty stream.

I am not unmindful that some of you have come here out of great trials and tribulations. Some of you have come fresh from narrow jail cells. Some of you have come from areas where your quest for freedom left you battered by the storms of persecution and staggered by the winds of police brutality. You have been the veterans of creative suffering. Continue to work with the faith that unearned suffering is redemptive.

Go back to Mississippi, go back to Alabama, go back to South Carolina, go back to Georgia, go back to Louisiana, go back to the slums and ghettos of our northern cities, knowing that somehow this situation can and will be changed. Let us not wallow in the valley of despair.

I say to you today, my friends, even though we face the difficulties of today and tomorrow, I still have a dream. It is a dream deeply rooted in the American dream.

I have a dream that one day this nation will rise up and live out the true meaning of its creed: "We hold these truths to be self-evident; that all men are created equal."

I have a dream that one day on the red hills of Georgia the sons of former slaves and the sons of former slaveowners will be able to sit down together at the table of brotherhood.

I have a dream that one day even the state of Mississippi, a state sweltering with the heat of injustice, sweltering with the heat of oppression, will be transformed into an oasis of freedom and justice.

I have a dream that my four little children will one day live in a nation where they will not be judged by the color of their skin but by the content of their character.

I have a dream today.

I have a dream that one day, down in Alabama, with its vicious racists, with its Governor having his lips dripping with the words of interposition and nullification, one day right there in Alabama little black boys and little black girls will be able to join hands with little white boys and white girls as sisters and brothers.

I have a dream today.

I have a dream that one day every valley shall be exalted, every hill and mountain shall be made low, the rough places will be made plane, and the crooked places will be made straight, and the glory of the Lord shall be revealed, and all flesh shall see it together.

This is our hope. This is the faith with which I return to the South. With this faith we will be able to hew out of the mountain of despair a stone of hope. With this faith we will be able to transform the jangling discords of our nation into a beautiful symphony of brotherhood. With this faith we will be able to work together, to pray together, to struggle together, to go to jail together, to stand up for freedom together, knowing that we will be free one day.

This will be the day when all of God's children will be able to sing with new meaning—

My country, 'tis of thee,
Sweet land of liberty,
   Of thee I sing
Land where my fathers died,
Land of the pilgrims' pride,
From every mountainside
   Let freedom ring.

And if America is to be a great nation this must become true. So let freedom ring from the prodigious hilltops of New Hampshire.

Let freedom ring from the mighty mountains of New York.

Let freedom ring from the heightening Alleghenies of Pennsylvania!

Let freedom ring from the snowcapped Rockies of Colorado!

Let freedom ring from the curvaceous slopes of California!

But not only that; let freedom ring from Stone Mountain of Georgia!

Let freedom ring from Lookout Mountain of Tennessee!

Let freedom ring from every hill and molehill of Mississippi. From every mountainside, let freedom ring. And when this happens—when we let freedom ring, when we let it ring from every village and every hamlet, from every state and every city, we will be able to speed up that day when all of God's children, black men and white men, Jews and Gentiles, Protestants and Catholics, will be able to join hands and sing in the words of the old Negro spiritual "Free at last! Free at last! Thank God almighty, we are free at last!"

ENDNOTES

1. Stephen Toulmin, *The Uses of Argument* (Cambridge, Mass.: At the University Press, 1958).
2. David Jabusch and Stephen Littlejohn, *Elements of Speech Communication* (Boston: Houghton Mifflin, 1981), p. 249.
3. John Douglas Gibb, "An Experimental Comparison of the Humorous Lecture and the Non Humorous Lecture in Informative Speaking," Master's Thesis, University of Utah, 1964.
4. "War Message to Congress," in *Franklin D. Roosevelt: Selected Speeches, Messages, Press Conferences and Letters* (New York: Holt, Rinehart, and Winston, 1947), p. 301.
5. *The Oxford Universal Dictionary*, 3d ed. (Oxford: Clarendon Press, 1955), p. 657.
6. Adapted from John A. Davis, "Making Visuals Aid," *Today's Speech*, January, 1958, pp. 31–32.

4
Organization Using the Transactional Focus

In this chapter:
General approaches
General principles
Introductions: transactional functions
Conclusions: transactional functions
Techniques of organization
Summary
Barbara Ward, "Only One Earth"

In 1970 the world was in turmoil. The United States was heavily involved in a frustrating war in Southeast Asia. Millions of dollars and thousands of lives were being spent in a cause that was not altogether clear to many Americans. Disenchantment with the war was growing. Simultaneously, great changes were occurring at home. The civil rights movement had been transformed into a human rights movement, which in turn was to spawn a renewal of a women's rights movement. Sophisticated chemical industries, which had produced seemingly miraculous new products, had also produced voluminous amounts of toxic waste. The arms race between the U.S. and the Soviet Union had resulted in the development and production of nuclear warheads 1000 times more powerful than those that destroyed the cities of Hiroshima and Nagasaki. A "war on poverty," declared by President Johnson at the time of the Vietnam War, placed great strain on the U.S. economy which had been growing steadily since World War II on successive waves of population increases, both at home and throughout the world. More babies created greater demand for all consumer goods, from baby oil to automobiles and homes. But with the "guns and butter" policy of the federal government came larger budget deficits, and higher inflation, cost overruns, and reports of corruption.

Meanwhile, science and technology had combined to produce space exploration, mining of the ocean floor, miracles of medicine, and a greatly accelerated development of the earth's natural resources.

By the early 1970s, a few intellectuals were beginning to warn of dangers ahead. One such warning was given during a distinguished lecture series sponsored by the International Institute for Environmental Affairs in cooperation with the Population Institute.

The speaker was Barbara Ward, the Albert Schweitzer Professor of International Economic Development at Columbia University. Her skillfully crafted speech seemed to be designed not only for her immediate audience but for the more universal audience of all humankind as well. The clarity and focus of the structure of this speech are exemplary of the principles of transactional organization that we discuss in this chapter.

Let us look at the process of structuring or organizing your materials. Until now we have been discussing an *analysis* process whereby you have torn apart the context and potential content of your speaking transaction to see how it all "ticked." Now we will look at a *synthesis* process whereby you select and arrange the materials in a way that will enhance your transaction with your audience. We first discuss some general approaches to this process, then some basic principles governing organization, and finally some specific techniques for structuring a message. The central question we address is: How can I structure my materials so as to maximize my listeners' ability to transact with me and my ideas?

GENERAL APPROACHES

There are two general approaches to structuring a message, the inductive and deductive. The *inductive approach* means that you work from the specific to the general, while the *deductive* means to work from the general to the specific.

Using the inductive approach you begin with all of the specific data and ideas you have gathered during your research. It may be a hodgepodge of examples, generalizations, arguments of different types, statistics, and the like. Working inductively, you begin to combine data that seem to support a particular claim. Soon you will see claims that cluster around a broader claim. Eventually all of the data will be grouped under some idea and claim, and all specific ideas will be found to support two or three more general ideas. Then you look for a thought that captures the whole thing, and you are back to the central idea we discussed earlier. An important consideration guiding this process is whether your scheme for clustering ideas makes sense to the audience. Will this organizational pattern serve to enhance their understanding, belief, or action?

The second general approach to outlining is the deductive approach. Typically, you are better able to use the deductive approach if you know your subject well. From our transactional perspective, you start with your central idea and ask (much as we did in the previous chapter on supporting ideas with ideas), "What ideas are crucial in supporting this central idea with this *particular audience?*" Both the information you gathered during your research and knowledge of your audience will provide answers to this question. After you have listed the main ideas that support the central idea, you ask the same question of each successively smaller idea until you have all of the ideas necessary to transact with this particular audience on your particular central idea. Then you ask what forms of support you need to get this audience to identify (understand, believe, etc.) with each idea. Again, your research should provide the appropriate data, but if not, you may have to return to the library for the clinching statistic, quotation, or other form of support.

For example, if you wanted to get your audience to be able to recognize good furniture when they see it and your central idea was "quality shows," you would probably come up with the main ideas that:

I. Quality shows in the materials.
II. Quality shows in the design.
III. Quality shows in the workmanship.

Having your main ideas, you would discover the materials that may vary in quality are:

A. the woods
B. the fabric
C. the finish

When you ask "How can I get this audience to recognize good wood?" you may want to use some comparisons of different woods, demonstrated by showing some specimens, and explain where some woods work better than others. After you have completed this process for each idea, the body of your speech is clearly organized. As you can see, whether using the inductive or deductive approach to synthesis, the overriding object is to discover a way of structuring your message that will provide the clearest transactional bond between your central idea and your audience.

GENERAL PRINCIPLES

In earlier chapters we have referred several times to *focus* in your preparation. Focus can be achieved by the application of three principles of organization, which you may recall from an English composition class—unity, coherence, and emphasis—as well as principles for the selection and use of supporting materials.

Unity

Unity is the characteristic of having everything in your message relate to the other parts of the message. Unity is based primarily on a clear, specific purpose and central idea. It results in a speech that marches, not meanders, toward a conclusion. Consider the difference between the following two approaches to a speech on first aid.

Speech I: Central Idea: The elements of first aid.
    Body
 I. The history of first aid
  A. The Crusades
  B. Clara Barton
 II. The need for first aid
  A. Statistics on untimely deaths
  B. Examples
 III. Meeting emergencies
  A. Stopping bleeding
  B. Get them breathing again
 IV. Shock—the big killer
  A. Statistics on shock
  B. Explain what shock is
 V. Setting broken bones
  A. Arms
  B. Legs
  C. Neck
 VI. Transporting the patient to the hospital

Speech II: Central Idea: Keep the patient alive.
    Body
 I. Stop the bleeding
  A. Identify pressure points
   1. Arms
    a. Show visual
   2. Legs
    a. Show visual
   3. Neck
    a. Show visual
  B. Demonstrate the technique for applying pressure
   1. Manually
   2. Tourniquets
 II. Restore breathing
  A. Describe the symptoms
  B. Demonstrate mouth-to-mouth resuscitation
  C. Demonstrate the Heimlich Maneuver

III. Treat for shock
    A. Shock occurs when blood leaves the head and limbs and collects in the viscera
        1. Explain symptoms
        2. Show pictures of people in shock
    B. Explain treatment for shock
        1. Elevate the feet
            a. Story of Mrs. Jones
            b. Show visual
        2. Keep the patient warm
            a. Demonstrate on a listener
            b. Show visual

As you compare these two organizational approaches, you will see that the first one is "a little speech" on first aid. It is a self-centered attempt to fill time. It attempts to do too much and so accomplishes nothing; it rambles. The second approach has unity, based on the need of listeners to know how to keep patients alive. It all relates to the purpose. It is detailed enough to accomplish the purpose. It transacts.

Coherence

Coherence in organization has to do with the way the various ideas and materials in the message relate to one another and to the audience. A coherent message hangs together; relationships are clear. In the first of the outlines above, the discussion of shock doesn't seem to relate to the other "emergencies," and the history doesn't seem to relate to anything. In the second message, the main ideas are unrelated to each other, but they all relate beautifully to the central idea. In III, "treating for shock," the explanation that blood rushes to the stomach and away from the head makes sense out of the treatment of elevating the legs. Each idea and its supporting materials have an integral part to play in the total explanation.

Emphasis

Emphasis is the third principle of organization. It seems obvious to say you must emphasize the most important points, but it is not so easily accomplished. Furthermore, what is important depends on the specific purpose of the transaction. For instance, we pointed out in Chapter 3 that you may have a choice of conceptual patterns (chronological, space, or problem-solution) from which to choose. Your choice has a great bearing on the ideas that receive emphasis. I teach two courses dealing with great historical speeches and debates. In one, my transactional purpose is to emphasize the issues and problems that have been argued over the years. In this class the major units are:

I. People's relationship to government
II. Racial and sexual discrimination
III. Religion
IV. War and peace

Within each unit I treat the debates in roughly historical order, but the emphasis is on the issues. In the other class, I want students to learn the historical development of both the issues and the styles of public discourse. In this course the units are chronological:

I. Colonial Period
II. Revolutionary Period
III. Constitutional Development
IV. Pre–Civil War
V. Civil War
VI. Post–Civil War and later

As I evaluate the outlines of student speakers, one of the most frequent problems I see is that the key points are buried in some third-order, subordinate position and need to be pulled out and elevated to the status of a main idea for proper emphasis.

Selection and Use of Supporting Materials

Not only is the structure of your ideas governed by guiding principles, but so are your selection and use of supporting materials. We will discuss (1) the Iceberg, (2) the Lasso, and (3) the Matrixing Principles.

Iceberg Principle. It is well known that the visible part of an iceberg represents but a small fraction of its total mass. Similarly, the content of your speech should represent only a small fraction of the mass of material you have assembled through experience and research. Your selection of specific examples, statistics, quotations, and so on should be governed by your assessment of what materials are required to share an idea with the *particular* audience you are addressing. You should have plenty of material in reserve, in the event the material you select does not accomplish the transaction. In this case, you can draw on the reserve until shared meaning is achieved. Although you may feel overprepared by doing this, it is a comforting feeling to know that you are ready for almost any unexpected response as the speaking transaction progresses.

Lasso Principle. Any fan of Western movies or rodeos is familiar with the way a cowboy ropes a calf by the skillful use of a lasso. Periodically, we even see a television commercial in which people lasso other people. Your forms of support can be used like lassos. A striking statistic can get a majority of the audience to identify your idea. A specific example may lasso a few more, and an apt quotation even more. Some are bound to get away, but the more varied lassos you have, the better your chance of transacting with most of your listeners.

Matrixing Principle. Every public communicator faces a frustrating problem. By the time you begin to speak you have extensive experience with your topic and have researched it thoroughly. If every member of your audience knew what you know about the topic, identification would already be achieved and the speech would be unnecessary. But how do you share all of your information with your listeners in the short five minutes or an hour that you might have for your speech?

Your first step is to establish priorities according to the *needs of your listeners*. Usually you should still have more material than you can share in the time available. Let this material represent a matrix, with the columns representing numerous detailed instances and the rows representing statistics or quotations that summarize those specifics. While it might take you days to describe the total matrix, you can quickly and accurately represent the content of the material to your listeners by giving a specific, concrete example in combination with a summarizing statistic or quotation. The concrete example communicates the vertical dimension of the matrix (the depth), while the statistic or quotation represents the horizontal dimension of the matrix (the breadth of the issue). If additional time is available, a second or third example can add more depth, and both statistics and quotations can be used for greater breadth. In any case, you can accurately and interestingly represent huge amounts of data by utilizing the Matrixing Principle.

INTRODUCTIONS: TRANSACTIONAL FUNCTIONS

Introductions to speeches can be problematic. Not knowing quite how to begin, some speakers start right off with their first main idea. Others clutter the opening of their messages with irrelevant history or dull and obvious definitions of terms.

As is the case with so many principles of public speaking, the overriding function of the introduction is deceptively simple: *to get the audience to listen to the rest of your message.* Viewed from a more traditional, transmissional perspective, instructors have suggested steps to follow in the introduction, or have urged that the introduction constitute some percent of the total time of the speech. From a transactional perspective, we recognize that the introduction takes as long as necessary to get the audience to listen, from zero to perhaps as much as half of the total time. Rather than steps to be followed, transactionally we prefer to think of *functions* to be accomplished in transaction with listeners. I will discuss the functions of (1) attention, (2) motivation, (3) accreditation, and (4) orientation. When these functions are accomplished, your audience will be ready to listen to the body of your speech.

Attention

While attention must be maintained throughout the entire talk, it must be either inherent in the situation or captured in the introduction. Viewed transactionally, it is possible that a well-known or controversial speaker would have the intense attention of the audience, making a "dramatic attention" step superfluous. Such was the case when Sonia Johnson, president of the Mormons for E.R.A., addressed an overflow crowd at Idaho State University in the autumn of 1980. For most of us, however, some means of gaining attention is necessary.

It is common for well-meaning but inexperienced speakers to want to use a gimmick such as a noisemaker, irrelevant joke, or stunt to gain attention. I discourage this. It is better to begin with a relevant but striking story, statistic, or quotation—one of those forms of support you have researched. You should select one that bears more on your central idea than on a particular main or subordinate idea.

Motivation

A second function of the introduction is that of motivating your listeners to *need* to listen to your message. This appeal to motivation usually takes two forms. The first is to point out why your topic is *significant* to your listeners. Earlier I recommended that you select topics significant to your listeners and limit them according to the *needs* of listeners. In the introduction, all you must do, then, is to reinforce the significance and need. In the introduction of his "Call to Arms," Patrick Henry reminded his listeners that

> This is no time for ceremony. The question before the House is one of awful moment to this country. For my own part I consider it as nothing less than a question of freedom or slavery....[1]

Another effective way of achieving motivation is to arouse *curiosity* about your topic in the introduction: "Have you ever wondered how a sky diver hits a small target from 10,000 feet?" Or, "Perhaps you are curious why a speck in your eye causes so much irritation and contact lenses do not." Both could be effective motivation devices for talks on these topics.

Accreditation

In order for people to want to listen to what you have to say, they must consider you to be a source worth listening to. We will discuss the question of source credibility more fully in Chapter 8. Here we will emphasize establishing your *qualifications* and *common ground* with your listeners.

Your qualifications for speaking on your topic can be established in several ways. First, if you have selected a topic you know and care about and you have researched it extensively, you will have the necessary qualifications. Most speakers are introduced by someone who highlights the salient qualifications, if they are not already known. If not introduced, you may allude briefly to your experience with the topic. Your qualifications can be established or ruined nonverbally as well. Some time ago some teaching assistants were complaining that their students wouldn't take their word for anything, challenged grading practices, and generally denied their authority as teachers. At the time, the teaching assistants dressed informally in blue jeans, sat on the table while lecturing, and generally treated the students as equals. I suggested that for the first week or two of the quarter they dress, groom, and conduct themselves more formally until they had established themselves as the teacher figure in that class. The problem did not recur.

The other aspect of your accreditation as a speaker is the *common ground* you establish with listeners. I will be referring to your identification with listeners throughout this book. Your initial identification must be established in the introduction, before the listeners will give full consideration to your message. A politician's statement that "I was a farm boy myself" is perhaps too obvious, but somehow you must establish your common ground with listeners. This can be done by identifying with known beliefs, attitudes, or values, on the one hand, or shared experiences, understandings, or friendships, on the other. In any case, listeners are likely to give your message a more receptive hearing if you have accredited yourself through your qualifications and common ground with them.

Orientation

Have you ever attempted to walk or drive in a dense fog only to become disoriented and perhaps end up going (quite literally) in circles? A general idea of where you are and where you're headed helps you not only to arrive more expeditiously, but also to get back on course if you become lost. So it is with listeners. They must be given a general orientation of where you are going in order to process the message effectively. Orientation can take several forms, depending on the type of transaction. The first is a general orientation to your topic. Listeners need to know whether you are talking about money management, personal development, or national defense. Sometimes the person who introduces you will mention this, but usually all the audience knows is the title of your talk, which may or may not reveal your topic. Which of the foregoing topics would a speech entitled "Acres of Diamonds" cover? Usually you can reveal your general topic, without saying too much about it, by using a striking example, statistic, or quotation, as I suggested earlier. Another way of orienting your listeners, however, is to provide an *overview* of the main ideas. You might say, "The value of a diamond is determined by the clarity, the cut, and the karat. Now let's look at clarity." You can also overview by actually stating your central idea. You must be cautious about being too specific in your overview with antagonistic audiences, however, or they may react by closing their minds and destroying the transaction before it begins.

In rare cases, orientation involves the definition of a key term such as *gun abuse* in a speech on gun control, or *human life* in a speech on abortion. In most cases, however, people either have a pretty good idea of the meaning, or (as in the examples above) the meaning is so significant to the topic that your definition may require development as a main idea in the body of the speech.

We have seen, then, that attention, motivation, accreditation, and orientation represent functions that may be inherent in the speaking situation, but if they are not they must be accomplished in the introduction before you can get a full hearing from your audience.

CONCLUSIONS: TRANSACTIONAL FUNCTIONS

As in the case of introductions, conclusions of speeches have important functions that must be accomplished before your speaking transaction can reach an optimum close. But how often have you heard a speaker either stop abruptly, leaving the audience wondering if that was it, or conclude the message several times while losing the impact of the right moment in the process? We will examine the functions of (1) reorientation, (2) remotivation, and (3) termination.

Reorientation

Recall that we said an overview of the direction of the message in the introduction helps the listeners maintain their bearings during the speech. Even more important is the assurance that they are clear about your central idea by the end of the speech. Reorientation usually takes two forms. The first is a summary of your main ideas. A person speaking against the deployment of a new weapons system might conclude, "We have seen that there is no need for this system; that it will be far too complex to work effectively; and that the extreme cost will result in damage to our economy, which will far outweigh any possible military advantage."

A second and complementary way of reorienting your audience is to state your central idea clearly. Obviously, if they don't have it by the end of the speech they never will, so you must state it as clearly and forcefully as possible in the conclusion.

Remotivation

As I suggested earlier, attention and motivation need to be captured in the introduction and maintained throughout the entire speech. We know from experience, however, that attention and interest do not remain constant, but fluctuate widely throughout all but the most intense public speaking transactions. But if ever you want the audience attentive and motivated, it is at the conclusion of your message. You should therefore save some of your most motivating material for the conclusion, in order to recapture attention and bring your message to a motivational climax. Most of the great speakers of history, including those quoted in this book, have been able to phrase their motivating appeals in their own words. You may be able to do this too. More commonly, however, you will want to save your most motivating story, statistic, or quotation for the conclusion. This enables you more easily and naturally to achieve motivation while maintaining your own natural and sincere style.

Termination

The final function of the conclusion is termination. It is not completely inappropriate to simply say thank you, but this should not be necessary in order to get the point across that you are finished. In persuasive speeches the forms of support you use to accomplish the remotivation function may provide a clear, climactic ending to your speech. In informative speeches the summary and central idea may do the same. In other instances, however, a concluding statement or final appeal is in order. Salespeople are fond of saying, "You never get the order if you don't ask for it." In persuasive speeches your final appeal is a way of getting your speech stopped and asking for the business at the same time. In his inaugural address, John F. Kennedy terminated with the following simple appeal:

> With a good conscience our only sure reward, with history the final judge of our deeds, let us go forth to lead the land we love, asking His blessing and His help, but knowing that here on earth God's work must truly be our own.[2]

In the conclusion to his speech on the fall of France during World War II, Winston Churchill was somewhat more dramatic:

> Let us therefore brace ourselves to our duty and so bear ourselves that if the British Commonwealth and Empire lasts for a thousand years men will still say, 'This was their finest hour.'[3]

These functions need not necessarily be accomplished in a step-by-step order, nor even separately. All may be accomplished by an appropriate summary combined with a striking form of support that illustrates the central idea. While there are a wide variety of techniques for accomplishing reorientation, remotivation, and termination, your speech will probably not be as effective if you do not take careful cognizance of these transactional functions.

Note how Winston Churchill skillfully combines these functions in the conclusion of his speech on Dunkirk:

At any rate, that is what we are going to try to do. That is the resolve of His Majesty's Government, every man of them. That is the will of Parliament and the nation. The British Empire and the French Republic, linked together in their cause and their need, will defend to the death their native soils, aiding each other like good comrades to the utmost of their strength, even though a large tract of Europe and many old and famous States have fallen or may fall into the grip of the Gestapo and all the odious apparatus of Nazi rule.

We shall not flag nor fail. We shall go on to the end. We shall fight in France and on the seas and oceans; we shall fight with growing confidence and growing strength in the air.

We shall defend our island whatever the cost may be; we shall fight on beaches, landing grounds, in fields, in streets, and on the hills. We shall never surrender and even if, which I do not for the moment believe, this island or a large part of it were subjugated and starving, then our empire beyond the seas, armed and guarded by the British Fleet, will carry on the struggle until in God's good time the New World, with all its power and might, set forth to the liberation and rescue of the Old.[4]

TECHNIQUES OF ORGANIZATION

Now that we have examined the principles of organization, let us look at some specific techniques for structuring your message. I will discuss (1) outlining and (2) charting.

Outlining

At one time we could assume that everyone learned the basic skill of outlining in their English composition classes in the public schools. No doubt some students still do, but I recently had a college class in argumentation where I assigned an outline of some arguments, without much explanation of outlines, and the majority of the class were hopelessly lost—not on the content, but on what is meant by an *outline*.

Before discussing some recommended principles of outlining, let me dispel some common misconceptions of the concept. First, it is not a string of prose in paragraphs that are indented now and then. True, outlines use indentation, but in a very special way. Second, an outline is not a series of key words, memory devices, or acronyms. True, an outline can be a very useful memory device and a source of key words which may be used as notes when you speak, but in themselves those do not constitute a complete outline.

In essence, an *outline* is a succinct, systematic picture or blueprint of your *conceptualization* or thought processes related to your topic. It is a clear, thorough representation of your ideas, the data supporting those ideas, and the intricate *relationships* among those ideas and supporting materials. Every symbol, every indentation, and every punctuation mark represent a conscious choice that helps to clarify your own thinking and subsequently the thinking of your listeners with regard to your central idea.

Furthermore, outlining is a dynamic process. Once you have gathered many of your materials, analyzed the situation and topic, and presumably have all of the ideas and materials you would ever need for your speech, you will still find that the process of outlining reveals gaps or weaknesses in your ideas and supports which will require further research and analysis as you proceed.

Mechanics of outlining. With this brief overview of outlining, let us proceed to the practical mechanics of preparing an outline that clearly represents your conceptualization of the topic.

Your first concern is with the selection of *symbols*. Although the primary consideration is that you use your symbol system *consistently*, the following symbol system has received widespread acceptance and is used extensively.

I.
II.
   A.
   B.
      1.
      2.
         a.
         b.
            (1)
            (2)
               (a)
               (b)

A second consideration is *indentation*, which represents the *relationships* among the ideas and supporting materials in your speech. These relationships are basically ones of coordination and subordination. *Coordination* means that the ideas are of comparable weight, either in magnitude or importance, and deserve comparable if not equal emphasis in the outline. Coordination is represented in the outline as the same level of indentation. Hence, in the following model ideas *I* and *II* are coordinate; *A* and *B* are coordinate with each other, but not with *I* and *II*:

I.
   A.
   B.
II.

Subordination means that an idea or form of support "comes under" and supports the idea immediately superior to it in your symbol system. In the model above *A* and *B* directly support *I*. While they may complement each other, they do not directly support each other.

You should carry the outline to the level of supporting material or data for every set of ideas. This means that outlines for lengthy speeches can become quite elaborate. Most classroom speeches, however, do not have outlines that go beyond the third level. Hence, an outline of the body of a fairly brief speech may look something like this:

    Body
I. Main idea
  A. Subordinate idea
    1. Example
    2. Statistic
    3. Etc.
  B. Subordinate idea
    1. Quotation
    2. Story
II. Main idea
  A. Example
  B. Statistic
  C. Quotation
  D. Etc.
III. Main idea
  A. Subordinate idea
    1. Statistic
    2. Quotation
  B. Subordinate idea
    1. Example
    2. Etc.

You may have heard of a "rule" of outlining that says "never a *I* without a *II*." I am not partial to rules, but they usually reveal some underlying principle that is very useful in clarifying not only your thinking, but that of your audience. Only one symbol at a given level of indentation can be a signal of two difficulties. The first is that a crucial idea is missing. It stands to reason that you cannot divide an idea into one part. Hence, an *A* without a *B* may indicate that you have overlooked an idea. This sign of faulty conceptualization is not foolproof, however. You may have both an *A* and a *B*, but you will need to check your outline and think carefully about the possibility of a missing *C* or *D* as well.

The other potential difficulty of having an *A* without a *B* is that idea *A* may be only a restatement of the idea (*I* or *II*) that *A* is supposed to support. While less serious than a missing idea, this unwitting redundancy is also a sign of unclear analysis and should be eliminated by more clearly stating the idea your lone *A* is supposed to support.

Principles of outlining. In addition to the mechanics, good outlining is guided by principles for phrasing your ideas.

The first such principle is that the number of ideas, at any level of coordination (that is, using the same symbols), should be few. Of course, we have just seen that you need at least two, but if you go beyond five you should examine the ideas to see if all are absolutely crucial. Some might be eliminated or combined into a broader concept. Psychologists have demonstrated what you have probably learned from experience: Several objects, instances, or ideas are easier to comprehend and remember if they are clustered into meaningful groups. In order to demonstrate the clarity of your own comprehension of the topic, aid in remembering what you are going to talk about, and facilitate the comprehension and memory of your listeners, keep the number of ideas or groups of ideas at a given level in your outline to a minimum.

Finally, the issue of the phrasing of each idea is quite important. Should you use key words, phrases, or complete sentences in your outline? I recommend *complete but succinct sentences* at the beginning. We discussed earlier that the overriding purpose for the outline is to represent as clearly and succinctly as possible the conceptualization of your *ideas*. An idea cannot be expressed in less than a sentence. If you had a section labeled "I. Need." in your outline, what would you mean? "There is a desperate need for my solution"? "There is no need"? "The need has been ignored"? "The need has been exaggerated"? Until you phrase your idea in a sentence, your idea has not been fully clarified in your own mind and cannot be shared with listeners. Some students argue that complete sentences in outlines are excessively time consuming. On the contrary, if your thinking is already clear, it will take only a few minutes to write it out. If, on the other hand, it takes considerable time to prepare a complete sentence outline, it is concrete evidence of the necessity of doing it. In fact, I would argue that the amount of time it takes (over, say, ten minutes) represents the degree to which the process was necessary. The second outline on first aid (p. 72) is a good example of an outline for a speech to inform. The following is an example of an outline for a more complex speech to persuade:

TITLE: YANQUI GO HOME!

Specific Purpose: To have my audience believe that the U.S. is presenting itself poorly in Latin America.

Central Idea: We in the U.S. have a talent for offending our Latin American neighbors.

Body

Main point	**I.** Huge American owned-and-operated businesses provide sources of bitter discontent.
Subpoint	**A.** Their very largeness is resented.
Example	**1.** Honduras—United Fruit—"The Octopus."
Subpoint	**B.** The companies' operational policies do not revolve around the best interests of the natives.
Subpoint	**1.** Natives are not encouraged to own stock.
	a. evidence

Subpoint	**2.** Top executives are seldom Latins.
Examples	**a.** United Fruit—local managers as well as most department heads are Americans.
	b. Recent token breakthrough—grads of Zamorano—company-endowed school
Subpoint	**C.** The American personnel live completely apart from the native population.
	1. The children go to English schools.
	2. Employees and their families seldom learn to speak the native language.
	3. There is virtually no social contact.
Example	**a.** description of Tegucigalpa—company town
Main point	**II.** A majority of American diplomats and other State Department officials are poorly equipped to do their jobs.
Subpoint	**A.** Few have a real knowledge of or interest in the people.
Example	**1.** Exception—Mexico—shortly transferred
Subpoint	**B.** The official attitude is one of detachment.
Contrast	**1.** Russian emissaries meet the real people, do not confine themselves to lofty diplomatic circles.
Data	**2.** Example
Subpoint	**C.** The university student, a powerful force in Latin American politics, is virtually ignored by U.S. diplomats.
Data	**1.** Quote Caracas student.
	2. Example of 1959 Honduran revolution
Subpoint	**D.** Even an observance of common courtesy is absent.
	1. Example of cocktail party
Main point	**III.** The average American tourist does everything possible to intensify the already-low esteem in which Latin Americans regard us.
Subpoint	**A.** The bulk of American tourists are badly informed.
	1. They know little of Latin American history, geography, politics, or economics.
	a. data
	2. They speak Spanish poorly or not at all.
	a. data
Subpoint	**B.** They show lack of courtesy and common regard for their hosts.
Example	**1.** Tourist at Independence parade
Example	**2.** Unnecessary opulence story
Subpoint	**C.** They show no interest in their neighbors as people.
Example	**1.** Mr. John Tourist's trip through Mexico

Charting

Some people hate to outline. Try as they may, they find the mechanics more of a hindrance than a help. If you find yourself hung up with outlining, you may want to consider an alternative method for systematizing your conceptualization, which I call *charting*. While outlining represents a general-to-specific approach to organization, charting works from the specific to the general.

To begin a rough draft of your chart, turn a piece of paper (the bigger the better) sideways and scribe a straight line horizontally through the middle. Below this line divide the paper into about a dozen columns. Above the dividing line draw a series of horizontal lines to the top of the paper. Your empty chart will look basically like this:

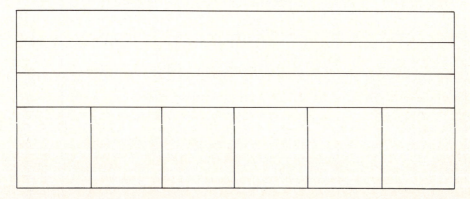

Now, skipping the first and last column, place your forms of support (examples, statistics, quotations, stories) in the columns, categorizing or "clumping" them as you go. Ask yourself "What are these examples of?" or "What do they prove?" Supports that clarify or prove the same things go in the same column. As you thus cluster your concrete materials, you may need to do some shifting around, as there is usually more than one scheme by which you can categorize the materials. When your supports are all listed below the dividing line, examine the column and decide what name characterizes the category or what idea is proven. Write this category or idea in the first space above the column it summarizes. Do this for all of the columns. Now look at the column topics and see if these can be clustered. Do two or more columns clarify or support a broader idea? If so, extend the line separating these columns from the others upward through the next row and label that cluster of columns. Continue this process until you can no longer cluster the clusters. Place the materials you want for your introduction in the first column and for your conclusion in the last column. Write your specific purpose and central idea at the top of the chart. Now the rough draft of your chart is complete.

This process sounds quick and simple, but do not be deceived. As your thinking clarifies you may switch materials from one column to another, relabel categories, and so on. You may find that you have parts of two or more clustering schemes resulting in clear categories that don't rationally relate to one another—the proverbial apples and

Specific Purpose: To have the audience understand the principles of first aid that are essential when ushering at a public meeting.

Central Idea: Keep the patient alive

Introduction	Stop the bleeding					Restore breathing			Treat for shock			Conclusion
	Pressure points			Applying pressure		Diagnosis	Treatments		Diagnose shock	Treatment for shock		
	Arms	Legs	Neck	Manual	Tourniquets		Mouth-to-mouth resuscitation	Heimlich maneuver		Elevate feet	Keep patient warm	
	Visual	Visual	Visual	Demo	Demo	a. Describe choking victim b. Visual	Demo procedure	Demo procedure	a. Explain symptoms b. Show pictures	a. Story b. Visual	a. Demo b. Visual	a. Summary b. Central idea c. Final statement

FIGURE 4–1
Chart of speech on first aid

oranges. Even when your rough draft is complete you should examine it carefully for misplaced ideas and materials in addition to seeing if the total scheme makes sense. Figure 4−1 is an example of a complete chart for the speech on first aid.

SUMMARY

In this chapter we have seen that you can approach organization either deductively or inductively. We discussed the importance of unity, coherence, and emphasis to the organization of your message.

Principles for the selection and use of supporting materials include the Iceberg Principle, the Lasso Principle, and the Matrixing Principle.

We then discussed organizing the introduction and the conclusion to fulfill functions rather than steps. The functions of the introduction are attention, motivation, accreditation, and orientation. The functions of the conclusion are reorientation, remotivation, and termination.

Outlining is a thorough blueprint of the conceptualization underlying your speech. Mechanics of outlining include the selection of a consistent symbol system and the accurate representation of relationships through proper coordination and subordination of symbols, and making sure more than one idea supports another idea.

Principles of outlining include developing as few ideas as possible at a given level of coordination, and expressing the ideas in complete sentences. Charting is an alternative way of conceptualizing your ideas.

"Only One Earth"

Barbara Ward

Are we present at one of those turning points when the human race begins to see itself and its concerns from a new angle of vision and, as a result, finds new openings for action, for courage, and for hope?

Condensed from ONLY ONE EARTH, by Barbara Ward and Rene Dubos, by permission of W.W. Norton & Company, Inc. and Andre Deutsch Ltd. Copyright © 1972 by Report on the Human Environment, Inc.

Over two millennia ago, intellectual ferment accompanied the end of China's feudal wars and the establishment of the first great centralized Han dynasty. In more recent history people had almost to stand on their heads to realize the sun did not go 'round the earth, but the reverse. This "Copernican Revolution" is the archetype of fundamental change by which people learn to rethink, totally, their place in the scheme of things.

Our own epoch is, I believe, such an age again. We belong to the generation that has used radio telescopes to uncover 100,000 million other suns. We belong to the generation that has brought nuclear energy to earth. Computers have made possible the simulation, acceleration, and forward projection of infinitely complicated human activities; instantaneous worldwide and interplanetary visible and audible communication has opened new horizons.

Above all, we are the generation to see through the eyes of the astronauts the astonishing "earthrise" of our small and beautiful planet above the barren horizons of the moon. Indeed, this generation would be some kind of psychological monstrosity if this were not an age of intense, passionate, committed debate and search.

So vast is the scale of change through which we live that there must be an equally vast range of competitors for first place as agents of upheaval. I want to suggest three areas in which, it seems to me, the concepts being virtually forced upon us offer a startling break from past patterns of thought and accepted wisdom.

A PLANET UNFIT FOR LIFE

The first is the possibility of making the planet unfit for life. Hitherto, people have known that they could do local damage. They could farm carelessly and lose top soil or deforest or overgraze or mine out a mineral. They also contrived to live through major natural disasters—earthquakes, tornadoes, ice ages. But nobody thought that the planet itself could be at risk.

Today our experts know something new. They know that air, soil, and water form a totally interdependent worldwide system or biosphere sustaining all life, transmitting all energy and, in spite of its rugged powers of survival, full of immensely delicate and vulnerable mechanisms, leaves, bacteria, plankton, catalysts, levels of dissolved oxygen, thermal balances—which alone permit the sun's searing energies to be transmuted and life to carry on.

Our experts also tell us what we do not know. Given our suddenly and vastly increasing numbers, our enormous rise in the use of energy, including nuclear energy, and our fabulous mastery of molecular chemistry, we impinge on the fine balances and mechanisms of the total system in ways and with consequences that we too often are in no position to judge.

For example, our traditional vision of the oceans is that they are boundless. But we have no idea of their capacity to absorb—as they ultimately must—virtually all the planet's wastes. In the last two or three decades, to give only one instance, a high percentage of the long-lived chlorinated hydrocarbons—including DDT—appears to have been absorbed into natural "sinks" in the biosphere. Recent sample taking suggests an unexpectedly high dosage appearing in the oceans.

Does this mean that natural storage systems are filling up? Will further effluents reinforce irreversible damage to marine species known to be susceptible to such substances as DDT? Is this part of a deeper risk of deterioration from a steadily widening range of chemical wastes? We do not know. Rivers and lakes teach us that there are limits to water's self-cleansing properties. Ultimately the oceans are one vast cistern with no outlet. This image is a safer one, perhaps, than that of infinite and "moving waters at their priestlike task of pure ablution round earth's human shores."

ECONOMIC GROWTH: NOT THE SOLUTION

This concept of newly understood limits is relevant to the second reversal of earlier concepts whose implications I would judge to be most revolutionary for the present age. For over a century now, and with increasing enthusiasm in the last twenty-five years, we have seen in economic growth, measured by the satisfaction of both ordinary and induced material needs, a prime aim of national policy and a powerful solvent of social conflict. Inside the nation, as output and incomes rise, the flow of goods will be great enough to reward effort and enterprise and provide on an upward scale for the needs of the mass of the people. In the world economy, international trade and investment will pull the developing peoples up in the wake of the already developed nations.

But this implicit assumption of unending expansion has two self-reinforcing flaws. Even within the wealthiest states, even with all the transfers of resources from richer to poorer citizens secured by tax and welfare and social insurance, "trickle down" economics do not ensure the ending of poverty at the base of society. The lowest 20 percent can have as little as 5 percent of national income; the top 20 percent as much as 40.

In the world at large, where no systematic social transfers occur, the richer states are pulling away from the less developed ones. Even if $10,000 a year per capita is a reasonable likelihood for developed societies by the year 2000, for two thirds of mankind, $400 a year looks like the utmost reach of optimism. For perhaps a third, malnutrition, illiteracy, shanty-town dwelling and unemployment—in other words, the worst of all human environments—could be the most likely fate.

But now we must add another constraint. Even if we assume unlimited resources with which to develop, the development is, as we have seen, grossly uneven. But suppose there are indeed strict physical "limits to growth"? Suppose that these delicate mechanisms and balances in the biosphere that make life possible cannot sustain 10 billion people all aiming to produce and consume and discard and pollute according to present developed standards?

Here, admittedly, the range of debate is very wide. Some experts believe that 20 billion people can live at America's present standards simply on the products of atomic energy, water and the minerals in common rock. Others postulate irretrievable damage in terms of exhausted resources, thermal pollution, and environmental disruption if even half that number secure the current standards of the rich. We are at the beginning of this debate. But one point is surely clear. There are limits. The biosphere is not infinite. Populations must become stable. So must the demands they make.

But in that case, whose upward aspirations must first be checked? Given finite resources, we cannot evade this basic social issue. Where are the restraints to be put? What is to be reduced, the luxuries of the rich or the necessities of the poor? What are the priorities—a decent human environment for the whole human species or riches for some and squalor for the majority? We can slide over this fundamental issue of environmental quality only if "trickle down" economics work within a context of unlimited resources. Neither assumption is correct. So, as nations, as a planet, we are compelled to confront the fundamental issues of choice and justice.

NATIONS ACTING TOGETHER TO AVERT DISASTER

But at this point we encounter a third basic challenge to our habits of thinking. Our effective instruments of judgment, decision, and action are separate national governments. The nations give our planet its color, its variety, its richness of life and experience. For those to whom full nationhood has come only in the last quarter of a century, it expresses the essence of their being and their hopes. None of this can be doubted. Yet it is also true that the cumulative effect of the separate actions of separate sovereign governments can, over time, injure the basic national needs of all of them.

If our air and oceans can stand only so much strain before they lose their capacity for self-purification, it will help no government to say that others were responsible. The most flagrant case is clearly the risk of nuclear conflict and planetary nuclear pollution. We may rejoice that a number of intergovernmental agreements now limit atomic testing in the air, keep nuclear weapons from the seabed, outer space, and Antarctica. We can welcome, too, the agreements between the United States and the Soviet Union to check the arms race and hope that such agreements may signal the beginning of a joint effort to wind it down.

But we could collectively pollute the planet not "with a bang but a whimper"—by the small, steady accumulation of long-lasting poisons and pesticides, of chemicals and tailings, of eroded soil and detritus—and reach, almost inadvertently, a creeping planetary disaster to which all have separately made their cumulative contribution. No single nation can avert this risk as numbers and activities rise. Its control will be achieved by nations acting together—or not at all.

This raises by another route the issue of planetary justice—which equally cannot be solved by nations acting alone. How do we ensure that the need to check pollution does not become an inhibition on the desperate need of two thirds of humanity for development? This is an area about which we do not know too much. It is certainly not clear that all non-pollutive technologies are more expensive. It is also possible that in opting straight away for pollution control, developing states could take full advantage of the greatest asset of late comers—to learn from other peoples' mistakes. Equally it is possible that to control wastes and effluents at an early stage of modernization would greatly add to costs and strains.

Should poorer countries then accept added costs for development or even their own modernization because developed nations have already, as it were, pre-empted so much of the biosphere's costless capacities for self-cleansing? We do not know the answers. But we do know that the relentless pursuit of separate national interest by rich and poor alike can, in a totally interdependent biosphere, produce global disasters of irreversible environmental damage.

A DESPERATE WRENCH FROM ACCEPTED THINKING

There are then, I suggest, three vital ways in which the reality we are beginning to perceive diverges from our habitual thinking. We normally consider Nature as a whole, the entire biosphere, to be safe from man, even if we can chip away at little bits of it. We have been taught to believe, with increasing intensity in recent decades, that we can modernize all our economies and settle most issues of distribution by our unlimited command of rising energy, technology, and resources. And by our millennial history we have been taught to expect final decision to be taken by separate sovereign states. It requires a desperate wrench from accepted thinking, a profound leap, a Copernican leap of the imagination, to begin to see that in stark physical and scientific reality none of these presuppositions are any longer true. We can damage the entire biosphere. Resources are not unlimited. States acting separately can produce planetary disaster.

We all know enough of history to realize how uncertain it is whether this change in the direction of our thinking will be made in time. Custom and habit hold us to the traditional themes. The sheer momentum of our present activities could well be enough to drive us on for another four or five decades on our present path. This is a possible "scenario." Realists might even call it the most likely one. But I want to give three reasons why I feel it is legitimate to entertain, shall we say, a modest hope?

The first is the United Nations Conference on the Human Environment in Stockholm. Once environmental concern moves nearer to the center of the nations' attention, I do not doubt that its fuller implications will inevitably unfold. Its whole message is that separate drives, ambitions, and policies have to be made compatible with the continuing common life of our single, shared planetary system.

My second reason is the scientific imperative. We can cheat on morals. We can cheat on politics. We can deceive ourselves with dreams and myths. But there is no monkeying about with DNA or photosynthesis or eutrophication or nuclear fusion or the impact on all living things of excessive radiation—from the sun or the hydrogen bomb.

To act without rapacity, to use knowledge with wisdom, to respect interdependence, to operate without hubris and greed are not simply moral imperatives. They are an accurate scientific description of the means of survival. This compelling force of fact may, I think, control our separatist ambitions before they have overturned our planetary life.

But man does not live by fact alone.

Our human environment has within it our perpetual striving to make it humane as well. In the past, historians tell us, there have been profound revulsions against the aggression, pride, and rapacity of human systems. The great ethical systems of mankind—in India, in China, in the Middle East, from the benign wisdom of Confucius to the passionate social protest of the Hebrew prophets—all sought to express an underlying moral reality: we live by moderation, by compassion, by justice; we die by aggression, by pride, by rapacity, and greed.

Now in these latter days, the planet itself in its underlying physical reality repeats the witness of the sages and the prophets. Our collective greeds can degrade and destroy our basic sources of life in air and soil and water. Our collective injustice can continue to create an intolerable imbalance between rich and poor. Envy and fear can unleash the nuclear holocaust. At last, in this age of ultimate scientific discovery, our facts and our morals have come together to tell us how we must live.

ENDNOTES

1. Glenn Capp, *Famous Speeches in American History* (New York: Bobbs-Merrill, 1963), p. 28.
2. Capp, p. 239.
3. James McBath and Walter R. Fisher, *British Public Addresses: 1928–1960* (Boston: Houghton Mifflin, 1971), p. 513.
4. McBath and Fisher, p. 505.

5

Transactional Style and Language

In this chapter:
The transactional nature of language
Transactional language variables
Characteristics of style
Developing oral style
Summary
Henry W. Grady, "The New South"

In December of 1886 the Civil War was still fresh in the memories of surviving combatants as well as their families and friends. The conclusion of the retributive reconstruction era in the South and the election of Grover Cleveland, first Democratic president of the U.S., had further intensified existing animosities toward the South. On December 22, the New England Society of New York City invited a young journalist, Henry W. Grady, to address their annual convention on post-war developments in the South. A native of Athens, Georgia, and editor of the Atlanta Constitution, Grady proved to be an excellent choice. He had lived through the war in which his father died. He was exceptionally well informed, broad minded, and conciliatory. He wrote beautifully.

    The situation Grady faced was a difficult one, to say the least. The audience was approximately 300 of New England's most influential and conservative business and professional leaders, including J.P. Morgan, Elihu Root, Seth Thomas, and Russell Sage. The prominent minister T. Dewitt Talmage and General William T. Sherman preceded Grady on the program. Talmage eulogized the returning Union armies and

Sherman further aroused anti-Southern sentiments with remarks disparaging to the South. At the conclusion of Sherman's remarks, the audience rose and lustily sang "Marching Through Georgia." Grady was next on the program with a speech entitled "The New South."

Although Grady used a variety of strategies for identifying with his audience, his language was particularly powerful and adaptive. When people speak of *style* they usually refer to some intangible, general charismatic quality with which many believe speakers are "born." In public speaking, however, we have a much more specific meaning for the word *style*. In this book we use style synonymously with the word *language*. That is to say, style constitutes the words you use and the way in which you combine words into sentences and larger segments of thought in order to share meaning with your listeners. As we see in this chapter, language is particularly transactional in its nature. We discuss the nature of language, language variables, and the characteristics of style that enhance communicative transactions in public speaking contexts.

THE TRANSACTIONAL NATURE OF LANGUAGE

When you read the word *father*, what image comes to your mind? Every different person has a slightly different one. Some of you see a surgeon, some a fisherman; others see a photographer, teacher, or ex-convict. It is only remotely possible that someone might see all of these. Furthermore, some of you experience feelings of warmth or attraction while others may feel fear and rejection. The vast majority probably experience a complex and slightly different combination of all of these feelings. We could extend this illustration indefinitely. Indeed, one could never finish a complete description of the word *father* or any other object. However, this example does serve to illustrate the transactional nature of language.

Words are symbols. They are not objects or things, but serve as substitutes for people, places, things, processes, feelings, and other aspects of our unique experiences with the objective universe. Obviously, the symbol *father* is not the objective reality of a person, but only stands for or represents the real person.

The symbolic nature of language has some interesting implications for how we use words. People vary in the degree to which they forget that the word is not the thing it represents. Thus, when different people hear the word *Chicano* or *handicapped*, to a greater or lesser degree they have preconceived notions, called *stereotypes*, about the people these words are designed to represent. The degree to which people believe that the word *is* the thing, or says all there is to say about the referent, is the degree to which people ignore important individual differences and fail to respond to each event on the basis of what they observe. It is even common to see people ignore or deny what they observe because it doesn't fit the preconceived image they associate with the label. As a public speaker, this can be used to your advantage or become a gross disadvantage,

THE TRANSACTIONAL NATURE OF LANGUAGE

depending on your awareness of the situation and your ability to adapt your language to the images of your listeners.

A second implication of our "father" illustration is the question of the meaning of words or, more properly, the locus of meaning in a given circumstance. Most of us were raised to believe that words "have" meaning. Much of our early education is devoted to learning new vocabulary, such as *erg, evolution,* or *existentialism.* We have dictionaries that tell us what words "mean." And yet our "father" illustration clearly demonstrates that a word elicits different meanings from different people. Indeed, meanings are in actuality the images, pictures, or feelings that people have in their minds. Meanings are *in people, not in words.* Hence, the degree to which people share the same meaning for a word is the degree to which the communication transaction has occurred. Having said that, let us hasten to add that meanings are elicited in people by several aspects of a communicative situation.

First, words elicit and contribute to the meanings people generate and share. When I say the word *mountain* you do not generate an image of a flat field of wheat. Nor if I say the word *automobile* do you picture an apple. Everyone may image a slightly different

How would you describe the language and style a speaker would use in this setting?

automobile, but the degree to which everyone images a vehicle of transportation is the degree to which the word *automobile* places a constraint on the choice of meanings we are likely to generate. This agreed-on constraint, which we learn from our culture, constitutes the "meaning" of a word. Linguists call this *denotative* meaning. These agreed-on denotative meanings are what make words useful in the communication transaction.

As we have seen, a portion of the meaning in a situation is a function of the prior experiences of the people involved. Your unique experiences with your father contribute significantly to the image you have when someone says *father*. If you have never seen a snail darter, you won't picture one if a person says *fish*.

Another aspect of a communication event which contributes to the meaning attributed to words by people is the *context* spoken of earlier. Instead of the word *father*, I frequently ask students to define the word *chair*. Definitions rarely incorporate the leopard-skin bean bag in my study. But imagine the surprise I received when I unthinkingly asked a public speaking class at the Utah State Prison what came to mind when I said the word *chair!* And this only a few months after the execution of Gary Gilmore, not 100 yards from where I was standing!

Another variable which contributes to the meaning generated in a communication situation is the *intent* or purpose that communicators attribute to one another. Not as important perhaps in a public speech as in dyadic contexts, attribution of intent contributes to the meaning people share or fail to share. How often have you over-reacted or reacted negatively to something said by a person you despised, or whom you perceived was "out to get you," when you would have accepted the same statement from a person whom you perceived "meant well"? How often have you excused a friend's remark by saying they really didn't mean it the way it sounded?

A final characteristic that contributes to meaning is the *medium* used to transmit the message. A telegram or phone call in the middle of the night "means" urgency and usually trouble. In a public speaking situation the medium is relatively standard. However, as we shall see in Chapter 6, your nonverbal delivery can significantly affect the way in which your listeners interpret your words.

We have seen, then, that the extent to which words constrain people to share similar images is called *denotative* meaning. The degree to which the experiences of people, the context, the attribution of intent, and the media result in similarities and differences in the way communicators generate meanings is referred to as *connotative* meaning. These are represented in Figure 5-1. As communicators transact, they can share both denotative and connotative meanings.

TRANSACTIONAL LANGUAGE VARIABLES

The use of language can vary in several ways. These variations can either aid or hinder your transaction in public communication. Let us examine the language variables of (1) specificity, (2) intensity, (3) immediacy, and (4) diversity.

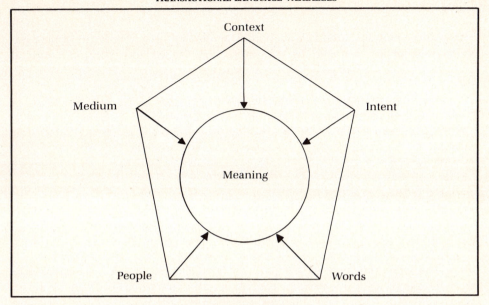

FIGURE 5–1
Sources of meaning

Specificity

Perhaps the most important language variable, especially to the public speaker, is specificity. *Specificity* is the degree to which your language is concrete, versus general, in nature. As we saw earlier, the symbolic nature of language makes it impossible to represent everything about an object or other referent. That is to say, language is an *abstraction* of reality, and hence can vary in its levels of abstraction. Consider the following words, which might refer to the same object, but vary in their levels of abstraction:

    plant
    tree
    evergreen
    redwood
    Sequoia semperviorn

Notice that the higher the level of abstraction, the more inclusive our language becomes. If, however, we are attempting to share specific meanings, generalities have the disadvantage of allowing listeners to generate significantly different meanings from our own. If we say *redwood* listeners may image different redwoods (if they have seen some, or even pictures), but if we say *evergreen* they may see something as different as a twisted juniper; and if we say *tree* they may see anything, from a desert joshua to a swamp mangrove.

In public communication specificity is generally desirable in order to achieve the instant intelligibility required by the transaction. Notice how Winston Churchill specifically states the war policy of Great Britain.

> You ask what is our policy? I say it is to wage war by land, sea, and air. War with all our might and with all the strength God has given us, and to wage war against a monstrous tyranny never surpassed in the dark and lamentable catalogue of human crime. That is our policy.
>
> You ask, what is our aim? I can answer in one word. It is victory. Victory at all costs—victory in spite of all terrors—victory, however long and hard the road may be, for without victory there is no survival.[1]

Intensity

Bowers has defined *intensity* as "the quality of language which indicates the degree to which the speaker's attitude toward a concept deviates from neutrality."[2] That is to say, language intensity is the relative blandness or vividness of both the words we select and the way we combine them for dramatic effect. Consider some examples of how language can vary in intensity. We could describe an obese person as significantly overweight (bland) or sloppy fat (intense). People who use cosmetics made of ambergris (bland) might be shocked to know that what they are spreading on their faces is really whale puke!

These examples illustrate an important transactional notion in the variation of language intensity in public speaking. Not only must a speaker be aware of the possibilities, but variation of intensity depends entirely on those aspects of the speaking situation we analyzed in Chapter 2. If you are dealing with an emotionally loaded topic in which your listeners may be highly ego-involved, then low-intensity language may be appropriate. If the audience is indifferent or complacent and you need to shock them in order to raise their awareness of the problem, then intense language may be necessary. In any case, it is your responsibility to be aware of the variable and apply it to the specific situation you discover during the analysis process.

Note the intensity of Robert G. Ingersoll as he attempts to convince his listeners that orthodox Christianity rewards the wrong people:

> Who are in heaven? How could there be much of a Heaven without the men I have mentioned—the great men that have endeavored to make the world grander—such men as Voltaire, such men as Diderot, such men as the Encyclopedists, such men as Hume, such men as Bruno, such men as Thomas Paine? If Christianity is true, that man who spent his life in breaking chains is now wearing the chains of God; that man who wished to break down the prison walls of tyranny is now in the prison of the most merciful Christ. It will not do. I can hardly express to you today my contempt for such a doctrine; and if it be true, I make my choice today, and I prefer Hell.[3]

Immediacy

Verbal *immediacy* "refers to the degree to which a source associates himself/herself with the topics of a message; that is, immediacy is the degree to which a source approaches or avoids a topic."[4] From a transactional perspective I might add that immediacy is the degree to which the source's language brings all co-communicators to associate with the topics of the message. In a way, immediacy is the opposite of aloofness or objectivity.

Differences in immediacy result from variations of verb tense (present versus past or future), probability (will versus may), mutuality (we together versus you and I separately or they) and articles (the versus that). Notice that I have attempted to enhance the immediacy of this book by referring to "you and I" or "we" rather than the more aloof "the writer" and "the reader" used in more "scholarly" writing.

As in the case of other language variables, immediacy must be adapted to the exigencies of each speaking transaction. This will vary with your own involvement with the topic and familiarity with the audience as well as the nature of the occasion. Notice how Woodrow Wilson varies the immediacy of his language in the two distinctly different situations below. In his declaration of war message he is the scholar—president setting forth a formal state message. He says:

> On the third of February last I officially laid before you the extra-ordinary announcement of the Imperial German Government that on and after the first day of February it was its purpose to put aside all restraints of law or of humanity and use its submarines to sink every vessel that sought to approach either the ports of Great Britain and Ireland or the western coasts of Europe or any of the parts controlled by the enemies of Germany within the Mediterranean.[5]

But late in his second term, when he was stumping the country on behalf of his beloved League of Nations, he sounds like a different person:

> I do not owe a report or the slightest responsibility to anybody but you. I do not mean only you in this hall, though I am free to admit that this is just as good a sample of America as you can find anywhere, and the sample looks mighty good to me. I mean you and the millions besides you, thoughtful, responsible American men and women all over this country. They are my bosses, and I am mightily glad to be their servant.[6]

In these two divergent contexts Wilson skillfully and sincerely adapts his language to meet the demands of the situation in order to create bonds of identification with his listeners.

Diversity

Diversity of language is the variety of words you use. Technically, it has been defined as "the manifest range of a source's vocabulary."[7] Diversity is quantified by dividing the number of different words in a message by the total number of words. In public speaking, diversity is a double-edged sword.

On the one hand, diversity or variety leads to greater interest. As we saw in Chapter 3, the instant intelligibility required in oral communication necessitates considerably more redundancy than does written prose. If this redundancy is to maintain attention and interest, however, it must be varied. Hence, subordinate ideas reinforce or qualify main ideas. Examples, statistics, quotations, and other forms of support restate the ideas they support in interesting and varied ways. Varieties of restatement occur frequently. The speaker is, therefore, walking a tightrope between unintelligibility and boredom. Usually, diversity of language can help solve this dilemma.

There is an exception to this generalization, however. If effectively managed, repetition and restatement can be not only interesting but motivating. With each repetition the effect tends to accumulate, and hence this phenomenon has been referred to by writers as *cumulation*. Recall how F.D.R. built a cumulative effect by repetition in his description of the Japanese attacks in the Pacific at the outbreak of World War II (see p. 57).

I suggest that you attempt to build your vocabulary in order to increase your ability for language diversity. You will then be ready to use diversity or repetition as the transaction demands.

CHARACTERISTICS OF STYLE

Now that we have examined the ways that language varies, let us look at some characteristics of oral style that can enhance your transaction with listeners. We will look at some characteristics of words and then the ways they are combined in sentences for greater effectiveness.

Words

As we have seen, words are fascinating substitutes for the real thing, to which people respond in interesting and individual ways. Some of the characteristics of your use of words which influence the ways listeners transact are (1) clarity, (2) correctness, (3) appropriateness, (4) interestingness, and (5) impressiveness.

Clarity. Perhaps the most universally accepted characteristic of language which is deemed desirable for effective communication is clarity. Transactionally, clarity implies shared meaning between speakers and listeners. Certainly it is at the heart of all speaking to gain understanding, and few people buy a product or concept they do not understand.

To a large degree, clarity is based upon common experiences or referents for a particular word. If you say the word *sunset*, your meaning will be clear to the degree that you and your listeners have experienced the same or similar sunsets. The degree to which those experiences have been different is the degree to which your meaning will be unclear. The same is true of our previous examples of *tree* and *automobile*.

A counterpoint on clarity is in order. While being clear is usually best, there are contexts in which vagueness or ambiguity is desirable. Oliver points out that in international diplomacy it is desirable to be clear enough so that the agreement is sound, but ambiguous enough so that the negotiators can save face with their constituents despite the compromises they have made.[8] We can all think of instances in our interpersonal dealings in which it is better to be vague and save a person's feelings than to be too clear and lose a friend. Politicians, of course, soon learn how vague or how clear they must be in order to satisfy a maximum number of their constituents.

Notice how beautifully clear and simple Abraham Lincoln's language is in the conclusion of his Second Inaugural Address:

> With malice toward none, with charity for all, with firmness in the right as God gives us to see the right, let us strive on to finish the work we are in, to bind up the nation's wounds, to care for him who shall have borne the battle and for his widow and his orphan, to do all which may achieve and cherish a just and lasting peace among ourselves and with all nations.[9]

Correctness. Correctness is the grammatical accuracy with which we use language. It has to do with noun–verb agreement, not ending sentences with prepositions, and the other rules of grammar you may have studied in high school English classes. Most of us learned our basic oral grammar from our parents, and hence what "sounds right" to us may not be correct. Radio and television also influence our grammar. Unfortunately, the care that was exercised in the early years of broadcasting to air only correct grammar and pronunciation is no longer observed.

One of the primary differences between written and oral communication is the emphasis placed on correct grammar. People have come to expect a higher level of correctness in written communication than in oral. Furthermore, the more formal the oral communication transaction, the more important it is to be correct. We pay little attention to incomplete sentences or other innocuous grammatical slips in conversation, but we expect better of people who are presumably qualified to speak to large audiences on significant occasions.

Transactionally, *not violating the linguistic expectations of your listeners or the event* is probably more important than any absolute standard of grammatical correctness. Improvement in grammar is not one of the major objectives of most beginning public speaking instruction, but your instructor or your audiences may give you feedback on your need to work on grammatical usage if it detracts from your message and diminishes the transaction. As a rule, it is rare for your grammar to be *too* correct for your listeners, so any improvement in your usage should help.

Appropriateness. Of far greater importance than grammatical correctness in oral communication is the appropriateness of your language usage to the expectations of your listeners. The story is told that Winston Churchill (a master of the English language) once ended a sentence with the preposition *with* in a manuscript he was writing. His secretary is said to have recast the sentence to correct the apparent error. Upon seeing the change Churchill wrote a brief note to his secretary: "This is the sort of impertinence, up with which I will not put!" He thereby demonstrated that he knew the correct usage but had intended the incorrect sentence for communicative effect—and appropriately so. Would you use the above sentence, albeit correct, in issuing a reprimand? You would probably say, "This is the sort of impertinence I won't put up with!" You would thereby sacrifice correctness for the more appropriate, emphatic, and probably more transactional usage.

This tension between correctness and appropriateness is one reason that I recommend (in the next chapter) that you not write out your speeches, but determine the wording by practicing out loud from your outline. Unless very skillfully done, written speeches tend to sound unnatural, stilted, aloof. Written language sounds inappropriately unconversational. The written speech has sarcastically been characterized as an "essay standing on its hind legs."

Whether written or extemporaneous, however, you should take care to make your language usage appropriate to the constraints of the speaking situation and, especially, to the expectations of listeners.

Interestingness. We spoke earlier of your concern for attention and interest in almost every stage of preparing yourself to speak. Your use of language can contribute to the interestingness of your speech.

Recall how the selection of your supporting materials can contribute to interest by emphasizing the vital, the familiar, conflict, suspense, curiosity, resolution, release, and humor. Now let us see how language can further promote interest by using words that are vivid, contrasting, novel, active, familiar, and concrete.

Earlier we spoke of intensity and specificity as language variables. More intense and specific language results in *vividness*, which listeners of course find more interesting than bland and dull language. Note the interestingness of the following vivid quotation from Patrick Henry's "Call to Arms":

> It is in vain, sir, to extenuate the matter. Gentlemen may cry peace, peace—but there is no peace. The war is actually begun! The next gale that sweeps from the North will bring to our ears the clash of resounding arms! Our brethren are already in the field! Why stand we here idle?[10]

Another characteristic of interesting language is *contrast*. Words can be used to bring two contrasting images to the listeners' minds in such a way as to enhance their interest in the transaction. Read Lincoln's discussion of the implications of the Dred Scott decision:

We shall lie down pleasantly dreaming that the people of Missouri are on the verge of making their state free; and we shall awake to the reality instead, that the Supreme Court has made Illinois a slave state.[11]

Similarly, Gregory Crompton describes the experience of floating down the Colorado River through the Grand Canyon:

You are close enough to the rock and the water to appreciate the power at work, and you can even come to grips now and then with the marvels and the beauty of its creation. The rhythm and tempo of the water, the rise and reach of the walls, the quality of air and light generate emotion and mood. On the rim you can take it or leave it. On the water you take it.[12]

Robert G. Ingersoll also uses interesting language in the following discussion of evil in the world by contrasting it with his listeners' belief that God forgives people's sins:

Now, when I read the history of this world, and when I think of the experience of my fellow men, when I think of the millions living in poverty and when I know that in the very air we breathe and in the sunlight that visits our homes there lurks an assassin ready to take our lives, and even when we believe we are in the fullness of health and joy, they are undermining us with their contagion—when I know that we are surrounded by all these evils, and when I think of what man has suffered, I do not wonder if God can forgive man, but I often ask myself, 'Can man forgive God?'[13]

A third way language can be used to generate interest is through the use of *novelty*. Providing it does not significantly violate the expectations or values of listeners, novel language can keep them interested. When Sonia Johnson, president of the Mormons for E.R.A., refers to her "Mother, God" she may offend some people and please others, but no one could claim she is not interesting! Another speaker used novelty by using words in incongruous contexts; she said of a local politician that "no one would ever accuse him of being honest."

Another way language can be used to create listeners' interest is to use *active* rather than passive language. Notice how Franklin Roosevelt describes money managers following the stock market crash of 1929.

The money changers have fled from their high seats in the temple of our civilization. We may now restore that temple to the ancient truths. The measure of the restoration lies in the extent to which we apply social values more noble than mere monetary profit.[14]

Later Roosevelt says:

Happiness lies not in the mere possession of money; it lies in the joy of achievement, in the thrill of creative effort.[15]

Similarly, note the active, vivid way William Pitt, First Earl of Chatham, articulates the abstract principle of "freedom from searches and seizures":

> The poorest man may in his cottage bid defiance to all the forces of the Crown. It may be frail—its roof may shake—the wind may blow through it—the storm may enter—the rain may enter—but the King of England cannot enter—all his force dares not cross the threshold of the ruined tenement![16]

Words and images which are *familiar* to us also capture and retain our attention and interest. Have you ever been disinterestedly scanning the newspaper and experienced a news story leap from the page at you because it was about a person or place with which you were familiar? Several years ago I was stationed aboard the U.S.S. Bremerton in Tokyo Bay. Being bored, I wandered down to the communication shack to see what was on the teletype. There was nothing very interesting. Suddenly a line hit me between the eyes which had completely missed the attention or interest of the other men. It said: "Pepperwood California destroyed by the rampaging Eel River." Why should that line interest me? Because Pepperwood was a small town located less than twenty miles from my home, which was located on the banks of that same river.

Earlier we discussed how language can vary in its level of abstraction, or specificity. The more specific and *concrete* your language is, the more *real* your message seems to your listeners. "Psychologists know . . ." sounds unreal and dull, whereas "B.F. Skinner has demonstrated . . ." sounds more interesting and more believable.

A speaker might make the following appeal: "Depend on us; we are interdependent." Booker T. Washington achieved interest by phrasing the same idea more concretely:

> As we have proved our loyalty to you in the past, in nursing your children, watching by the sick bed of our mothers and fathers, and often following them with their tear-dimmed eyes to their graves, so in the future . . . we shall stand by with a devotion that no foreigner can approach, ready to lay down our lives, if need be, in defense of yours, interlacing our industrial, commercial, civil, and religious life with yours in a way that shall make the interests of both races one. In all things that are purely social we can be as separate as fingers, yet one as the hand in all things essential to mutual progress.[17]

Impressiveness. Have you ever listened to a speaker and murmured to yourself, "I wish I'd said that"? What you probably meant was "I wish I could express my ideas that impressively." Impressiveness of style is derived from the beauty or colorfulness of the words you use and the memorability of the phrases you couch. We discuss here the use of metaphors, imagery, allusions, and "quotable quotes."

Earlier we discussed metaphor and simile as types of comparisons. They are quick and colorful; sometimes they are even elegant. Note the elegant use of metaphor as Edmund Burke describes the execution of Marie Antoinette:

> I saw her just above the horizon, decorating and cheering the elevated sphere she had just begun to move in, glittering like the morning star, full of life and splendor and joy. . . .

Little did I dream that I should have lived to see such disasters fallen upon her, in a nation of gallant men, in a nation of men of honor, and of cavaliers! I thought ten thousand swords must have leaped from their scabbards, to avenge even a look that threatened her with insult.[18]

Of course, it takes a very linguistically sophisticated person to create such elegant metaphors and they probably would not transact with most audiences today anyway. But metaphor and colorful language need be neither complicated nor elegant. Recall how Booker T. Washington and Abraham Lincoln used relatively simple language and comparisons to create impressive style.

Imagery. *Imagery* is the use of the spoken or written word to appeal to the five senses—sight, sound, taste, touch, and smell. That is to say, it is a way of "painting pictures" or creating vicarious experiences with words. One of the most impressive uses of imagery with which I am familiar is Henry W. Grady's description of the returning Confederate army (see p. 113).

As I read or hear that passage, I can see "the graves that dot the old Virginia hills," feel the weariness and desperation of "footsore Confederate soldiers," and experience the pride and exhilaration of the people who made the "fields that ran red with blood in April" become "green with the harvest in June."

Imagine the fear felt by the listeners who personally identified with the following combination of metaphor and imagery, used by Jonathan Edwards in his famous sermon "Sinners in the Hands of an Angry God":

O sinner! Consider the fearful danger you are in: 'Tis a great furnace of wrath, a wide and bottomless pit, full of the fire of wrath, that you are held over in the hand of that God, whose wrath is provoked and incensed as much against you, as against many of the damned in hell. You hang by a slender thread, with the flames of divine wrath flashing about it, and ready every moment to singe it, and burn it asunder....[19]

Allusion. An *allusion* is the use of language to bring to mind an image that is already familiar to the audience. When Patrick Henry said, "Our chains are forged, their clanking can be heard on the plains of Boston," he was calling to mind recent oppressive events in the Massachusetts Colony with which his listeners were well familiar. As you read "The Cross of Gold," by W. J. Bryan, you will notice numerous allusions to historical events, Biblical passages, and natural phenomena which would have brought to his listeners' minds vivid images he did not need to describe in detail. In fact, to have done so would have bored them and insulted their intelligence. The use of allusion is, therefore, one of the most transactional techniques you can use, since it depends so greatly on the audience supplying most of the content of the transaction.

Quotable Quotes. A final means of achieving impressiveness or beauty in your use of language is by phrasing "quotable quotes." When you hear a well-known person speak, what phrases stick out in your mind? Certainly, some of the characteristics of impressiveness we have just discussed constitute quotable quotes. But there are others, not so easily categorized, which are repeated over and over again. They are usually brief but striking. Phrases like "I have a dream" (Martin Luther King), "Make the world safe for democracy" (Woodrow Wilson), "The only thing we have to fear is fear itself" (F.D.R.), "An iron curtain has descended" (Winston Churchill), and "Give me liberty or give me death" (Patrick Henry) have been so often quoted as to become trite. Anyway, the authors were famous people, and you and I are not famous. In some cases, however, the people were not famous until they coined these phrases; it is their language that is their legacy.

Other phrases not so easily attributable to famous people have also had an impact on the way we talk and think. "Black is beautiful," "Better red than dead," "My country right or wrong"—the list is endless.

As you begin your study of public speaking, the aspects of impressiveness or beauty discussed above will probably be the least of your worries. But this characteristic constitutes the difference between a merely superior and truly eloquent public speaker; and your early understanding of impressive and beautiful language may allow you to become one of those rare individuals who use language elegantly whenever it is appropriate.

Sentences

The style of public speakers can be characterized by not only its use of words but also the way those words are arranged in sentences. We will discuss sentence length and sentence structure.

Sentence Length. One of the primary differences between oral and written communication is the length of sentences used in each. Written communication uses relatively long, complex sentences. When we talk we use not only shorter sentences but even sentence fragments. It makes our talk more intelligible—more easily assimilated. It sounds "chatty."

Note in the Woodrow Wilson quotes above that the first quote, on unrestricted submarine warfare, is a single sentence! It sounds formal and, appropriately, official. Note in the second quote that the sentences are shorter, more personal, and hence more appropriate to the oral communication transaction.

Sentence Structure. Sentences can also be varied in the way the are structured. Although sentence structure can vary in many ways, we discuss here only the variables of antithesis and parallelism because of the frequency with which they are used in public speaking.

Earlier we spoke of using words for contrast to arouse interest. *Antithesis* is the method of putting contrasting ideas together in contiguous sentences or clauses within a sentence. Perhaps the most familiar use of antithesis was made by John F. Kennedy when he said, "Ask not what your country can do for you, but what you can do for your country."

Recall Barbara Ward's use of antithesis to pose a set of choices in her address, "Only One Earth":

> What is to be reduced, the luxuries of the rich or the necessities of the poor? What are the priorities—a decent human environment for the whole human species or riches for some and squalor for the majority?[20]

As in the case of impressiveness, you should be aware of antithesis, but not worry too much about using it until you have developed considerable experience in public speaking.

A second aspect of sentence structure that enhances your style and competence in public communication is *parallelism*. Parallel sentence structure is the device of phrasing a series of sentences with an identical structure and, frequently, with nearly identical words. In his keynote speech for the "March on Washington," Martin Luther King used parallelism extensively, but most strikingly in his "I have a dream" and "Let freedom ring" series.

Two of the most skillful and extensive users of parallelism were Franklin Roosevelt and Winston Churchill. Recall how F.D.R. dramatically describes the Japanese attacks at the opening of World War II (p. 57).

Similarly, Winston Churchill made effective use of parallelism in several of his great speeches of the same period. Following is an example:

> Even though large tracts of Europe and many old and famous states have fallen or may fall into the grip of the Gestapo and all the odious apparatus of Nazi rule, we shall not flag or fail. We shall go on to the end. We shall fight in France, we shall fight on the seas and oceans, we shall fight with growing confidence and growing strength in the air, we shall defend our island, whatever the cost may be. We shall fight on the beaches, we shall fight on the landing grounds, we shall fight in the fields and in the streets, we shall fight in the hills. We shall never surrender. . . .[21]

DEVELOPING ORAL STYLE

During the discussion of the nature, variables, and characteristics of language, you have probably been asking, "All well and good, but how do I develop the ability to *do* this?" The bad news is that, in my opinion, style is the most difficult of all of the competencies in public communication to achieve. The good news is that virtually every scholar in this field agrees that language behavior is *learned*.

Initially, we learn our most basic language skills from our parents or "mothering ones." You have probably noticed among your classmates that some already use more correct and perhaps even more impressive language than others. This is probably because their parents have exposed them to that kind of language since their early childhood.

"But," you say, "I have no control over what I was exposed to up until now, and in any case it's too late to change that." I agree. There are two things that I can suggest at this point, however.

The first is *exposure*. Generally speaking, we learn to use the kind of language to which we are exposed. Lord Chatham is said to have actually *studied* the dictionary. Various popular publications have sections on vocabulary building or developing "word power." Probably the best way to expose yourself to superior language usage is to read *good* books. Perhaps even better for developing oral style is to read great speeches, and this is one reason I have included a few of the greatest in this book. If you wish to read more contemporary examples of significant public speeches, *Vital Speeches of the Day* is a periodical that selects and publishes many of them; I know professional public speakers who subscribe to it regularly. However you do it, by exposing yourself to eloquent prose, either oral or written, you will absorb, virtually by osmosis, greater facility with language.

The other major way of developing your style is through practice. Most of us have a much larger vocabulary and knowledge of semantic rules than we use in daily conversation. By practicing, it simply becomes easier to mobilize and use the language ability we have stored in our brains. I will say more about practice in the next chapter, but suffice it to say here that you should not only accept every opportunity to speak, when you feel appropriately qualified, but also practice as much before each speaking opportunity as you possibly can.

SUMMARY

In this chapter we define public speaking style as your use of language. As symbols, words are not objects but substitutes in place of the objects or concepts they represent. Language is particularly transactional because it carries not only the denotative (definitional) meaning but also connotative meaning. Connotative meanings are derived from the experiences of listeners as well as their attribution of intent to speakers. Meaning is constrained by the context within which the communication event occurs and the medium through which it is transmitted.

Your use of language can vary along several spectra, including intensity, immediacy or objectivity, diversity and specificity, and level of abstraction.

Public speaking style can also exhibit different characteristics depending on word usage or sentence construction. Word clarity can vary according to simplicity, familiarity, and technicality. Correct grammar may be important in a speech but you must also be concerned about appropriateness (identification) in your use of words. Style can add interest to your speech by being vivid, familiar, active, novel, concrete, and contrasting. Words can add impressiveness or beauty to your message through metaphors, imagery, allusions, and quotable quotes.

Sentence construction can contribute to the quality of style by using sentence length that is appropriate to the oral communication transaction. Antithesis and parallel sentence structure provide linguistic identification with listeners.

Oral style can be developed by exposing yourself to superior language usage through reading and listening to skillful practitioners, as well as by extensive practice.

"The New South"

Henry W. Grady

"There was a South of slavery and secession—that South is dead. There is a South of union and freedom—that South, thank God, is living, breathing, growing every hour." These words, delivered from the immortal lips of Benjamin H. Hill, at Tammany Hall in 1866, true then, and truer now, I shall make my text tonight.

Mr. President and Gentlemen:

Let me express to you my appreciation of the kindness by which I am permitted to address you. I make this abrupt acknowledgement advisedly, for I feel that if, when I raise my provincial voice in this ancient and august presence, I could find courage for no more than the opening sentence, it would be well if, in that sentence, I had met in a rough sense my obligation as a guest, and had perished, so to speak, with courtesy on my lips and grace in my heart. [laughter] Permitted through your kindness to catch my second wind, let me say that I appreciate the significance of being the first Southerner to speak at this board, which bears the substance, if it surpasses the semblance, of original New England hospitality [applause], and honors a sentiment that in turn honors you, but in which my personality is lost, and the compliment to my people made plain. [laughter]

I bespeak the utmost stretch of your courtesy tonight. I am not troubled about those from whom I come. You remember the man whose wife sent him to a neighbor with a pitcher of milk, and who, tripping on the top step, fell, with such

Source: From Joel Chandler Harris, *Henry W. Grady: His Life, Writings, and Speeches* (New York: Cassell Publishing, 1890), pp. 15–16.

casual interruptions as the landing afforded, into the basement; and while picking himself up had the pleasure of hearing his wife call out: "John, did you break the pitcher?"

"No, I didn't," said John, "but I be dinged if I don't!" [laughter]

So, while those who call to me from behind may inspire me with energy if not with courage, I ask an indulgent hearing from you. I beg that you will bring your full faith in American fairness and frankness to judgment upon what I shall say. There was an old preacher once who told some boys of the Bible lesson he was going to read in the morning. The boys finding the place, glued together the connecting pages. [laughter] The next morning he read on the bottom of one page: "When Noah was one hundred and twenty years old he took unto himself a wife, who was"—then turning the page—"one hundred and forty cubits long [laughter], forty cubits wide, built of gopher-wood [laughter], and covered with pitch inside and out." [loud and continued laughter] He was naturally puzzled at this. He read it again, verified it, and then said: "My friends, this is the first time I ever met this in the Bible, but I accept it as an evidence of the assertion that we are fearfully and wonderfully made." [immense laughter] If I could get you to hold such faith tonight I could proceed cheerfully to the task I otherwise approach with a sense of consecration.

Pardon me one word, Mr. President, spoken for the sole purpose of getting into the volumes that go out annually freighted with the right eloquence of your speakers—the fact that the Cavalier as well as the Puritan was on the continent in its early days, and that he was "up and able to be about." [laughter] I have read your books carefully and I find no mention of that fact, which seems to me an important one for preserving a sort of historical equilibrium if for nothing else.

Let me remind you that the Virginia Cavalier first challenged France on this continent—that Cavalier John Smith gave New England its very name, and was so pleased with the job that he has been handing his own name around ever since—and that while Miles Standish was cutting off men's ears for courting a girl without her parents' consent, and forbade men to kiss their wives on Sunday, the Cavalier was courting everything in sight, and that the Almighty had vouchsafed great increase to the Cavalier colonies, the huts in the wilderness being full as the nests in the woods.

But having incorporated the Cavalier as a fact in your charming little books I shall let him work out his own salvation, as he has always done with engaging gallantry, and we will hold no controversy as to his merits. Why should we? Neither Puritan nor Cavalier long survived as such. The virtues and traditions of both happily still live for the inspiration of their sons and the saving of the old fashion. [applause] But both Puritan and Cavalier were lost in the storm of the first Revolution; and the American citizen, supplanting both and stronger than either, took possession of the Republic bought by their common blood and fashioned to wisdom, and charged himself with teaching men government and establishing the voice of the people as the voice of God. [applause]

HENRY W. GRADY: THE NEW SOUTH

My friend Dr. Talmage has told you that the typical American has yet to come. Let me tell you that he has already come. [applause] Great types like valuable plants are slow to flower and fruit. But from the union of these colonist Puritans and Cavaliers, from the straightening of their purposes and the crossing of their blood, slow perfecting through a century, came he who stands as the first typical American, the first who comprehended within himself all the strength and gentleness, all the majesty and grace of this Republic—Abraham Lincoln. [loud and continued applause] He was the sum of Puritan and Cavalier, for in his ardent nature were fused the virtues of both, and in the depths of his great soul the faults of both were lost. [renewed applause] He was greater than Puritan, greater than Cavalier, in that he was American [renewed applause] and that in his homely form were first gathered the vast and thrilling forces of his ideal government—charging it with such tremendous meaning and so elevating it above human suffering that martyrdom, though infamously aimed, came as a fitting crown to a life consecrated from the cradle to human liberty. [loud and prolonged cheering] Let us, each cherishing the traditions and honoring his fathers, build with reverent hands to the type of this simple but sublime life, in which all types are honored; and in our common glory as Americans there will be plenty and to spare for your forefathers and for mine. [renewed cheering]

In speaking to the toast with which you have honored me, I accept the term, "The New South," as in no sense disparaging to the Old. Dear to me, sir, is the home of my childhood and the traditions of my people. I would not, if I could, dim the glory they won in peace and war, or by word or deed take aught from the splendor and grace of their civilization—never equaled and, perhaps, never to be equaled in its chivalric strength and grace. There is a New South, not through protest against the Old, but because of new conditions, new adjustments and, if you please, new ideas and aspirations. It is to this that I address myself, and to the consideration of which I hasten lest it become the Old South before I get to it. Age does not endow all things with strength and virtue, nor are all new things to be despised. The shoemaker who put over his door "John Smith's shop. Founded in 1760," was more than matched by his young rival across the street who hung out this sign: "Bill Jones. Established 1886. No old stock kept in this shop."

Dr. Talmage has drawn for you, with a master's hand, the picture of your returning armies. He has told you how, in the pomp and circumstance of war, they came back to you, marching with proud and victorious tread, reading their glory in a nation's eyes! Will you bear with me while I tell you of another army that sought its home at the close of the late war—an army that marched home in defeat and not in victory—in pathos and not in splendor, but in glory that equaled yours, and to hearts as loving as ever welcomed heroes home. Let me picture to you the footsore Confederate soldier, as, buttoning up in his faded gray jacket the parole which was to bear testimony to his children of his fidelity and faith, he turned his face southward from Appomattox in April, 1865. Think of him as ragged, half-starved, heavy-hearted, enfeebled by want and wounds; having fought to exhaustion, he surrenders his gun, wrings the hands of his comrades in silence, and lifting his tear-stained and pallid face for the last time to the graves that dot the old Virginia hills, pulls his gray cap over his brow and begins the slow and painful journey. What does he find—let me ask you, who went to your homes eager to find in the welcome you had justly earned, full payment for four years' sacrifice—what does he find when, having followed the battle-stained cross against overwhelming odds, dreading death not half so much as surrender, he reaches the home he left so prosperous and beautiful? He finds his house in ruins, his farm devastated, his slaves free, his stock killed, his barns empty, his trade destroyed, his money worthless; his social system, feudal in its magnificence, swept away; his people without law or legal status, his comrades slain, and the burdens of others heavy on his shoulders. Crushed by defeat, his very traditions are gone; without money, credit, employment, material or training; and, besides all this, confronted with the gravest problem that ever met human intelligence—the establishing of a status for the vast body of his liberated slaves.

What does he do—this hero in gray with a heart of gold? Does he sit down in sullenness and despair? Not for a day. Surely God, who had stripped him of his prosperity, inspired him in his adversity. As ruin was never before so overwhelming, never was restoration swifter. The soldier stepped from the trenches into the furrow; horses that had charged Federal guns march before the plow, and fields that ran red with human blood in April were green with the harvest in June; women reared in luxury cut up their dresses and made breeches for their husbands, and, with a patience and heroism that fit women always as a garment, gave their hands to work. There was little bitterness in all this. Cheerfulness and frankness prevailed. "Bill Arp" struck the keynote when he said: "Well, I killed as many of them as they did of me, and now I am going to work." [laughter and applause] Or the soldier returning home after defeat and roasting some corn on the roadside, who made the remark to his comrades: "You may leave the South if you want to, but I am going to Sandersville, kiss my wife and raise a crop, and if the Yankees fool with me any more I will whip 'em again." [renewed applause] I want to say to General Sherman—who is considered an able man in our hearts, though some people think he is a kind of careless man about fire—that from the ashes he left us in 1864 we have raised a brave and beautiful city; that somehow or other we have caught the sunshine in the bricks and mortar of our homes, and have built therein not one ignoble prejudice or memory. [applause]

But in all this what have we accomplished? What is the sum of our work? We have found out that in the general summary the free Negro counts more than he did as a slave. We have planted the schoolhouse on the hilltop and make it free to white and black. We have sowed towns and cities in the place of theories and put business above politics. [applause] We have challenged your spinners in Massachusetts and your iron-makers in Pennsylvania. We have learned that the $400,000,000 annually received from our cotton crop will make us rich, when the supplies that make it are home-raised. We have reduced the commercial rate of interest from twenty-four to six percent, and are floating four percent bonds. We have learned that one Northern immigrant is worth fifty foreigners, and have smoothed the path to southward, wiped out the place where Mason and Dixon's line used to be, and hung our latch-string out to you and yours. [prolonged cheers] We have reached the point that marks perfect harmony in every household, when the husband confesses that the pies which his wife cooks are as good as those his mother used to bake; and we admit that the sun shines as brightly and the moon as softly as it did "before the war." [laughter] We have established thrift in city and country. We have fallen in love with work. We have restored comfort to homes from which culture and elegance never departed. We have let economy take root and spread among us as rank as the crabgrass which sprang from Sherman's cavalry camps, until we are ready to lay odds on the Georgia Yankee, as he manufactures relics of the battlefield in a one-story shanty and squeezes pure olive oil out of his cotton-seed, against any Down-easter that ever swapped wooden nutmegs for flannel sausages in the valley of Vermont. [loud and continuous laughter] Above all, we know that we have achieved in these "piping times of peace" a fuller independence for the South than that which our fathers sought to win in the forum by their eloquence or compel on the field by their swords. [loud applause]

It is a rare privilege, sir, to have had part, however humble, in this work. Never was nobler duty confided to human hands than the uplifting and upbuilding of the prostrate and bleeding South, misguided perhaps, but beautiful in her suffering, and honest, brave and generous always. [applause] In the record of her social, industrial, and political illustrations we await with confidence the verdict of the world.

But what of the Negro? Have we solved the problem he presents or progressed in honor and equity towards the solution? Let the record speak to the point. No section shows a more prosperous laboring population than the Negros of the South; none in fuller sympathy with the employing and land-owning class. He shares our school fund, has the fullest protection of our laws and the friendship of our people. Self-interest, as well as honor, demand that he should have this. Our future, our very existence depend upon our working out this problem in full and exact justice. We understand that when Lincoln signed the Emancipation Proclamation, your victory was assured; for he then committed you to the cause of human liberty, against which the arms of man cannot prevail [applause]; while those of our statemen who trusted to make slavery the cornerstone of the Confederacy doomed us to defeat as far as they could, committing us to a cause that reason could not defend or the sword maintain in the sight of advancing civilization. [renewed applause] Had Mr. Toombs said, which he did not say, that he would call the roll of his slaves at the foot of Bunker Hill, he would have been foolish, for he might have known that whenever slavery became entangled in war it must perish, and that the chattel in human flesh ended forever in New England when your fathers—not to be blamed for parting with what didn't pay—sold their slaves to our fathers—not to be praised for knowing a paying thing when they saw it. [laughter] The relations of the Southern people with the Negro are close and cordial. We remember with what fidelity for four years he guarded our defenseless women and children, whose husbands and fathers were fighting against his freedom. To his eternal credit be it said that whenever he struck a blow for his own liberty he fought in open battle, and when at last he raised his black and humble hands that the shackles might be struck off, those hands were innocent of wrong against his helpless charges, and worthy to be taken in loving grasp by every man who honors loyalty and devotion. [applause] Ruffians have maltreated him, rascals have misled him, philanthropists established a bank for him, but the South, with the North, protects against injustice to this simple and sincere people. To liberty and enfranchisement is as far as law can carry the Negro. The rest must be left to conscience and common sense. It should be left to those among whom his lot is cast, with whom he is indissolubly connected and whose prosperity depends upon their possessing his intelligent sympathy and confidence. Faith has been kept with him in spite of calumnious assertions to the contrary by those who assume to speak for us or by frank opponents. Faith will be kept with him in the future, if the South holds her reason and integrity. [applause]

But have we kept faith with you? In the fullest sense, yes. When Lee surrendered—I don't say when Johnston surrendered, because I understand he still alludes to the time when he met General Sherman last as the time when he "determined to abandon any further prosecution of the struggle"—when Lee surrendered, I say, and Johnston quit, the South became, and has since been, loyal to this Union. We fought hard enough to know that we were whipped, and in perfect frankness accepted as final the arbitrament of the sword to which we had appealed. The South found her jewel in the toad's head of defeat. The shackles that had held her in narrow limitations fell forever when the shackles of the Negro slave were broken.[applause] Under the old regime the Negros were slaves to the South, the South was a slave to the system. The old plantation, with its simple police regulation and its feudal habit, was the only type possible under slavery. Thus we gathered in the hands of a splendid and chivalric oligarchy the substance that should have been diffused among the people, as the rich blood, under certain artificial conditions, is gathered at the heart, filling that with affluent rapture, but leaving the body chill and colorless. [applause]

The Old South rested everything on slavery and agriculture, unconscious that these could neither give nor maintain healthy growth. The New South presents a perfect democracy, the oligarchs leading in the popular movement—a social system compact and closely knitted, less splendid on the surface but stronger at the core—a hundred farms for every plantation, fifty homes for every palace, and a diversified industry that meets the complex needs of this complex age.

The New South is enamored of her new work. Her soul is stirred with the breath of a new life. The light of a grander day is falling fair on her face. She is thrilling with the consciousness of growing power and prosperity. As she stands upright, full-statured and equal among the people of the earth, breathing the keen air and looking out upon the expanding horizon, she understands that her emancipation came because in the inscrutable wisdom of God her honest purpose was crossed and her brave armies were beaten. [applause]

This is said in no spirit of time-serving or apology. The South has nothing for which to apologize. She believes that the late struggle between the States was war and not rebellion, revolution and not conspiracy, and that her convictions were as honest as yours. I should be unjust to the dauntless spirit of the South and to my own convictions if I did not make this plain in this presence. The South has nothing to take back. In my native town of Athens is a monument that crowns its central hills—a plain, white shaft. Deep cut into its shining side is a name dear to me above the names of men, that of a brave and simple man who died in a brave and simple faith. Not for all the glories of New England—from Plymouth Rock all the way—would I exchange the heritage he left me in his soldier's death. To the foot of that shaft I shall send my children's children to reverence him who ennobled their name with his heroic blood. But, sir, speaking from the shadow of that memory, which I honor as I do nothing else on earth, I say that the cause in which he suffered and for which he gave his life was adjudged by higher and fuller wisdom than his or mine, and I am glad that the omniscient God held the balance of battle in His Almighty hand, and that human slavery was swept forever from American soil—the American Union saved from the wreck of war. [loud applause]

This message, Mr. President, comes to you from consecrated ground. Every foot of the soil about the city in which I live is sacred as a battleground of the Republic. Every hill that invests it is hallowed to you by the blood of your brothers, who died for your victory, and doubly hallowed to us by the blood of those who died hopeless, but undaunted, in defeat—sacred soil to all of us, rich with memories that make us purer and stronger and better, silent but staunch witnesses in its red desolation of the matchless valor of American hearts and the deathless glory of American arms—speaking an eloquent witness in its white peace and prosperity to the indissoluble union of American States and the imperishable brotherhood of the American people. [immense cheering]

Now, what answer has New England to this message? Will she permit the prejudices of war to remain in the hearts of the conquerors, when it has died in the hearts of the conquered? [cries of "No! No!"] Will she transmit this prejudice to the next generation, that in their hearts, which never felt the generous ardor of conflict, it may perpetuate itself? ["No! No!"] Will she withhold, save in strained courtesy, the hand which straight from his soldier's heart Grant offered to Lee at Appomattox? Will she make the vision of a restored and happy people, which gathered above the couch of your dying captain, filling his heart with grace, touching his lips with praise and glorifying his path to the grave; will she make this vision on which the last sight of his expiring soul breathed a benediction, a cheat and a delusion? [tumultuous cheering and shouts of "No! No!"] If she does,

> the South, never abject in asking for comradeship, must accept with dignity its refusal; but if she does not; if she accepts in frankness and sincerity this message of goodwill and friendship, then will the prophecy of Webster, delivered in this very Society forty years ago amid tremendous applause, be verified in its fullest and final sense, when he said:
>
>> Standing hand to hand and clasping hands, we should remain united as we have been for sixty years, citizens of the same country, members of the same government, united, all united now and united forever.
>
> There have been difficulties, contentions, and controversies, but I tell you that in my judgement
>
>> Those opposed eyes,
>> Which like the meteors of a troubled heaven,
>> All of one nature, of one substance bred,
>> Did lately meet in th' intestine shock,
>> Shall now, in mutual well-beseeming ranks,
>> March all one way. [prolonged applause]

ENDNOTES

1. James H. McBath and Walter R. Fisher, *British Public Addresses: 1828–1960* (Boston: Houghton Mifflin, 1971), p. 505.
2. James J. Bradac, John Waite Bowers, and John A. Cartright, "Three Language Variables in Communication Research: Intensity, Immediacy, and Diversity," *Human Communication Research* 3 (Spring 1979): 257.
3. Ernest Wrage and Barnet Baskerville, *American Forum* (New York: Harper and Row, 1960), p. 305.
4. Bradac et al., p. 262.
5. Glenn R. Capp, *Famous Speeches in American History* (New York: Bobbs-Merrill), p. 151.
6. Capp, pp. 179–180.
7. Bradac et al., p. 263.
8. See Robert T. Oliver, "Speech in International Affairs", *Quarterly Journal of Speech* 2 (April 1952): 173–174; and Oliver, "The Rhetoric of Power in Diplomatic Conferences," *Quarterly Journal of Speech* 3 (October 1954): 289.
9. A. Craig Baird, *American Public Addresses 1740–1952,* (New York: McGraw Hill, 1956), p. 117.
10. Baird, p. 32.
11. Wrage and Baskerville, p. 186.
12. C. Gregory Crampton, *Land of Living Rock* (New York: Alfred A. Knopf, 1972), p. 40.

ENDNOTES

13. Wrage and Baskerville, p. 305.
14. Ernest Wrage and Barnet Baskerville, *Contemporary Forum* (New York: Harper & Brothers, 1962), p. 158.
15. Wrage and Baskerville, p. 158.
16. *The Oxford Dictionary of Quotations*, 2d ed. (London: Oxford University Press, 1953), p. 379.
17. Baird, p. 191.
18. David J. Brewer, ed. *The World's Best Orations* Vol. II (Chicago: F.P. Kaiser, 1923), p. 417.
19. Baird, p. 23.
20. Barbara Ward, "Only One Earth," *Engage*, September, 1972, p. 17.
21. McBath and Fisher, p. 505.

6

Delivery: Transactional Synthesis

In this chapter:
Transactional functions of delivery
Traditional characteristics
Transactional characteristics
Preparing for delivery
Summary
William Jennings Bryan, "Cross of Gold"

It was blazing hot as well as muggy in Chicago on July 8, 1896. Many of the raucous crowd in attendance at the Democratic National Convention were involved in the debate over the Platform. Four speakers had been selected to debate the plank on the money question, that is, the gold standard versus the free coinage of silver. As in most political conventions attention was mixed—until William Jennings Bryan, a two-term congressman and editor of the Omaha *World Herald,* began speaking against the gold standard. Speaking without a public-address system, Bryan riveted the attention of his listeners with his precise articulation and clear, powerful voice. The shirt-sleeved delegates were electrified by his now-famous final appeal:

> If they dare to come out in the open field and defend the gold standard as a good thing, we will fight them to the uttermost. Having behind us the producing masses of this nation and the world, supported by the commercial interests, the laboring interests, and the toilers everywhere, we will answer their demand for a gold standard by saying to them: You shall not press down upon the brow of labor this crown of thorns, you shall not crucify mankind upon a cross of gold.[1]

The next day the delegates nominated Bryan as the Democratic candidate for President of the United States.

Few public speakers are as well endowed as Bryan with a voice and other physical attributes that enhance the success of a public speaking transaction. Indeed, several of the most eloquent orators in history have been poorly equipped for effective delivery—Burke, Lincoln, and Churchill among them.

When asked about a public speech, either as a speaker or critic, most inexperienced public speakers concentrate their concerns and criticisms on the overt, physical, nonverbal (transmissional) characteristics of delivery. The fact that we have discussed the public communication process for five chapters without concentrating on delivery suggests that I do not consider it all there is to know about public speaking. But it is indeed important and, skillfully practiced, can contribute significantly to your success (or failure) in a public communication transaction. We will discuss (1) modes of delivery, (2) functions of delivery, (3) traditional transmissional characteristics, (4) transactional characteristics, and (5) techniques for preparing for delivery.

TRANSACTIONAL FUNCTIONS OF DELIVERY

Before we discuss the characteristics and techniques of effective delivery, let us look at the functions or transactional goals you are attempting to accomplish. We will discuss attention, intelligibility, credibility, and identification.

Attention

As pointed out earlier, attention must be maintained throughout an entire speech. In previous chapters we have discussed how this can be done verbally, by both your selection of forms of support and the style or language you use to phrase your ideas and supports. Attention can be maintained nonverbally as well, by means of the way you deliver the speech. By use of eye contact with your listeners, the dynamism and variety with which you move your body, and the way you vary the intensity and quality of your voice, your delivery can help gain and retain the attention of your listeners.

Intelligibility

As is the case with gimmicky attention-getting devices in an introduction, variety leading to attention for its own sake is not enough. Meaningless activity only detracts. The variety and intensity of your delivery must be carefully directed toward the ideas you are attempting to communicate. Indeed, some comic routines are based on the incongruity of serious subjects being treated as common, mundane experiences or light, trivial subjects being delivered as earthshaking catastrophes. Your delivery must be correlated with the meaning of your message in order to enhance and not detract from intelligibility.

Intelligibility can be enhanced by not only the correlation of your delivery with your message, but also your articulation and pronunciation. We discuss these in more detail below, but the care with which you form your words can add immeasurably to your listeners' ability to hear and comprehend your message. William Jennings Bryan's wife, Mary, testifies that on some occasions she could understand at great distances every word the great orator spoke, not only because of his powerful voice, but because of the precision and clarity with which he articulated every speech sound. Yet who has not had the experience of needing to ask someone sitting nearby to repeat a comment because it was spoken in such a soft voice or with such inflexible lips and jaw that the sounds were blurred and unintelligible?

Credibility

Another function of delivery is to help to establish your credibility as a speaker. Your listeners must feel that you are a person worth listening to. However, there are nonverbal factors that relate to credibility, and in interesting ways. Some are beyond your control, such as sex, race, and even height, and since there is not much you can do about these, we now turn to those over which you have some control.

Perhaps the most important credibility factor that stems from delivery is *dynamism*. This is the degree to which you are active rather than passive, involved versus uninvolved, or intense rather than bland in your presentation. There is no "quick fix" for being dynamic. If you are involved in your topic (having correctly chosen a subject you really care about), you should have less trouble with dynamism.

Perhaps you have had the experience at a social gathering of seeing someone who said very little, and when they did say something it was bland and uninteresting. Then someone broached a subject in which the "wallflower" was involved. Suddenly the person began to talk in an animated, active, and interesting way; he or she seemed like a different person. This is what you do for your own dynamism, and hence credibility, when you choose a topic in the way recommended in Chapter 2.

Another factor affecting dynamism is your own self-confidence—or lack of it. Lack of self-confidence can be overcome through experience in speaking. In the preparation of your early speeches this means practice: the more you practice, the more confident you will become that your speech will go well, and the more of your natural dynamism you will release for your speech.

The way you dress and groom can also contribute to, or detract from, your credibility. This variable is greatly dependent on the audience and occasion or context within which the speech occurs. However, you should take care to communicate nonverbally to your audience that you are not only a well-qualified person, but also that you respect the listeners and consider the particular speaking event important. Sloppy dress and slovenly grooming as well as posture, bodily activity, and articulation, may communicate quite the opposite.

Identification

Credibility is not so much a matter of source variables as it is a bond of identification between speakers and listeners. Identification can, of course, be achieved or hindered by everything you do in preparation for a speaking event, but your delivery can also add or detract. The way you dress and groom, the way you stand or move, your gestures or facial expressions, all contribute to your identification with listeners.

Identification results, in part, from meeting expectations of listeners. In some cases those expectations are anticipated similarities—similarities in dress, grooming, or even tone of voice. One is expected to dress, groom, and talk differently at funerals or the symphony than one does at a New Year's Eve party or the Super Bowl.

I place the emphasis on listener expectations rather than the more obvious similarities in identification because, from our transactional perspective, the listener frequently *expects* dissimilarities. Recall the example of the teaching assistants who dressed in blue jeans. Both credibility and identification were diminished because that group of students expected nonverbal behavior from a teacher different from that of a student. The same may be true of priests, politicians, or plumbers, depending on the particular audience and context in which the communication occurs.

In summary, then, you can enhance your communicative effectiveness by keeping in mind the transactional goals of good delivery: capturing and maintaining listeners' attention, transmitting your message intelligibly, establishing and maintaining your credibility, and identification with your listeners. Now let us turn to the characteristics of delivery that lead to the accomplishment of these transactions.

TRADITIONAL CHARACTERISTICS

Traditionally we have focused on transmissional characteristics possessed by speakers, which have contributed to their skill in public communication. Today we are more concerned with patterns or combinations of these characteristics with which listeners identify, and hence transact. However, in order to fully appreciate the transactional properties of delivery, let us look at some of the individual transmissional characteristics of delivery that combine to make up the patterns and combinations contributing to the delivery transaction. They include characteristics of the voice, body movement, facial expression, and articulation and pronunciation.

Voice

One of the most obvious and useful components of delivery is your voice. The voice is, of course, the instrument that produces the sound waves that carry your message to your listeners. Your voice has four characteristics that can be controlled in such a way as to vary and enhance the meaning of your message. Writers in the area of nonverbal communication have called this *paralanguage*. We will discuss these variable characteristics of the voice as (1) pitch, (2) rate, (3) volume, and (4) quality.[2]

Pitch. *Pitch* is the relative highness or lowness of your voice. Everyone has a basic pitch, which listeners interpret as a generally high or low voice. In singing, this distinguishes a soprano from a bass. Pitch, however, can be varied to convey meaning. For instance, if you let the pitch of your voice fall at the end of a sentence you convey a positive statement, or even command, and you sound like a decisive, assertive person. If you let the pitch of your voice rise at the end of a sentence, you convey a question or doubt, regardless of the content of the message. If you allow the pitch to vary in certain ways you can convey the impression of weakness or indecisiveness.

Rate. *Rate* is the speed at which you talk. Some people habitually talk faster than others—some so fast you can hardly understand them, and some so slow you want to finish every sentence for them. Rate, however, can also be varied to convey meaning. If you talk faster you may communicate excitement, while slower speech may reflect calm or seriousness. Some people speak faster on less important ideas and subjects, but slow down on the more important points.

A common problem among inexperienced public speakers is talking too fast. This results from excitement and anxiety as well as a desire to fill the air with sound. Beginners tend to feel embarrassed about periods of silence when they are the focus of attention. If you watch experienced speakers, however, you will see that they speak at a moderate rate and frequently use pauses with great effect.

Volume. A third variable characteristic of the voice is *volume*. This is the loudness with which you speak. In the extreme, it is the difference between a whisper and a shout. Most of us have been taught from early childhood not to shout. This is good advice during normal conversation, but in public speaking you must speak loudly enough to be heard. Without a public address system most people initially feel like they are shouting, and yet many can't be heard beyond the third row. With the use of a P.A. system, of course, you can use a much more normal volume. In either case, it is good to arrive early, check the situation, and practice briefly to assess the volume you will need to "carry" to the farthest listener.

Volume can also be varied for meaning. For example, in combination with other variables, greater volume may be interpreted as excitement, or even anger, while lower volume (yet still intelligible) can connote seriousness or calm.

Quality. The final variable characteristic of your voice is quality. *Quality* is the sound of your voice that distinguishes it from others'. Quality is determined by the sound waves produced by your vocal folds resonating through the cavities and "off the walls" of your throat, nose, mouth, and sinuses. Since everyone's resonating cavities are different sizes and shapes, the quality of each voice is unique.

But quality, too, can be altered. Our resonating cavities are somewhat flexible. This is what allows impressionists to make their voices sound like celebrities such as Johnny Carson or John Wayne. While you and I may not be impressionists, we can indeed vary the quality of our voices to communicate feelings of anger, doubt, caring, envy, and the like.

Quality is perhaps the most difficult characteristic of voice to intentionally vary in a way that sounds natural. Sometimes it ends up sounding like a poor actor, artificial or unnatural, and can result in drawing attention away from our message or reducing our credibility.

I do not recommend that you try to vary the quality of your voice intentionally. Rather, if you concentrate on the meaning of what you are saying and allow yourself to be as natural as possible, the quality of your voice will vary naturally and enhance the meaning of your message.

We have seen, then, that the voice can be varied in pitch, rate, volume, and quality, and that these variations can contribute to or detract from the communication transaction.

Bodily Activity

In public speaking, your message can be enhanced by not only your voice but also the way you move your body. It is important to communicate with not only your listeners' ears, but their eyes as well. Appearance, bodily movement, and gestures all communicate in a visual way.

Appearance. The way you appear to your listeners is an important part of the visual cues you communicate to an audience. Your appearance is a combination of posture, clothing, and grooming.

The way you stand (or don't stand) can elicit meaning. If you stand erect you can convey energy, vibrance, and interest, thereby enhancing the attention of your listeners and their evaluation of your dynamism. If you slouch or sit on the table or podium, you can convey dullness or even indifference to the occasion. Many inexperienced speakers want to sit or slouch in order to compensate for their feelings of anxiety. What they don't realize is that it is not so important that you *feel* comfortable as it is that you *look* comfortable and energetic. Many newly acquired skills, such as an overlapping golf grip, *feel* unnatural at first but they provide the technique that will produce the best results in the long run.

The same can be said for your dress and grooming. There was a time when people were expected to dress formally for public events; today these restrictions have relaxed somewhat. The key is to dress and groom in a way that is *appropriate* to the occasion—which meets the expectations of your listeners.

You need to convey to your audience by your posture, dress, and grooming that you consider this occasion an important one. As a general rule, people still expect a more formal appearance at a public event than in a private encounter. You can rarely detract from your communication by overdressing, but you can surely hurt your effectiveness by appearing slovenly or indifferent in relation to the expectations of your listeners.

Bodily movement. By *bodily movement* I mean the more or less large movements of your body while you are speaking. Usually this takes the form of walking or pacing. Random activity can be distracting. As a listener, you can concentrate on this meaningless activity and allow yourself to become distracted or, on the other hand, you can force yourself to concentrate on the message.

As a speaker, you should try to both vary and coordinate your activity with your message. Vary the direction and distance you walk. Don't pace incessantly or in regular patterns. By coordinating your movement with your message, you can punctuate your speech. You make relatively larger movements between the introduction, body, and conclusion. Progressively smaller movements can be made between main ideas, subordinate ideas, and forms of support. Emphasis and clarity can thus be provided simply by the way you move.

Body movement can also be used to great advantage to burn off some of the nervous energy most speakers experience and can also enhance your listeners' perception of your dynamism. At the beginning, it is best not to worry too much about these considerations in order to concentrate on your content and audience, but as you gain experience you will be able to add this type of refinement.

Gestures. By *gestures* I mean the movement of your hands. This is, of course, a specialized form of body movement, but it constitutes such an important aspect to your delivery that I treat it separately. In a study of classroom behavior, one of the more common public communication settings, Krout identified 7,777 distinct gestures.[3]

We have all known people who talk so much with their hands that you might think they would be silenced if their hands were held at their sides. And yet in public speaking we frequently encounter those same people standing motionless as they speak with their audience.

Gestures can serve to both augment your verbal message and substitute or add to it. Gestures can be used to add emphasis or intensity, on the one hand, or to subdue or mollify, on the other.

Your hands can also be used to transmit messages nonverbally. Called *emblems* by researchers, no less than thirty-three gestures have been identified correctly by 100 percent of the listeners who observed them. Numbering your points with your fingers is unmistakable, but so are the gestures for "shame on you," "be calm," and "who knows?"

As is the case with your voice and body, it is difficult to plan your gestures. I think it is better to leave your hands free to gesture (at your side or waist—not in your pockets nor clasped together), and then "let them go" as the meaning of your message dictates.

A speaker gestures for emphasis

From our transactional perspective, then, the visual cues of appearance, bodily activity, and gestures should be appropriate to the occasion, conform to the expectations of listeners, be coordinated with your message, and be spontaneously motivated.

Facial Expression

In addition to appearance and bodily activity, facial expression provides visual cues of great importance in the delivery of public speeches. By *facial expression* I mean the way you move your face and eyes to create identification with your audience. The meaning of a scowl or a friendly smile has almost universal acceptance and comprehension.

TRADITIONAL CHARACTERISTICS

Facial expression and body movement augment the verbal message

Facial expression is particularly effective in generating connotative meanings as well as certain emotions in listeners. Researchers in nonverbal communication have found a high degree of consistency in listeners' interpretation of facial expressions connotating surprise, anger, fear, happiness, sadness, and disgust.[4] As in the case of gestures, however, facial expression should not be practiced in isolation; it should flow naturally from what you are saying.

Of particular importance to the public speaker is *eye contact*. Some people have been given the misleading advice to pick out a friendly face in the audience or to look at the back wall. Either of these practices is not only transmissional but terribly counterproductive. In order to transact, you should watch your audience at all times. Let your eyes move slowly from one section of the audience to another.

Look particular members directly in the eye, especially those who look bored or inattentive.

The objectives of eye contact in public speaking are significant. Watching your listeners carefully not only helps gain and maintain their attention, but allows you to monitor their feedback. This allows you to tell if they strongly agree or disagree, and understand or are confused by what you are saying, which in turn enable you to adjust your transaction accordingly.

Articulation and Pronunciation

A final transmissional aspect of delivery is the way you form your words.

Articulation. This is the care and precision with which you form speech sounds. The major articulators are your tongue, lips, teeth and mouth, and jaw. In the extreme, misarticulation results in speech disorders such as a lisp, where the speaker mushes an *s* or *t* into an *sh*. Most people do not have severe articulation problems and function very well in normal conversation. In public speaking, however, it is useful to have clearer-than-average articulation in order to be clearly intelligible to your listeners. This can be accomplished by practicing, taking more care with the way you form your speech sounds. If your instructor does not bring this to your attention, you probably articulate with sufficient clarity. If you require improvement, ask your instructor for specific exercises for the particular sounds that need improvement.

There are two common articulation difficulties among students today. The first is an inflexible jaw, which results in mumbling words so that listeners cannot understand. The other is the dropping of final sounds in words like *thinkin'*, *feelin'*, or *actin'*. While these practices are probably learned from peers in the lower grades of public school in order to appear "cool," in public speaking they create the impression of ignorance and carelessness, and may detract significantly from your listeners' perception of your competence.

Pronunciation. This is the way you accent or place stress on different syllables within a word, as well as the way you form the vowel sounds. If you have an uncommon name, like mine, you are already well aware of the many different ways people can mispronounce your name. Common words are pronounced differently by different communities and subcultures. Of course, there are preferred, dictionary pronunciations for most words, and you should try to avoid gross mispronunciations. However, the best rule of thumb is to adapt to the pronunciation of the educated or professional social class of the subculture or community of your audience. This procedure will best help you fulfill the functions of credibility and identification.

TRANSACTIONAL CHARACTERISTICS

As a listener, you almost never hear the transmissional or "part" characteristics of delivery in isolation. What you normally hear are *combinations* of variations in pitch, rate, volume, and quality; as well as body movement, gestures, facial expression, and so forth. These combinations form transactional characteristics of delivery, which listeners hear and see, to which they attribute meanings, and which in turn fulfill the functions of delivery discussed earlier. Here we will discuss variety, emphasis, intensity, sincerity, and appropriateness.

Variety

The first transactional characteristic of delivery is variety. We have all heard speakers who spoke in a monotone. We have also observed speakers who either stood as immovable as statues or, perhaps worse, used the same facial expression, gesture, or body movement repeatedly—to the point that you became entranced by the repeated visual cue and forgot to listen to the message!

As a student, I had a professor who removed his glasses and put them back on again, over and over again. This monotonous behavior was a severe distraction to his listeners—so much so that a few students even counted the number of times he did it during a lecture. Surely they were not learning much of the subject matter. This example illustrates the transactional nature of delivery. As speakers we should avoid repetitive, monotonous, or distracting behavior, but as listeners we should try to avoid letting these behaviors get in the way of processing the message.

Emphasis

The foregoing discussion of variety leads us to the next transactional characteristic of delivery: emphasis. Emphasis results from placing *stress* on a syllable, word, or idea.

Varying the stress on a syllable within a word varies our pronunciation of the word, as discussed earlier. What I am emphasizing here is the way we can alter the meaning of a sentence by varying the stress on a word or words. Take a simple sentence like "Please bring me the newspaper." Note the different meanings that can be conyeyed just by varying the emphasis place on different words:

Stress	Meaning
"*Please* bring me the newspaper."	Emphatic. I really want it.
"Please *bring* me the newspaper."	Don't take it away.
"Please bring *me* the newspaper."	Don't give it to someone else.
"Please bring me the *newspaper*."	Not the magazine.

It is important to emphasize not only words but ideas and forms of support as well. You can in effect underline your most important ideas by varying the speed and volume of your voice, combined with an emphatic gesture and a serious facial expression. These variations, of course, cannot be rehearsed. By leaving your voice, hands, and body ready, and thinking about the meaning behind what you are saying, this type of emphasis will develop somewhat naturally with experience.

Intensity

It has been my observation over the years that one of the prime characteristics which distinguishes casual conversation from public speaking is the *intensity* with which public speakers communicate. Whether it is a well-known public figure arguing for or against legalized abortion, or a young parent vehemently opposing a proposed halfway house in the neighborhood, competent public speakers seem to speak with a level of intensity commensurate with the seriousness of their subject. I have even heard it claimed that student evaluations of their teachers may be related more to the excitement that the teacher shows for the subject than the amount of information the students learn.

Intensity seems to come quite naturally to people who are ego-involved enough in an issue to risk speaking in a public meeting. Being assigned to speak in a class, however, creates the possibility of your being indifferent, and hence not very intense; but only if you ignore my previous injunction to speak on topics you genuinely *care* about.

Sincerity

Although somewhat less tangible than variety, emphasis, and general intensity, sincerity seems to me to be one of those characteristics of delivery in which facial expression, vocal quality, posture, and bodily movement combine to meet the functions of delivery stated earlier.

The *Oxford Universal Dictionary* defines *sincere* as "characterized by the absence of all dissimulation or pretense; honest, straightforward . . . not falsified or perverted in any way; genuine, pure." Although sincerity is difficult to describe, most people agree that Presidents Reagan and Carter projected it to a high degree—Nixon and Johnson less so.

Actors and con artists may be able to fake sincerity, but for most of us the easiest way to appear to others as sincere is to believe strongly in the ideas we advocate. Most sales managers I know insist that their sales representatives own the products they sell, on the assumption that their sales presentations will be more sincere if they do.

Appropriateness

A final transactional characteristic of delivery is appropriateness. As suggested earlier, our dress, grooming, and pronunciation should be congruent with the expectations of listeners. Using delivery which is appropriate to the expectations of your audience is

TRANSACTIONAL CHARACTERISTICS

also important in the use of your voice, body movements, and gestures as well. A raucous use of the voice and body, which would be appropriate to a pep rally or celebration, might be offensive to a professional organization or service club. Some religious organizations expect a pious demeanor and even a special tone of voice, while others do not.

Violating the expectations of listeners by combining the transmissional variables of delivery in inappropriate ways can cost you dearly in credibility, identification, and even attention and intelligibility.

We have seen, then, that your message can be delivered by use of nonverbal cues, transmitted by your voice, bodily movement, facial expression, and gestures. These combine in patterns of variety, emphasis, intensity, sincerity, and appropriateness; which in turn create transactions with your audience fulfilling the functions of attention, intelligibility, credibility, and identification. Figure 6−1 represents these relationships.

FIGURE 6−1
Delivery

Traditional characteristics	Transactional characteristics	Objectives

1. Voice
   Pitch
   Rate
   Volume
   Quality
	Emphasis
	
	Variety
		Intelligibility
		
		Attention

2. Bodily Activity
   Posture
   Gestures
   Facial expression
	Intensity
	
	Sincerity
		
		Credibility

3. Articulation and Pronunciation	Appropriateness	Identification

Source: From Jabusch and Littlejohn, ELEMENTS OF SPEECH COMMUNICATION, p. 227. Copyright © 1981 by Houghton Mifflin Company. Used by permission.

PREPARING FOR DELIVERY

Now that we have discussed the principles underlying competent delivery, let us look at the way your prepare yourself to deliver public speeches. We will discuss the modes of transactional delivery and the techniques of preparation.

Transactional Delivery Modes

All speeches should be well prepared. You owe it to yourself and to your listeners to ensure that a public speaking event goes well. While you should be well prepared for every speech, specific preparation for specific speaking events varies rather widely. I will discuss impromptu, extemporaneous, and manuscript speeches.

Impromptu. Speeches that *appear* to be unprepared are called *impromptu* speeches. You have probably been at a meeting or celebration and observed people who were either "called on to say a few words" or who became involved in a heated debate without having intended to do so—and without having prepared to do so. We will discuss some of these occasions in Chapter 9. In terms of preparation, however, I contend that these speeches should be well prepared, even if *not for the specific time and place* in which they occur. When asked how he could have spoken so eloquently, apparently with no preparation, a great orator once responded, "I've been preparing that speech all my life!" Preparation for impromptu speeches takes two forms.

First is your general level of competence as a public speaker. Reading this book and practicing speaking with the critical feedback of your instructor should contribute to your preparation for unexpected speaking responsibilities. The more experienced you become, the less you will be preoccupied with how your speech is going, and the more you will be able to concentrate on the content of what you are saying as you "think on your feet."

The second area of preparation for impromptu speeches is in the preparation of content. By definition, you cannot prepare the specific content for a specific impromptu speaking occasion. You can, however, make yourself a competent, knowledgeable person in those topic areas on which you are mostly likely to speak.

You can acquire information for impromptu speeches in much the same way that I recommended that you research a specific speaking event. By reading, or watching TV documentaries and reports, you can become not only a generally well-informed person but an expert on topics of importance to you.

Before the widespread availability of libraries, newspapers, TV, and data retrieval systems we enjoy today, one of the primary qualifications of a competent public speaker was *memory*. Memory is no longer as crucial in other modes of delivery, but it is just as important as ever in impromptu speaking. By jotting down key statistics, practicing telling and retelling pertinent stories in addition to simply attending carefully to relevant information, you can have pertinent information readily available to your memory during impromptu speaking. Certainly whatever work you do in memory training will help.

Finally, I suggest that you be careful to speak only when you have something substantive to say. Generally, you will not be called upon unexpectedly to speak on a subject or to commemorate a person or event about which you know little or nothing. Do yourself and your listeners a favor by not volunteering to speak impromptu unless you have something worthwhile to say.

Extempore. Probably the most commonly used mode of delivery in public speaking, and the one I recommend whenever possible, is the extempore or extemporaneous speech. Contrary to popular belief, the extempore speech is extremely well prepared for each specific speaking event. With the exception of writing down the words, all of the principles and practices of preparation discussed in this book apply to extempore speaking. You do all of the situation analysis, research, and organization you would do for any speech. Having completed a detailed, complete sentence outline, you determine the wording, not by writing it out verbatim, but by practicing aloud.

This mode of delivery has several advantages. First, it leaves you flexible to transactionally adapt both your wording and ideas to audience feedback. Second, it precludes the necessity of either memorizing the words or losing eye contact when you read them. Finally, it makes you more confident of your preparation than in the case of the impromptu speech.

Written manuscript. The preparation of a manuscript speech is identical to an extemporaneous speech up to the point of completing your outline. At this point, instead of practicing the wording of your speech, you write it word for word.

This mode of delivery has the advantage of allowing you to select your wording with great care. It is particularly useful if you are in a position of responsibility, like the President of the United States, where subtle nuances of your language are closely watched and could be misinterpreted—with significant consequences. Another context in which manuscript speaking is required is the mass media. Radio and television schedules require precise timing, which is possible only with a written manuscript.

The disadvantages of cutting off feedback, reducing flexibility and conversationality, have been discussed above. I do not recommend writing your speeches unless your instructor (or in later life, a superior or a special situation) requires you to do so.

Techniques of Preparation

As I suggested earlier, *practice* is the primary technique for preparing for the final synthesis of your speech that occurs during delivery. As I also pointed out, you cannot, by definition, practice for a specific impromptu event, but you can gain general experience that will serve you well in impromptu situations. In preparation for extempore and manuscript speaking events you can enhance your delivery with practice.

In practicing for an extempore speaking transaction, you simply take your complete sentence outline, and *with your audience in mind*, begin to talk through the speech. Even though your outline is in sentence form, you do not use the exact wording in the outline. Transitions and other details are not provided in the outline and must be developed in practice. For instance, your outline may say "I. Tell the story of the stained shoes." During practice you will actually tell the story. It will take time and, while the specific words will be slightly different, the telling should improve with each practice.

Between the last subpoint under your first main point and the second main point, your outline should show blank space, as follows:

I. Main idea: Tabloid format
  A. Subpoint
  B. Subpoint
    1. data
    2. data

    (here)
II. Main point: Style of writing

The wording of the transition here will be developed in practice and could sound like this: "Not only does the format make yellow journalism sensational but so does its style of writing." Then you proceed to develop the second main idea, "Style of writing."

The number of practices required varies with your experience. Very experienced speakers may require only one or two practices. Less experienced speakers usually require a *minimum* of three practices, and some a dozen or more.

Some of my students have sounded as if they had memorized their speeches when actually they had not. They complained that they practiced it too much. That is impossible. Russell Conwell delivered his famous speech "Acres of Diamonds" thousands of times, and each time it sounded spontaneous and unrehearsed. The feeling and sound of memorization results from faulty practice, not from too much of it. When you practice, concentrate on the ideas in your outline and on your potential audience—not the specific words. The words will come more easily with each practice, and they will eventually sound pretty similar. But if you concentrate on the ideas and audience, the words will not sound memorized and will not cut you off from the flexibility to transact discussed earlier.

Another characteristic of your practice is that it be oral—out loud. Some people say they practice by thinking to themselves. While this procedure has some merit, it is no substitute for practicing out loud. By not only selecting your words but practicing them, you can release your voice and body to nonverbally augment the verbal message.

As you practice, try to provide for some feedback. One way to do this is to practice in front of a full-length mirror. Another means of feedback, not only for the visual cues but also your content, is to get a roommate, friend, or spouse to listen and comment. A very effective way to receive feedback is to record or videotape your practice. This, of course, requires access to special equipment, but these are becoming readily available in homes as well as schools.

Practicing for manuscript speaking transactions is similar to practicing for extempore speeches, with some significant exceptions. The most obvious is that your wording is already determined. Your primary concern is with making your reading or memorizing of the manuscript feel and sound conversational and spontaneous. You must free yourself of the manuscript so that you can transact with the audience.

As you practice reading a manuscript, concentrate on the thought so that your timing and stress convey the meaning you originally intended when you wrote the manuscript. Keep practicing so that you know the manuscript well enough not only to make it sound conversational but to think more about the audience and ideas, and less about the words. If you cannot memorize perfectly, you will become preoccupied with remembering the words and lose audience contact. It is best to read it well and maintain contact with the audience. Personally, I have not had occasion to deliver a speech from memory since participating in highly restricted public speaking contests twenty-five years ago!

From our transactional perspective, then, regardless of the mode of delivery, your preparation and practice should be designed to maximize your ability to concentrate on ideas, monitor audience feedback, and remain flexible to adjust to contingencies arising during the actual delivery of the speech.

SUMMARY

In this chapter we have looked at delivery as the final synthesis of your speech as it evolves during the dynamic transactional process with your listeners.

We found that delivery serves the transactional functions of getting and maintaining attention, achieving intelligibility for your ideas, building your credibility as a speaker, and creating identification with your listeners.

Traditional considerations of delivery focused on nonverbal cues. The voice can be varied in pitch, rate, volume, and quality to enhance or even change the verbal message. Bodily activity, in terms of appearance, body movement, and gestures, can also communicate nonverbal messages. Facial expressions—especially eye contact—are particularly important transmittors of affective messages. Articulation and pronunciation also contribute to the nonverbal communication in your speech.

These transmissional variables are combined and patterned to achieve transactional characteristics such as variety, emphasis, intensity, sincerity, and approrpriateness with which your audience can readily identify.

In preparing for delivery you select from among the impromptu, extempore, or written modes. Extensive oral practice prepares you to monitor audience feedback and adjust to contingencies.

"Cross of Gold"

William Jennings Bryan

I would be presumptuous, indeed, to present myself against the distinguished gentlemen to whom you have listened if this were a mere measuring of abilities; but this is not a contest between persons. The humblest citizen in all the land, when clad in the armor of a righteous cause, is stronger than all the hosts of error. I come to speak to you in defense of a cause as holy as the cause of liberty—the cause of humanity.

When this debate is concluded, a motion will be made to lay upon the table the resolution offered in commendation of the administration, and also the resolution offered in comdemnation of the administration. We object to bringing this question down to the level of persons. The individual is but an atom; he is born, he acts, he dies; but principles are eternal; and this has been a contest over a princille.

Never before in the history of this country has there been witnessed such a contest as that through which we have just passed. Never before in the history of American politics has a great issue been fought out as this issue has been, by the voters of a great party. On the fourth of March, 1895, a few Democrats, most of them members of Congress, issued an address to the Democrats of the nation, asserting that the money question was the paramount issue of the hour; declaring that a majority of the Democratic party had the right to control the action of the party on this paramount issue; and concluding with the request that the believers in the free coinage of silver in the Democratic party should organize, take charge of, and control the policy of the Democratic party. Three months later, at Memphis, an organization was perfected, and the silver Democrats went forth openly and courageously proclaiming their belief, and declaring that, if success-

Source: From *Speeches of William Jennings Bryan*, vol. 1 (New York: Funk and Wagnalls, 1909), pp. 238–249.

ful, they would crystallize into a platform the declaration which they had made. Then began the conflict. With a zeal approaching the zeal which inspired the Crusaders who followed Peter the Hermit, oursilver Democrats went forth from victory unto victory until they are now assembled, not to discuss, not to debate, but to enter up the judgment already rendered by the plain people of this country. In this contest brother has been arrayed against brother, father against son. The warmest ties of love, acquaintance and association have been disregarded; old leaders have been cast aside when they have refused to give expression to the sentiments of those whom they would lead, and new leaders have sprung up to give direction to this cause of truth. Thus has the contest been waged, and we have assembled here under as binding and solemn instructions as were ever imposed upon representatives of the people.

We do not come as individuals. As individuals we might have been glad to compliment the gentleman from New York [Senator Hill], but we know that the people for whom we speak would never be willing to put him in a position where he could thwart the will of the Democratic party. I say it was not a question of persons, it was a question of principle, and it is not with gladness, my friends, that we find ourselves brought into conflict with those who are now arrayed on the other side.

The gentleman who preceded me [ex-Governor Russell] spoke of the State of Massachusetts; let me assure him that not one present in all this convention entertains the least hostility to the people of the State of Massachusetts, but we stand here representing the people who are the equals, before the law, of the greatest citizens in the State of Massachusetts. When you [turning to the gold delegates] come before us and tell us that we are about to disturb your business interests, we reply that you have disturbed our business interests by your course.

We say to you that you have made the definition of a business man too limited in its application. The man who is employed for wages is as much a business man as his employer, the attorney in a country town is as much a business man as the corporation counsel in a great metropolis; the merchant at the cross-roads store is as much a business man as the merchant of New York; the farmer who goes forth in the morning and toils all day—who begins in the spring and toils all summer—and who by the application of brain and muscle to the natural resources of the country creates wealth, is as much a business man as the man who goes upon the board of trade and bets upon the price of grain; the miners who go down a thousand feet into the earth, or climb two thousand feet upon the cliffs, and bring forth from their hiding places the precious metals to be poured into the channels of trade are as much business men as the few financial magnates who, in a back room, corner the money of the world. We come to speak for this broader class of business men.

Ah, my friends, we say not one word against those who live upon the Atlantic coast, but the hardy pioneers who have braved all the dangers of the wilderness, who have made the desert to blossom as the rose—the pioneers away out there [pointing to the west], who rear their children near to Nature's heart, where they can mingle their voices with the voices of the birds—out there where they have erected school houses for the education of their young, churches where they praise their Creator, and cemeteries where rest the ashes of their dead—these people, we say, are as deserving of the consideration of our party as any people in this country. It is for these that we speak. We do not come as aggressors. Our war is not a war of conquest; we are fighting in the defense of our homes, our families, and posterity. We have petitioned, and our petitions have been scorned; we have entreated, and our entreaties have been disregarded; we have begged, and they have mocked when our calamity came. We beg no longer; we petition no more. We defy them.

The gentleman from Wisconsin has said that he fears a Robespierre. My friends, in this land of the free you need not fear that a tyrant will spring up from among the people. What we need is an Andrew Jackson to stand, as Jackson stood, against the encroachments of organized wealth.

They tell us that this platform was made to catch votes. We reply to them that changing conditions make new issues; that the principles on which Democracy rests are as everlasting as the hills, but that they must be applied to new conditions as they arise. Conditions have arisen, and we are here to meet those conditions. They tell us that the income tax ought not be brought in here; that it is a new idea. They criticize us for our criticism of the Supreme Court of the United States. My friends, we have not criticized; we have simply called attention to what you already know. If you want criticisms, read the dissenting opinions of the court. There you will find criticisms. They say that we passed an unconstitutional law; we deny it. The income tax law was not unconstitutional when it was passed; it was not unconstitutional when it went before the Supreme Court for the first time; it did not become unconstitutional until one of the judges changed his mind, and we cannot be expected to know when a judge will change his mind. The income tax is just. It simply intends to put the burdens of government upon the backs of the people. I am in favor of an income tax. When I find a man who is not willing to bear his share of the burdens of the government which protects him, I find a man who is unworthy to enjoy the blessings of a government like ours.

They say that we are opposing national bank currency; it is true. If you will read what Thomas Benton said, you will find he said that, in searching history, he could find but one parallel to Andrew Jackson; that was Cicero, who destroyed the conspiracy of Cataline and saved Rome. Benton said that Cicero only did for Rome what Jackson did for us when he destroyed the bank conspiracy and saved America. We say in our platform that we believe that the right to coin and issue money is a function of government. We believe it. We believe that it is a part of sovereignty, and can no more with safety be delegated to private individuals than we can afford to delegate to private individuals the power to make penal statutes or levy taxes. Mr. Jefferson, who was once regarded as good Democratic authority, seems to have differed in opinion from the gentleman who has addressed us on the part of the minority. Those who are opposed to this proposition tell us that the issue of paper money is a function of the bank, and that the Government ought to go out of the banking business. I stand with Jefferson rather than with them, and tell them, as he did, that the issue of money is a function of government, and that banks ought to go out of the governing business.

They complain about the plank which declares against life tenure in office. They have tried to strain it to mean that which it does not mean. What we oppose by that plank is the life tenure which is being built up in Washington, and which excludes from participation in official benefits the humbler members of society.

Let me call your attention to two or three important things. The gentleman from New York says that he will propose an amendment to the platform providing that the proposed change in our monetary system shall not affect contracts already made. Let me remind you that there is no intention of affecting those contracts which according to present laws are made payable in gold; but if he means to say that we cannot change our monetary system without protecting those who have loaned money before the change was made, I desire to ask him where, in law or in morals, he can find justification for not protecting the debtors when the act of 1873 was passed, if he now insists that we must protect the creditors.

He says he will also propose an amendment which will provide for the suspension of free coinage if we fail to maintain the parity within a year. We reply that when we advocate a policy which we believe will be successful, we are not compelled to raise a doubt as to our own sincerity by suggesting what we shall do if we fail. I ask him, if he would apply his logic to us, why he does not apply it to himself. He says he wants this country to try to secure an international agreement. Why does he not tell us whathe is going to do if he fails to secure an international agreement? There is more reason for him to do that than there is for us to provide against the failure to maintain the parity. Our opponents have tried for twenty years to secure an international agreement, and those are waiting for it most patiently who do not want it at all.

And now, my friends, let me come to the paramount issue. If they ask us why it is that we say more on the money question than we say upon the tariff question, I reply that, if protection has slain its thousands, the gold standard has slain its tens of thousands. If they ask us why we do not embody in our platform all the things that we believe in, we reply that when we have restored the money of the Constitution all other necessary reforms will be possible; but that until this is done there is no other reform that can be accomplished.

Why is it that within three months such a change has come over the country? Three months ago, when it was confidently asserted that those who believe in the gold standard would frame our platform and nominate our candidate, even the advocates of the gold standard did not think that we could elect a President. And they had good reason for their doubt, because there is scarcely a State here today asking for the gold standard which is not in the absolute control of the Republican party. But note the change. Mr. McKinley was nominated at St. Louis upon a platform which declared for the maintenance of the gold standard until it can be changed into bimetalism by international agreement. Mr. McKinley was the most popular man among the Republicans, and three months ago everybody in the Republican party prophesied his election. How is it today? Why, the man who was once pleased to think that he looked like Napoleon—that man shudders today when he remembers that he was nominated on the anniversary of the battle of Waterloo. Not only that, but as he listens he can hear with ever-increasing distinctness the sounds of the waves as they beat upon the lonely shores of St. Helena.

Why this change? Ah, my friends, is not the reason for the change evidence to any one who will look at the matter? No private character, however pure, no personal popularity, however great, can protect from the avenging wrath of an indignant people a man who will declare that he is in favor of fastening the gold standard upon this country, or who is willing to surrender the right of self-government and place the legislative control of our affairs in the hands of foreign potentates and powers.

We go forth confident that we shall win. Why? Because upon the paramount issue of this campaign there is not a spot of ground upon which the enemy will dare to challenge battle. If they tell us that the gold standard is a good thing, we shall point to their platform and tell them that their platform pledges the party to get rid of the gold standard and substitute bimetalism. If the gold standard is a good thing, why try to get rid of it? I call your attention to the fact that some of the very people who are in this convention today and who tell us that we ought to declare in favor of international bimetalism—thereby declaring that the gold standard is wrong and that the principle of bimetalism is better—these very people four months ago were open and avowed advocates of the gold standard, and were then telling us that we could not legislate two metals together, even with the aid of all the world. If the gold standard is a good thing, we ought to declare in favor of its retention and not in favor of abandoning it; and if the gold standard is a bad thing, why should we wait until other nations are willing to help us to let go? Here is the line of battle, and we care not upon which issue they force the fight; we are prepared to meet them on either issue or on both. If they tell us that the gold standard is the standard of civilization, we reply to them that this, the most enlightened of all the nations of the earth, has never declared for a gold standard and that both the great parties this year are declaring against it. If the gold standard is the standard of civilization, why, my friends, should we not have it? If they come to meet us on that issue we can present the history of our nation. More than that; we can tell them that they will search the pages of history in vain to find a single instance where the common people have ever declared themselves in favor of the gold standard. They can find where the holders of fixed investments have declared for a gold standard, but not where the masses have.

Mr. Carlisle said in 1878 that this was a struggle between "the idle holders of idle capital" and "the struggling masses, who produce the wealth and pay the taxes of the country"; and, my friends, the question we are to decide is: Upon which side will the Democratic party fight; upon the side of "the idle holders of idle capital" or upon the side of "the struggling masses"? That is the question which the party must answer first, and then it must be answered by each individual hereafter. The sympathies of the Democratic party, as shown by the platform, are on the side of the struggling masses who have ever been the foundation of the Democratic party. There are two ideas of government. There are those who believe that, if you will only legislate to make the well-to-do prosperous, their prosperity will leak through on those below. The Democratic idea, however, is that if you legislate to make the masses prosperous, their prosperity will find its way up through every class which rests upon them.

You come to us and tell us that the great cities are in favor of the gold standard; we reply that the great cities rest upon our broad and fertile prairies. Burn down your cities and leave our farms, and your cities will spring up again as if by magic; but destroy our farms and the grass will grow in the streets of every city in the country.

My friends, we declare that this nation is able to legislate for its own people on every question, without waiting for the aid or consent of any other nation on earth; and upon that issue we expect to carry every State in the Union. I shall not slander the inhabitants of the fair State of Massachusetts nor the inhabitants of the State of New York by saying that, when they are confronted with the proposition, they will declare that this nation is not able to attend to its own business. It is the issue of 1776 over again. Our ancestors, when but three millions in number, had the courage to declare their political independence of every other nation; shall we, their descendants, when we have grown to seventy millions, declare that we are less independent than our forefathers? No, my friends, that will never be the verdict of our people. Therefore, we care not upon what lines the battle is fought. If they say bimetalism is good, but that we cannot have it until the other nations help us, we reply that, instead of having a gold standard because England has, we will restore bimetalism, and then let England have bimetalism because the United States has it. If they care to come out in the open field and defend the gold standard as a good thing, we will fight them to the uttermost. Having behind us the producing masses of this nation and the world, supported by the commercial interests, the laboring interests, and the toilers everywhere, we will answer their demand for a gold standard by saying to them: You shall not press down upon the brow of labor this crown of thorns, you shall not crucify mankind upon a cross of gold.

DELIVERY: TRANSACTIONAL SYNTHESIS

ENDNOTES

1. Glenn R. Capp, *Famous Speeches in American History* (New York: Bobbs-Merrill, 1963), pp. 129–130.

2. For a complete discussion, see Virgil A. Anderson, *Training the Speaking Voice* (New York: Oxford University Press, 1942).

3. Judy Burgoon and Thomas Saine, *The Unspoken Dialogue* (Boston: Houghton Mifflin, 1978), p. 54.

4. Mark Knapp, *Non Verbal Communication in Human Interaction* 2d ed. (New York: Holt, Rinehart, and Winston, 1978), pp. 270–277.

7

Informative Transactions

In this chapter:
Analyzing informative transactions
The content of informative transactions
Organizing informative transactions
Language in informative transactions
Summary
Chase Peterson, Post-Operation News Conferences

Shortly before Christmas in 1982, medical history was made when Dr. William DeVries implanted an artificial heart into the chest of a dying Seattle dentist named Barney Clark. Public attention was focused on the University of Utah Medical Center and reporters from around the globe descended on Salt Lake City. Doctors and dog-catchers, architects and astronauts, Muslims and Moonies alike wanted to know the details. How was Dr. Clark? How did the heart work? What was the operation like? As with any experimental procedure, unforeseen problems arose. Dr. Clark's condition was changing constantly, as was the information to be disseminated to the public.

The University had planned carefully, not only for the medical procedure, but also for the complex public communication. Reporters were treated fairly and equally. With one exception, no information was leaked to local insiders. Regular briefing sessions were scheduled, and special sessions were held when events demanded it.

Although several carefully selected people were interviewed from time to time, the primary spokesperson was not a local media personality, nor a trained public relations expert—he was the knowledgeable and articulate University of Utah Vice-President for Medical Affairs, Dr. Chase Peterson, a physician.

The problem he faced was not an easy one. How do you communicate to a large, highly heterogeneous audience a very complex, sophisticated medical procedure with profound emotional, personal, and ethical implications? It would have been easy to have leaped into specialized explanations and technical jargon, as so many "experts" do—impressive, perhaps, but confusing and frustrating to listeners. Chase Peterson made a far more difficult task look easy: that of clearly sharing the complexities of the situation in terms anyone could understand.

Sharing understanding is a public communication transaction with which we are frequently confronted. Teachers face it daily. Business people need to explain their product. Teenagers need to understand their sexuality. Politicians and other public figures often need to "set the record straight."

In Chapter 2 we spoke of several kinds of communication gaps or differences that can be bridged with transactional ideas and supporting materials. Of particular importance in informative transactions are sharing comprehension or understanding, interest, clarity, and memory. We will discuss how these transactions can be enhanced by the analysis of informative ideas, content, organization, and language.

Chase Peterson explains the artificial-heart surgery

ANALYZING INFORMATIVE TRANSACTIONS

While sharing understanding is an important part of all communication transactions, there are some kinds of ideas that are particularly germane to informative transactions. We will discuss analysis of abstract concepts, processes, history, distinguishing characteristics, space relations, common misconceptions, functions, perspectives, and categories.

Abstract Concepts

One of the most difficult types of understandings to share is an *abstract concept*. Philosophers are particularly known for discussing the meanings and ramifications of ethics, aesthetics, or beauty. Scientists and mathematicians are also concerned with concepts such as momentum, infinity, or zero. But intellectuals are not the only ones concerned with abstract concepts. What person has not struggled with the concepts of love, discrimination, or inflation?

Ideas as well as words can be viewed as being at different levels of abstraction. Hence an idea which is difficult to understand because it represents a relatively high level of abstraction can be clarified by dividing it into its components or characteristics which are at a lower level of abstraction, and hence closer to our human experience. Thus Dietrich Bonhoffer once discussed *responsibility* as being a balance between freedom and obedience. The concept of God has frequently been described in terms of love, justice, power, intelligence, or influence.

Abstract concepts can also be shared by discussing how people experience them. Thus you may hear people share the meaning of automation, beauty, or procrastination by the way they feel, or the way these concepts have affected their lives. In either case, abstract concepts can be supported, clarified, and shared by other, less abstract, ideas that are closer to your listeners' experience.

Processes

A second kind of information you may wish to share with listeners is a *process*. At one time the "how to" speech was very popular; unfortunately, these became centered more on the process than the needs of listeners and were frequently devoted to insignificant topics such as "how to build a campfire" or "how to swing a tennis racket." In recent years, however, an increase in leisure time, as well as rising labor costs, have seen a growing interest in "doing it yourself." Night classes teaching everything from stained glass to oriental cooking are enriching people's lives.

A physicist communicates an abstract concept with a lively demonstration

"How to" processes can usually be broken down into smaller, more manageable steps. A woodworking project, for instance, usually involves planning, rough cutting, fine cutting or shaping, gluing, sanding, and finishing. If you speak on this "how-to" subject you will probably find that the short time you have may require you to limit your speech to only one of the subprocesses, but I'm sure a competent woodworking teacher could talk about the fine points of wood finishing for hours.

Other processes simply pose curiosities. For instance, people may wonder how a particular product is manufactured, how a volcano is formed, or how a city disposes of its sewage. In analyzing a process or procedure you should ask questions such as the following:

1. What is the input or raw material for the process?
2. What is the result or product?
3. What are the major stages of the process?
4. What is the general character of the process? (Does it grow, build, disintegrate, reduce, restore, beautify, or alter in some way?)

The answer to the last question is sometimes the most difficult, but it should provide you with a more sharply focused central idea.

History

It is common for inexperienced speakers to begin both informative and persuasive messages with a little historical background. This is usually inappropriate—it is rarely relevant to the specific purpose—but there are times when the historical development of the topic is the most significant way of focusing the entire speech.

As I have traveled in the U.S., Japan, and Mexico, I have been struck by how much more meaningful the experience can be, both during and after, if I know some of the historical development of the cultures and geographic areas I am seeing.

When tracing the historical development of your topic, it is relatively easy to identify ideas from chronological steps, stages, eras, epochs, or phases which enhance the clarity and ease of understanding of your audience.

Distinguishing Characteristics

Sometimes an idea can be better understood by understanding its distinguishing characteristics. The student who wants his classmates to recognize good furniture when they see it supports his central idea, "quality shows," with a discussion of the distinguishing characteristics of quality design, quality materials, and quality workmanship. Likewise, a student who wants her listeners to understand the meaning of *yellow journalism* develops the characteristics of (1) the tabloid format, (2) selection of articles, (3) abrupt style of writing, (4) "scare" headlines, and (5) sensationalized photography as the things that contribute to the sensationalism (her theme) of the yellow press.

Space Relations

Still other ideas can be developed and clarified by *space relations*. Geography can be covered north-to-south or east-to-west; the architecture of a new building from top-to-bottom or vice versa. Travelogues frequently move from city-to-city or historical site–to–cultural center. The description of a war can be developed chronologically or spatially by "theaters" or battle areas.

149

Common Misconceptions

Earlier, when we discussed your motivation to speak, we described how misunderstandings or listeners' misconceptions can motivate you to speak; I know a Lincoln expert, for example, who gives a popular lecture on "Common misconceptions about Lincoln." Every few years the school teachers in the communities in which I have lived get into seemingly impossible contract impasses with their school boards. In most cases, both parties are operating on major misconceptions—the teachers about the budgeting process and the school board about the meaning of professionalism and the nature of the teachers' work. The sharing of information, designed to overcome these misconceptions and based on the needs of your listeners, can provide transactional focus for your entire talk.

Functions

Informative ideas can also be developed by discussing their functions. A *function* is something that is done or accomplished. If you want your listeners to understand the nature of a foreign diplomat's job, you might discuss it in terms of the functions the diplomat performs for the government represented, not the least of which may be intelligence gathering. And recall that earlier we discussed the functions of the conclusion of a message, which are reorientation, remotivation, and termination.

Perspectives

Greater insight and understanding can be accomplished by developing an idea or concept from different perspectives. A *perspective* is a point of view. The same idea or object can appear somewhat different depending on the angle from which you look at it. Mount St. Helens certainly looked different to people before and after its eruption, from the north or south side of the mountain, or depending on whether the viewers were residents, tourists, or geologists. Similarly, human personality or American culture can be explained from different points of view, usually called *theories*. Indeed, all of the ways of developing an informative topic constitute perspectives from which it may be viewed, and several could apply to the same topic. At any rate, your listeners' understanding can usually be enhanced by getting them to look at your subject from a different perspective, or better yet, from several.

Categories

While all of the foregoing approaches to analysis of an informative topic may be viewed as categories, some categorical breakdowns do not fall neatly into the above "categories of categories." Traditionally we have referred to the use of categories as developing your subject *topically*. Recall the informative central idea I mentioned earlier on first aid, "Keep the patient alive." This was developed by sharing the topics (1) "Stop the bleeding," (2) "Restore breathing," and (3) "Treat for shock." These topics need be treated in no particular chronology nor space relations. They are simply topics that, taken together, constitute the whole and fully clarify the central idea.

A final word about transactional focus is in order. As mentioned before, more than one—or all—of the methods for developing a central idea with other ideas might be applied to any particular topic. However, the one you select can add substantially to the *focus* or unity of the transaction. I have heard speeches that combined ideas from several of these methods of development, and the listeners were frequently more confused after the speech than before. Your selection of a single method of development will be governed by your specific purpose. Which method of development will meet the listeners' greatest needs regarding your topic? Focusing on the most appropriate of the approaches will meet your purpose by greatly enhancing the understanding of your topic by your audience.

THE CONTENT OF INFORMATIVE TRANSACTIONS

As we saw in Chapter 3, the actual job of transacting in public communication contexts is accomplished by concrete, substantial materials which support and amplify your main and supporting ideas. Any of the supporting materials described in Chapter 3 may be used, but of particular importance in informative contexts are examples, comparisons, and reiteration. In order to reinforce their importance in informative transactions, we will relate these supporting materials to the way psychologists believe people learn new information.

Examples

One of the most useful types of supporting material in any communication transaction is the example or specific instance. In informative transactions examples are particularly important because of people's tendency to learn by *modeling* the behavior of others. We have all seen small children mimic the walk or talk of their parents; and every generation of young athletes seems to become more skilled by modeling the "moves" of Bob Cousy, "Dr. J," or the Fosbery "flop."

Psychologist Albert Bandura demonstrated that under certain conditions children will model violent behavior. Likewise, my own research has demonstrated that some people can learn public speaking or the use of visual aids more effectively by observing good models or examples. Examples can be incorporated into informative speeches by the description of specific stories, demonstrations, or prepared models.

But how does this apply to your public speaking? I have seen golf and skiing instructors demonstrate the correct golf grip or mogul technique and then have students either imitate it or pose in the correct position until it looks and feels right. I have seen a student speaker illustrate a point about ballet by first explaining it and then demonstrating it by dancing. I have seen art and graphics teachers lift the aspiration level of their students, as well as clarify what they meant, by showing students examples of superior paintings or graphics. I have seen young people learn how to cook, build houses, and raise vegetables by watching their skillful parents. You can substantially enhance your ability to share comprehension, interest, clarity, and memory by using specific instances that listeners can model, by either describing or demonstrating those examples.

Comparisons

In Chapter 3 we discussed analogies, similes, and metaphors as comparisons which interpret that which is unknown in terms of that which is known, or the unfamiliar in terms of the familiar. One of the most researched ways of learning is learning by *association*. The psychologist Pavlov was able to train his dog to salivate at the sound of a bell by associating the bell with food.

Similarly, teachers help students understand new ideas by comparing them to concepts or experiences with which the students are already familiar. As we saw earlier, my child was able to grasp the abstract concept of energy acting upon mass by associating it with the familiar experience of the effort required to move a large rock. I have heard our human circulatory system compared to a complex freeway, carrying food and supplies to the extremities and picking up waste on the return trip.

Finally, note that the use of association or comparison is highly transactional. It requires an understanding of what listeners already know, followed by a conscious effort to share new information by relating it to existing knowledge and experience.

Reiteration

Repetition and restatement, or redundancy, are characteristic of oral communication. "I'm going to make you do it until you get it right," admonish some parents and teachers.

The efficacy of reiteration in sharing information is soundly based in learning theory. A prominent method of learning is by *exposure*. It is as if exposure to a given idea or skill predisposes us to "catch" it or understand it eventually. This is the presupposition on which such learning techniques as drill, practice, and recitation are based. Reiteration is also one of the bases for the effects of advertising. Whether you are playing a piano, shooting a basketball, or speaking in public, the more you practice the recommended techniques, the more skillful you will become.

In the information transaction, reiteration takes many forms. In our organization of introduction, body, and conclusion, we tell them what we are going to tell them; we tell them; and then we tell them what we told them. Transitions are a form of reiteration. The point of a transition is "not only does this point support the main idea but so does my next point."

Illustrations and other forms of support are also methods for building redundancy; and finally, our language can be used in such a way as to say the same thing in a variety of interesting ways.

Multisensory Aids

Although not a distinct form of support or content, multisensory aids are particularly important in communicating our content in informative transactions. Both models and demonstrations are themselves multisensory methods of sharing specific instances with listeners.

I have seen both students and teachers use, to great advantage, such multisensory aids as pictures and slides of plants and animals; specimens of rocks, flowers, and archeological artifacts; equipment that illustrated a principle of physics or engineering; as well as graphs and charts that illustrated a plethora of other informative ideas.

Multisensory aids enhance the information transaction by identifying your ideas with listeners on all five sensory dimensions—sight, sound, taste, touch, and smell.

ORGANIZING INFORMATIVE TRANSACTIONS

While the organization of messages for informative transactions is not unique, the application of principles of organization to informative contexts (discussed in Chapter 4) merits some attention. We will discuss the principles of organizing the introduction, body, and conclusion as they apply to information transactions.

Introduction

In Chapter 4 we introduced the functions of attention, motivation, accreditation, and orientation. Attention and motivation are important in information transactions, but not particularly distinctive; in a sense, you simply want to create a "need to *know*" the central idea you are going to develop in the body. This can be done with striking examples, statistics, or quotations; or by posing a curiosity you think your audience may share.

Accrediting yourself as a dependable source of information is important. Most speakers in information contexts (teachers, for example) are selected because they are qualified. If you are a special visitor to a group, the person who introduces you will most likely establish your qualifications. However, if you speak with an audience without the establishment of your credentials in advance, you may need to briefly mention your involvement with the topic in the introduction.

The orientation of the audience to the topic is of particular importance in an informative transaction. It usually takes the form of a straightforward statement of your central idea and an initial summary of your main ideas. This will serve as an overview of where you are going, and will give the audience a perspective to which they can relate specific information.

Body

Our earlier discussion of analyzing different types of information transactions, such as abstract concepts, processes, and the like, suggested approaches for organizing informative messages. For instance, the development of a process would probably take the major steps of the process and organize them chronologically or in the order they occur over time.

In organizing information transactions we are much more direct, even obvious, than we may be in persuasive or specialized transactions. There is no need to be indirect or suggestive. The relationships among ideas, between ideas and supports, and the general view of where we are going should be obvious to the listeners at all times.

A particularly effective way of keeping our organization clear to listeners is through *transitions*. As we go from point to point we give the audience "sign posts" telling them where we are going. Recall the informative speech on first aid. The central idea was "Keep the patient alive"; the first main idea was "Stop the bleeding"; while the second was "Restore breathing." Your transition between the two main ideas might sound like this: "In order to keep the patient alive you must not only stop the bleeding, but also restore breathing, if it has stopped." In this way, you are giving the listener a sign post that says, "Leave point one and go on to point two." There is nothing subtle about it, but it is *clear*.

Conclusion

The functions of the conclusion (reorientation, remotivation, termination) are all important in informative transactions. *Reorientation* takes the form of a summary of the main ideas and a reiteration of the central idea. The conclusion for a speech on the golf swing might sound like this:

> We have seen that in order to develop a consistent, repeating golf swing [central idea] we need a grip that bonds our body to the club, a comfortable stance, a controlled backswing, and a high follow-through.

Remotivation is necessary to be sure that the audience is at least awake when you tie the entire speech together. This can be accomplished with a particularly striking story or some other form of support.

Termination in informative contexts is less complex than in other situations and is usually a matter of stopping without being abrupt or inordinately repetitious. Many informative speakers simply end with a summary like the above. Others combine remotivation and termination with one clinching example or story. Still others make a concluding statement like "I hope these tips on the golf swing will make your next round more enjoyable."

As you can see, due to the need for clarity, reorientation is probably the most important function of conclusions in informative transactions.

LANGUAGE IN INFORMATIVE TRANSACTIONS

Of all the characteristics of language we discussed in Chapter 5, perhaps the most crucial in informative transactions is clarity. Here we discuss how you can enhance the clarity of your message by using language that is familiar, specific, and simple.

One way of achieving clarity through language is by using words that are familiar to listeners, or by using new words in familiar contexts which makes their meaning clear. As we pointed out earlier, words like *parity* or *ethnoarcheology* may be the subject of an entire speech to inform, but if the meaning of unfamiliar terms is not the primary focus of the speech, then you should avoid the use of too many of them unless they can be explained quickly without distracting from your main line of reasoning, or unless the context makes them immediately clear.

Notice in the speech at the end of this chapter how Chase Peterson either uses familiar words or relates his words to experiences and images that are familiar to listeners.

Another way of enhancing clarity in the absence of shared experiences is to be as *specific* as possible. It is more likely that your listeners will misperceive your intended meaning if you say the word *tree* than if you say *majestic redwood*.

If you were to ask an acquaintance what he or she thought of a person you had never met, which answer would share more information?—"He's real cool, man," or "He is sensitive, attractive, intelligent, and fun to be with"? In order to avoid misunderstandings and enhance clarity, you should be as specific with your language as possible.

Another factor contributing to clarity is *simplicity* of language. The simpler your language, the clearer it is likely to be with less specialized audiences.

An important aspect of simplicity is the technicality of the language you use. Every field has its jargon. No doubt the use of highly technical language is both necessary and efficient when used within a group whose members understand the denotative meaning of the highly technical words being used. However, when communicating with people outside the technical "in" groups, as public speakers frequently do, great care must be taken to interpret the concepts of nontechnical language with which the listener can identify.

Consider the following story in which clarity is lost or achieved depending on the simplicity, familiarity, and technicality of the words used by the communicator:

> A plumber wrote to a governmnt agency, saying he found that hydrochloric acid quickly opened drain pipes. Was this a good thing to use? A scientist et the agency replied that "the efficacy of hydrochloric acid is indisputable, but the corrosive residue is incompatible with metallic permanence." The plumber wrote back, thanking him for assurances that hydrochloric acid was all right. Disturbed by this turn of affairs, the scientist showed the letter to his boss—another scientist—who then wrote to the plumber: "We cannot assume responsibility for the production of toxic and noxious residue with hydrochloric acid and suggest you use an alternative procedure." The plumber wrote back that he agreed, hydrochloric acid worked fine. Greatly disturbed by this misunderstanding, the scientists took their problem to the top boss. He broke with jargon and wrote to the plumber: "Don't use hydrochloric acid. It eats hell out of the pipes."[1]

SUMMARY

In this chapter we have examined public communication transactions designed to share information or understanding.

We looked at how speakers and listeners analyze ideas that relate to abstract concepts, processes, historical or chronological development, distinguishing characteristics, space relations, common misconceptions, functions, perspectives, and categories.

Developing informative content relates forms of support to the way people learn. Concrete examples can enhance understanding through modeling; comparisons foster learning by association; and reiteration encourages learning by simple exposure. Multisensory aids enhance understanding by communicating information through more than one medium.

In organizing informative information, the function of orientation is particularly important in both the introduction and conclusion of a speech. A direct approach, combined with clear transitions, enhances the sharing of information in the body of a speech. Clarity of language is particularly desirable in information transactions. Clarity can be enhanced by using language that is familiar to listeners, as well as both specific and simple.

Post-Operation News Conferences

Chase Peterson

DECEMBER 2, 1982

Dr. DeVries has been in surgery now for 5½ hours. The patient is doing well at the present time, and I am pleased to say that it has been now 50 minutes since the patient was off the heart-lung machine, namely the last 50 minutes the patient has been sustained by his own new heart. There were considerable difficulties the last two or three hours associated with, on the one hand, pulmonary edema which is swelling of the lung caused by his previous congestive heart failure. That was corrected by maneuvers that were taken, and secondly there has been difficulty with fiable or delicate tissues which bled easily. This is a consequence of a cortisone therapy he has been on the last two or three years which was given in an attempt to arrest the deterioration of the heart muscle. Cortisone makes tissues delicate and bleed easily. This has led to some oozing which has taken considerable time to simply mop up and control but this now appears to be under control. The third problem the last two or three hours was getting the outflow track functioning properly and now we can report that the pressures that are coming out of the artificial heart are entirely normal and satisfactory to support him. We're hopeful therefore that in the next fifteen minutes to a half hour they'll be able to close, and he will be moving into the care of the acute nursing team and after a period of observation in the operating room he'll move with that team into the intensive care unit. That's really all that really needs to be said right now. The parameters of the pumping of the artificial heart now appear to be normal. We'll get right back to you. [pause of some time]

I had a chance to talk to Dr. DeVries just now and they are in the final stages of surgery, the patient is on his own artificial heart. He has a blood pressure equivalent to an eighteen-year-old man, and essentially doing very well. Now he is obviously not conscious, he's still under anesthesia and we won't know for a number of hours exactly how he is. As soon as they close, and this should be in the next fifteen, twenty, thirty minutes, whatever. Dr. DeVries doesn't want to close

---

These press conferences were transcribed from audio tapes recorded by Mark Sands, University of Utah Medical Center, and are printed with his permission.

until he's sure all the bleeding has been taken care of. But when it's closed he'll be moved into the surgical intensive care unit and Dr. DeVries is going to go right with him. And he'll be with him for the morning and then sometime around noon or 1:00 I think. Mr. Dwan says that we'll be able to bring Dr. DeVries down as well as the surgical staff and you have the intensive questioning for them as to all they've done.

I'll be glad to entertain questions but in essence we can say that they have been through hard work; they had delicate tissues to work with because of the use of cortisone, to suppress his disease in the past years that led to a lot of oozing [which] had to be meticulously mopped up, so to speak, and stopped before they wanted to close the chest. Otherwise there would be collections of blood in the chest which can lead to infection. I told you about the problem with the pressure on the artificial heart when they first got it going, there was something that simply wasn't giving the right pressures coming out of the left heart; the valve, the kinking of the artery or something simply wasn't working right and they watched it, it didn't improve itself so they went back and corrected it.

Question: [inaudible]

Well they don't know for sure but the beauty is that they had parts. And they simply went back and put another part in. They put another left side in. Here's the system. [Peterson refers to a visual.] This is the left and right side and when they couldn't make the one work to their satisfaction they simply got another one, put it in.

Question: How long will it be before Mr. Clark is conscious, do you know?

Anywhere from one to three hours. It all depends on his own response to anesthesia and how quickly he metabolizes the drugs that are in him.

Question: What's the feeling in there now?

Well, enormous fatigue on the part of the surgeons but somehow that doesn't affect him and he's going to be with him and awake all through the morning. I would say cautious optimism. Optimism because things are working well now, cautious because we'll never be satisfied and Dr. DeVries especially until he sees that man talking and moving his legs, etc. These vessels are opened up that allows all kinds of problems to develop theoretically; we think we've taken care of them all but you never know for sure until you see the man alert.

Question: Where is his family at now?

His family has been here through the night.

Question: Can you give us an idea how bad the bleeding was, how much blood did you have to give him?

I don't know, but it was not arterial spurting bleeding, the kind that you see on some of the shows that you people put on. [laughter] But it was simply an ooze, an oozing from many surfaces. And it was mixed with wash water saline, etc. so it was difficult from watching from afar to actually measure the quantity.

Question: Was there a moment when it was touch and go at any time?

No, it was never tense because at the time when they were working with outflow pressures on the original process he was on a heart-lung machine. So he has that alternative, that fall-back position, and it was only after they were fully satisfied with what the artificial heart was doing that they took him off the heart-lung machine, and that was at 4:09; so he's now been off pumping with his own new artificial heart for the two hours and five minutes.

Question: [inaudible]

Well, I simply asked Dr. DeVries how he felt and he said he'd had a lot of hard work and there was a great deal of simply digging hard during the middle part of the operation while they solved these problems I've talked about. But he felt now that they had them all solved, that he was eager to have him get into intensive care unit, he wanted to be with him until he woke up, watch him carefully. There's so many things, you know you all ask yourself, why do I get a cold, why do I have a sore knee, the question you ought to ask is why don't I always have a cold, why don't my knees always hurt? The body is so complex that it's amazing that it operates as well as it does. And that's [why] I'm answering by saying that there [are] so many things that could go wrong that Dr. DeVries simply doesn't dare say "things are fine" until much more time has gone by.

Question: Could you tell us a bit about the critical period, how long will it be before you really [feel he is] temporarily out of the woods?

The first critical period will be the next three hours until he wakes up and tells us the nature of his nervous system and his general condition. After that it would be probably two or three days. You'll have to ask Dr. DeVries this afternoon to get a more accurate answer but two or three days to be sure we're not developing pneumonia, that the pump is continuing to work well and other complications don't occur. We would hope to see [that] the liver function is improving hourly now, that he is now profusing his liver properly [pause], his lungs, I told you he had pulmonary edema, which is excess fluid in the lungs, and that's already corrected itself with the help of the heart so all these things that they'll keep going in this direction. So I'd say first critical period, three hours, the next one, two or three days and then we'll see.

Question: What was his blood pressure before surgery, was it hypertensive or hypotensive?

Hypotensive, because his heart was not beating strong enough to generate any pressure. A normal pressure for a man 61 years of age should be something like 135 over 85. That's normal and a lot of people are slightly hypertensive about that age. His pressure was 85 to 90 systolic over a lower diastolic. I don't know what that figure was. That's very low for him and consistent with the fact that his heart was really not pumping. It was just almost quivering. Now his blood pressure is 119 over 75. Which is what it ought to be.

Question: To what degree can you call it a success at this point?

The question was what degree can we call success. It's mechanically entirely successful right now. This thing is doing what it is supposed to do and his pressures are normal. Beyond that we have no right to say anything is a success because we don't know how he is doing.

DECEMBER 15, 1982, FOLLOWING FURTHER SURGERY

At 9:45 this morning which was five hours into his 13th day of the artificial heart, Dr. Clark had a sudden drop in his blood pressure. Dr. Jarvik was in the room, Cheryl Perkins was there, the nurse who was watching the drive mechanism. The pressure dropped down to about 80/40, where it had been in the range of 140/80; he was alert during this time; in fact became more alert as if aware himself that something had changed within his body physiology. The cardiac output dropped to a range of about 1.8 to 3 liters, at different times. Immediately Dr. Jarvik and others and Dr. Hastings came in and Dr. Joyce came back to the room; they were just down the hall. And they tried the other heart driver, you recall there are two drivers that are available. So they switched to the other one to see if by any chance that was responsible. An X-ray was taken, and there was no change with the alternate heart driver and so the conclusion was drawn that there was something abnormal about a valve function on the left side of the heart, the right side appeared to be pumping correctly, the left side was overpumping, [there was] regurgitation of some sort. And was reported to you we felt this [was due to a] clot formation blocking the valve function. The valve itself could have been malfunctioning. Or there could have been a tissue flap in some way impinging upon the function of the valve. Mrs. Clark came in the room, Mr. Clark was really very alert at that time, still had the tube in so he wasn't speaking with spoken words but was mouthing words to her and they had considerable discussion. He was aware that the recommendation by Dr. DeVries was to return to surgery. He approved of that decision, although Mrs. Clark was formally the person that signed the permission, she approved of it, was very supportive as a matter of fact. He kissed his wife, at least in the act of blowing a kiss toward her, and was taken to surgery. He was prepped, put on the by-pass, and a break was found in the wirehousing of the mitro-valve, which is the valve on the left side of the heart, which regulates the flow that drops down through the left atrium into the left artificial ventricle. And it allows one-way circulation of the blood and because of the break in the brace on this valve, it allowed the blood to regurgitate in part backup into the atrium with the pumping of the heart. It wasn't a complete rupture of that valve but it was sufficient to change the pressures and require testing. Dr. DeVries had the patient on the by-pass for 46 minutes which compares to almost 4 hours, 13 days ago, and the actual replacement of the left heart was accomplished in 25 minutes. So the man now has a new left heart and a new air drive tube which is placed in a new fresh position in [the] left lower part of the chest and abdomen and that heart has now been functioning normally. Smears were taken, wipings were taken of the inside of the old heart and the right heart was also examined to be sure it was functioning well and it was found to be functioning perfectly, and smears and cultures were taken and no bacteria were seen anywhere on the inner surface of the heart or the great vessels. Cultures will take two or three days to show. But it gives us reassurance that in fact there appears to be no endocarditis, that is, no infection in the heart. There were also no clots anywhere in the hearts, of [the] right one that was left in and or of the old left one that was taken out. Nor were there any clots along the great vessels. So the new left heart was attached, the same Velcro attachment was used, the new drive line was put in, and Dr. Clark has now come through surgery.

Now what can be said about this process with respect to Dr. Clark's prognosis? He was on the by-pass only a very short period of time. That's good. The amount of time when the heart had to be opened was very brief, 25 minutes. He's clearly gone through another stress in terms of his respiratory system and we're concerned, have been all along, you recall; that's the reason the tube's been in so long, about his respiratory condition. He developed some fever yesterday and the fever almost certainly is associated with the focal pneumonia in the left lower part of the lung. None of that is made better by this kind of a process. At the same time it's been cultured, appropriate antibiotics have been given, and there's no special [reason] why it can't be attended to. His white cells have been responding as best they can even though he's been on the cortisone medication, as you remember, and that suppresses white cell response but his white cells have responded appropriately by the putting out of what we call bands or the kind of cells that are best suited to attack this infection. His platelets were returning this morning before surgery and so that process seems to have gone through. So the damage to the blood system and so forth from the by-pass should be minimal.

But he's had his third anesthesia now in 13 days and he does have some degree of pneumonia in the left lower lobe. Now he'll be given a tracheostomy, and probably has been by now, which is a small incision made in the anterior part of the neck to open up access to the trachea directly rather than through the tubing. The tubing has been used because we hoped at all times to be able to take it out tomorrow. Take it out tomorrow was our hope. But it is a temporary thing. And actually it is more irritating to the patient than would be a tracheostomy, which is a hole made for any length of time, and it's a small slit into which is put a small metal tube, about the size of your little finger, and he breathes through that tube. It is less traumatic, less harmful to the trachea, actually, than the intubation tube. It of course is longer lasting but at any time when the need for that opening into the lungs is gone, this thing heals spontaneously; you take the tube out and the tissues close around it, and generally speaking you don't even have to suture it. It closes on its own. This tracheostomy is done so we can have the best possible access to his lungs. To keep him cleaned out, sucked out, with this possible or likely pneumonia and the general secretions he has, and then he's able to talk if he chooses to by simply putting his finger over the opening of the metal tube and that diverts the air up through his normal vocal cords and he's able to speak that way. We think that would be good for him in terms of his communication and his contact. [Pause] Now that's a reasonable summary of what's gone on in these last 5½ hours.

ENDNOTE

1. *The Chicago Sun*, February 17, 1947, p. 10. In McBurney and Wrage, *The Art of Good Speech*, 1953, pp. 360–361. News Group, Inc., 1947. Reprinted with the permission of the *Chicago Sun-Times*.

8

Persuasive Transactions

In this chapter:
Defining persuasion
Sharing rationality
Sharing motivation (affective appeals)
Sharing trust (ethos)
Building resistance to change
Organizing persuasive transactions
Summary
Ronald Reagan, "Stay the Course"

The summer of 1982 was a hot one for the Republican Party. The economic policies of President Reagan were controversial. Substantial shifts in federal expenditures had been made from social service programs to military preparedness. Inflation was down, but unemployment had risen to over 10 percent, the highest since the Great Depression, and in some communities it was even worse. Although the President was not running for re-election, the campaign was seen by many as a referendum on his policies. Many of his supporters in Congress were slipping behind in the polls.

It was decided that the President would appear on television to explain his policies and urge Americans to "stay the course," by giving his policies more time to work and returning his supporters to Congress. Reagan's identification with the voters had been largely personal—that is, they trusted him. However, during the campaign he had been attacked as being ill-informed and out of control of the vast machinery of government.

In his speech, he appealed to American values and human emotions. Most of all, he appeared to appeal to people's reason. Was this designed to convince them with logic or to restore their eroding trust by demonstrating his competent command of circumstances?

Perhaps it was both. In any case, the trend was reversed: on election night the Republicans achieved a standoff in the U.S. Senate races and experienced a nominal loss of votes in the House of Representatives. Reagan and the Republicans had dodged yet another bullet.

With the exception of transactions that take place in your classes, the vast majority of the public communication situations in which you participate could be called persuasive events. Consider the following: a religious leader exhorts worshippers to greater faith or commitment; two presidential candidates vie for votes in a televised debate; a business representative presents a project proposal in hopes that his company will receive a contract; a teacher tries to get the local members of the N.E.A. to oppose some recent budget cuts; a citizen appeals to a neighborhood meeting to support the location of a half-way house in their neighborhood. In this chapter we examine what we mean by persuasion, some of the variables that affect persuasive change, and resistance to change.

DEFINING PERSUASION

Until recently, *persuasion* has typically been defined as "human communication designed to influence others by modifying their beliefs, values, or attitudes."[1] Close examination of this definition reveals that it focuses primarily on the communication strategies one person devises to influence another person to change attitude. As a transactional perspective has been applied to persuasion, our concept has been broadened to include influence on changes in people's decision-making and other behaviors, as well as attitude. It has further caused us to look at these variables as less transmitted or manipulated by one communicator and more *shared* by communicators, or at least *simultaneously* manipulated, transmitted, and received by all active participants in a communication event. Smith has recently gone a step further to define persuasion as self-influence when she says,

> Persuasion is best viewed as a symbolic activity whose purpose is to effect the internalization or voluntary acceptance of new cognitive states or patterns of overt behavior through exchange of messages.[2]

We have attempted to incorporate the reciprocal, simultaneous nature of persuasion when we defined it elsewhere as "responsible communication leading to mutually desirable change or resistance to change."[3]

Note that this approach to persuasion implies several distinguishing characteristics[4]:

1. It is *interpersonal.*
2. It results in a response or *effect*, that is, change or decision to change beliefs, attitudes, values, or behavior; or it enhances resistance to change these variables.
3. It is accomplished by *messages* or symbolic interaction.
4. Communicators perceive a *choice* among alternatives.
5. Effects are those *intended* by the communicators.

With this general overview of persuasion, let us look at variables people share in persuasive transactions in the rational, affective, and personal domains.

SHARING RATIONALITY

Everyone considers herself or himself to be a reasonable person. Indeed, our ability to think abstractly is one of the things that characterizes us as human beings. It follows, then, that we influence one another by appearing to be rational ourselves as well as appealing to the reasonableness of others.

Earlier we spoke of the relationship between claims and the data on which they are based. We also discussed in some detail the types of data or forms of support (examples, statistics, testimony, comparisons, stories, reiteration, and explanation). Now let us look at the reasoning processes by which we arrive at claims on the basis of these data.

Traditional Model

At the heart of reasoning, both formal and informal, is the establishment of *probabilities*, or the likelihood of the claim. With the formal use of sophisticated statistics researchers express their results in terms of the probability that the results could have happened by chance. In public communication we must share with listeners the reasonable likelihood of our claims. In a sense, you gamble on the odds of a particular conclusion. Every time we climb behind the wheel of an automobile, we bet our lives that we will not be the "statistic" that is killed or injured in an accident that day. Establishing the reasonableness of a claim is the process of demonstrating its probability (both logical and psychological) to a level that is acceptable to your listeners. From our transactional perspective, this involves a complex interaction among the topic, people's mind-set (analyzed in Chapter 2), their willingness to risk, their trust in you, and a plethora of other variables. There are, however, characteristics of the reasoning process that generally tend to give your communication a more reasonable basis.

Note how members of the audience pay close attention as former Utah governor Scott Matheson shares rationality

Traditionally we have classified reasoning as being either inductive or deductive. *Deductive* reasoning is that which begins with a generalization, or *premise*, and proceeds to a conclusion that is more specific. If you and your audience believe the general premise that the Soviets cannot be trusted to keep their word in international agreements, you might conclude that since SALT II is an international agreement, the Soviets are likely to break it (if it were ratified). These *major premises*, as they are called, can be beliefs, attitudes, or values you share with your listeners. Unless your listeners share the premise from which you reason, however, they cannot be expected to accept the reasonableness of your conclusion.

The other type of reasoning we find in oral discourse is called *inductive* reasoning. This is the process of drawing a general claim from a body of more specific data. When F.D.R. cited the Japanese attacks on Pearl Harbor, Guam, the Philippines, Hong Kong, Wake, and Midway, and then concluded, "The Japanese have, therefore, undertaken a surprise offensive throughout the Pacific area," he was reasoning inductively. Likewise, when the Surgeon General claims that smoking causes lung cancer, he is reasoning inductively, from dozens of experiments involving millions of specific animals as well as human subjects. The results, incidentally, are reported not in terms of certainties, but probabilities, or the likelihood of your contracting lung cancer if you continue to smoke throughout your lifetime.

Examples of "pure" deduction are difficult to identify in public discourse, but examples of pure induction, like those above, are relatively common. Furthermore, there is an interesting relationship between the two. The generalizations used in deduction are established, either formally or informally, by induction.

In the example above, if you asked yourself, "Why do we believe that the Russians can't be trusted to keep their word?", you would probably find that their record in numerous international agreements in the past was poor, or that someone you trusted told you that. This is basically an inductive process. Similarly, when you accept the Surgeon General's claim, "Smoking causes lung cancer," and then you reason, "Good grief, I smoke cigarettes, I'm likely to get it!", you are reasoning deductively from a premise that was established inductively.

The important thing to remember is that, traditionally, reasonableness has been viewed as the care with which claims are made, which can ultimately be traced to substantive data; that is, the data-claim relationship.

Toulman Model

Another way of looking at the relationship between reasoning, evidence or data, and claim has been advanced by Stephen Toulman and qualified by Rieke and Sillars.[5] Whether one reasons from specific to general or general to specific, they maintain that you begin with an *assertion* of some form of *data* and proceed to make a *claim* from those data. They further maintain that this reasoning process utilizes an assumption that connects the data and claim, which they name the *warrant*.

In diagram form, their model would look like this:

Assume you have discovered that the U.S. and the U.S.S.R. have signed fifty international agreements and that the Soviets have violated or broken their word in all but two of those agreements. This is your assertion of data. You then might claim that the Soviets would also break the SALT II agreement. The warrant would be the assumption that the Soviets are consistent over time in their behavior toward international agreements. Your reasoning might proceed like this: "Since the Soviets have broken forty-eight out of fifty of their international agreements with the U.S., they would also break SALT II." Note that this model provides for reasoning from the specific (data) to specific (SALT II) in addition to the traditional forms discussed earlier.

Toulman's model provides for other important aspects of the reasoning process as well. If you wish to include the level of probability or likelihood you believe your claim carries, you can add a *qualifier*, such as very likely, highly probable, extremely remote, unlikely, and the like.

You can also provide for extenuating circumstances or contingencies within which your claim would not hold. These statements are called *reservations* and are preceded by phrases like *unless*, *provided that*, *except for*, and so forth.

Finally, if your listeners do not accept your data, or disbelieve your warrant, you may have to provide documentation in support of these two aspects of your reasoning process. Our model would now look like this:

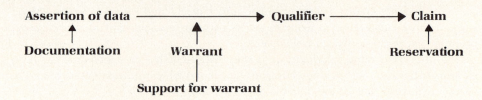

And your reasoning on SALT II might now sound like this: "Since the Soviets have broken forty-eight of fifty international agreements with the U.S., they are *very likely* to break SALT II *unless* it is in their best interest to keep it."

In any case, we are looking at the ways people reason from concrete (more probable) data to claims that represent varying degrees of probability. Let us now turn to ways of testing the reasonableness of not only our own thinking but that of public communicators to whom we listen.

Testing Data

The quality of the claims we make from any data are no better than the quality of the data themselves. The quality of data can be tested by asking certain analytical questions which bear generally on all data or on specific types of data.

General tests. The three tests which can be applied to all forms of data involve questions of consistency, specificity, and recency.

The first question we ask is "Are the data *consistent* with themselves and with other data we know about?" Surely a serious internal contradiction or inconsistency would negate the data in the minds of most people. Similarly, you have probably heard data cited that contradicted what you thought you "knew" about a subject. These data are immediately suspect and probably will not be believed without further verification. Not long ago my son asked if frozen animals could be brought back to life. I recalled from my biology classes, years ago, that freezing preserved tissue, but killed it irreversibly in the process. I said no, only to find that he had just seen a television documentary on scientists who were close to solving the problem of freezing living cells without killing them. This experience demonstrates both sides of the consistency test. That is to say, if a speaker's assertion of data is inconsistent with the listener's current "knowledge," it will be received with appropriate skepticism. On the other hand, the test is not infallible since new discoveries are made continually.

168

A second question we ask ourselves about data is "How *recent* is it?" Generally, the more recent the data the more probable or dependable they are. The state of the art in scientific research continues to improve, and new discoveries are changing the way we look at most things these days. Even when ancient documents, archeological sites, or medical treatments are rediscovered, they represent a more recent change than what we have accepted in the meantime. Recent sources usually include the best of the older wisdom which has stood the test of time as well as the more recent discoveries.

Finally, we can look at the *specificity* of the data. Whether we are dealing with examples, statistics, quotations, comparisons, or stories, the more specific we can be, the better chance we have of transacting with listeners. Specific examples are easier to identify with than hypothetical examples. Specific citation of a statistic (for example, mean versus average) can be not only clearer but more credible than vague statistical references. Quotations are more powerful and more real to listeners than vague references or paraphrases.

If a speaker says, "Scientists have discovered . . ." don't you want to say, "What scientists? When? Where can I read more about this?" Specific bibliographic notation (for example, *U.S. News and World Report*, December 1979, p.12) is not necessary, but a specific statement by a specific individual is desirable.

Both as speakers and listeners, we should be concerned with the consistency, recency, and specificity of the data used in the public communication transaction.

Testing examples and statistics. As we pointed out in Chapter 3, examples and statistics constitute the same type of evidence or data. That is to say, statistics constitute numerical summaries of many specific instances. We can test both types of data, therefore, with questions related to representativeness, sufficient numbers, and accounting for exceptional cases.

The *representativeness* of either your examples or statistics is, of course, the crucial question. Do they accurately represent the group they are used to illustrate? Earlier, when we spoke of the Matrixing Principle, we demonstrated that you cannot use all of the data in a single speech; indeed, you could probably not even research all of the possible examples and statistics on a given claim. Therefore you must select or sample only a few to represent the entire "population." The question you must ask yourself about your own data as well as those of speakers to whom you listen is, "How well does this welfare family or international treaty represent all of the others?" Surely the more homogeneous or similar they all are, the more likely a few instances or statistics are to represent the whole. A hand gun which has been hand-crafted will be more representative of its class than a "Saturday Night Special" that has been hand-made.

One way of increasing the likelihood of representativeness is by increasing the *numbers* in your sample. Whether using statistics or examples, the larger the sample, the less likely you are to be using exceptional cases.

Accounting for *exceptional cases* is the third question we ask when testing examples and statistics. Almost no population is so homogeneous that there are no exceptions—especially when you're dealing with people and their problems. That is why we deal in probabilities, not certainties. Expressing a conclusion as a probability and accounting for the exceptions increases the rationality of your data and reduces the likelihood of the listeners' rejecting your claim on the basis of a single exceptional case. You might say, as Ronald Reagan did, in effect, during the recession of 1982, "Of course, a few people are suffering from unemployment, but in the long run they and everyone else will be better off."

Whether the issue is sufficient numbers or allowing for exceptional cases, the primary issue in the use of examples and statistics remains the representativeness of the data you have selected.

Testing data from authority. Earlier we distinguished testimony from other quotations on the basis of the *authority* of the source. When we test the quality of authority, we ask questions about the source's qualifications, ability to observe, and bias.

The *qualifications* of the authority are crucial. Sometimes the claim requires specific expertise, as in the case of a scientist making claims about genetic damage resulting from atomic fallout. But some scientists are more qualified than others, and given equal qualifications, it could make a difference whether the scientist is an engineer, physicist, or geneticist. Any jury that attempts to judge the sanity of a murderer will hear testimony from psychiatrists on both sides of the question. Although sometimes difficult to distinguish, I think it helps if we are at least aware of the issue of qualifications when, as speakers or listeners, we evaluate authority as data.

A second issue relative to authoritative data is the *ability* of the source *to observe* the event under question. Eyewitness accounts are more believable than second-hand reports. People who have experienced the phenomena under discussion are more credible than people who have merely heard about it. Some care must be taken here, however, that the reporter has not had one of those exceptional experiences we spoke of earlier. In any case, when sources have comparable credentials, it is usually the one who is closest to the event on whom we rely, and sometimes otherwise unqualified observers may provide the more trustworthy testimony if they were closer to the event than the so-called expert.

A final test of authority is *bias*. If a source has a vested interest in the case, his or her testimony should be somewhat suspect. In some cases, a businessman's profit will be greater on the recommended product than the one you prefer. Politicians frequently have an interest in programs that will benefit their constituents or contributors. A branch of the military service has a vested interest in the deployment of new weapons systems. All of these biases and many more subtle ones cause the careful speaker or listener to weigh carefully the testimony provided by such sources. We have seen in recent decades such frequent distortion or withholding of data by government agencies and their representatives that people have, regrettably, developed a suspicion of data provided by any agent of the government—especially when the bias of the source is apparent.

We see, then, that the quality of data from authoritative sources can be tested by questions of qualification, ability to observe, and bias.

Tests of comparison. In our discussion of forms of support we cited analogies, similies, and metaphors as methods of supporting an idea or claim. Since all of these forms of support involve a comparison, the key test of their quality as data is the question of the quality of the comparison upon which they are based. Whether an extended literal analogy or an implied metaphor, we must ascertain whether the two things being compared are alike in the *essential variables*. We might ask whether the two systems of state medicine we are discussing are alike in their organization, their benefit schedule, the quality of treatment, and so on. As we saw in the card-playing example in Chapter 3, even a figurative analogy can be reasonably used as data if the comparison is accurate on the crucial variable—the effect of prior knowledge on one's objectivity.

Now that we have discussed the testing of data, let us turn to the way we test the claims we make on the basis of those data.

Testing Claims

In addition to the tests of data, you can also check the reasonableness of your arguments by applying tests to the claims you make. We will discuss testing (1) reasoning from examples and statistics, (2) causal reasoning, and (3) diversions or substitutions.

Testing generalizations. As we have pointed out, there is a close relationship between your data and the claims you make. Problems which occur from the misuse of examples or statistics are called *faulty generalizations*. This problem is, of course, the use of data that are not representative of the class from which they are drawn and from which your claim generalizes. Most often this is a result of using too few examples, or statistics based on too small a sample. Recall my story about being robbed in Mexico. For me to generalize that all Mexicans are thieves on the basis of that one experience would be tenuous indeed. But how often do you hear a friend or even a prominent politician indict a social service program because he or she knows one person who has taken unfair advantage of it? It has been said that jumping to conclusions on the basis of insufficient data is the only exercise some people get! As both speakers and listeners, we should carefully weigh not only the size of the data base upon which claims are made, but its representativeness as well.

This, of course, is where the Matrixing Principle comes into play. By using a few examples your research has shown to be representative, combined with statistics or quotations that demonstrate the breadth of the data base, you can quickly share with listeners the degree of rationality of your claim.

Testing causation. One of the most difficult processes in public transactions is establishing a causal connection between two phenomena. Many things relate to one another (co-relate) either through time or in amount, so that it seems that one *causes* the other. For instance, different archeologists who study the rise and fall of ancient civilizations have posited such variables as increase in population, technological advances, warfare, trade, and development of certain institutions as the cause of the development of civilizations. And yet civilizations can be found where each of these variables followed, not preceded, the rise of the civilization. Even if a variable did precede all civilizations, it would not categorically prove that the variable was the cause.

The first main problem with causation is that most complex social phenomena cannot be attributed to a single cause. Such problems as poverty, crime, and inflation could be attributed to a wide variety of causes. To select any one as the cause is not a reasonable way of making claims. This is also the way many disagreements occur. One special interest group will blame one cause, while the opposing group will blame another. In reality, they are both part right and part wrong. There would be fewer disagreements and more rational public communication if all would recognize the fallacy of *part cause*.

Another difficulty with causal reasoning is assuming that when something follows something else, it has been caused by it. "After this; therefore, because of this" is a common problem in causal reasoning. All of our common superstitions are based on it. You walk under a ladder, or a black cat runs in front of you, and later you have an unfortunate accident. You therefore assume that the ladder or cat caused the accident. Of course effects follow causes, but not everything that comes later has been caused by the earlier.

Another problem with causal reasoning is the confusion of causation with correlation. *Correlation* means that two things change together. When interest rates go up, the sale of houses usually goes down. There is an increase in the growth of some plants with an increase in the sunlight they receive. In these cases there is probably some causal connection between the two changes. But one might also find a positive correlation between an increase in population and the development of computers. Does this mean that one caused the other? If so, which is the cause and which the effect? Correlations are interesting and sometimes give us a hint about causation, but in the absence of supporting data do not in themselves adequately support a claim of causation.

Diversions and substitutions. Another way that speakers and listeners get into trouble with their persuasive claims is by diversions and substitutions. This means that in one way or another they make a claim that seems relevant to the data or topic but which, in fact, changes the subject. We will discuss (1) attacking the source, (2) substituting questions for data, (3) appealing to tradition or custom, (4) emotional language, and (5) psychological diversions.

One of the most common diversions is to *attack a person* instead of his or her ideas. What speakers and listeners fail to realize is that discrediting the source does not necessarily disprove their claim. This diversion has been called by logicians "you too!" or *ad hominum* argument. How often have you heard it said, "You have no right to criticize; you're no better!" Wait a minute; should a person's poor driving record discredit testimony in a traffic accident he or she observed? Of course, the testimony of a convict in the case of another's crime might be somewhat suspect, but only on the basis of the tests discussed earlier under testing authoritative claims.

Another diversion or substitution is the substitution of *questions for data*. In his call to arms, Patrick Henry said, "They say thet we are weak, but when will we be stronger?" His question, of course, is a substitution for the proof of the colonies' strength. Substituting questions for data essentially throws the responsibility from the speaker to the listener—a shift that a reasonable listener should not accept.

A third diversion or substitution is *appeal to tradition or custom*. Have you ever suggested a new activity or approach only to be told, "We've always done it this way, and as long as I'm in charge we always will"? The popular musical "Fiddler on the Roof" is in part a story of the struggle between innovation and tradition. Rationally, there is a certain presumption in favor of the status quo. Why give up an activity or solution that has proved effective over the years for some unknown, untried scheme? On the other hand, if a problem exists and a new solution has been proposed and supported with data, it should not be so easily brushed aside because "we've always done it this way."

Emotional language is another way to divert attention away from inadequate claims. We will see later in this chapter that emotional language can be effective, but not necessarily from a rational point of view. When speakers either have a weak argument or lack data, it is not uncommon for them to divert attention from the fact by substituting emotional language. Of course, there is nothing irrational about a well-prepared speaker communicating substantial data and reasoning with emotional language. Both speakers and listeners, however, should avoid being deluded by claims clothed in emotional language when the data are inadeqsate or missing altogether.

Another diversion or substitution is *repeated affirmation*. It has been said that if you repeat a lie often enough people may begin to believe it. So it is with unsupported claims. Not that they are necessarily lies, but claims which have no support are no more rational after the tenth repetition than they are at first. Advertisers are the most common users of repeated affirmation ("Western Airlines: the *only* way to fly"), but public speakers such as Adolph Hitler have used it with great effect also. As in the case of emotional language, you need not be shy about repeating a well-established claim, but both as a speaker and listener you should remember repeated affirmation is no substitute for data.

Speakers also use *psychological appeals to divert* our attention from the topic, or as a substitute for missing data. One psychological appeal is what advertisers call *plain folks*. Later in this chapter we will discuss building personal identifications with listeners. Appearing to be a "common person" sometimes enhances that identification. It may also enhance listeners' evaluations of speakers' honesty. The argument would be: "Surely, anyone as down-to-earth and simple as that could not be dishonest too!" But there are no data to show that "plain folks" are any more trustworthy than their more urbane counterparts. Further, when a speaker uses this appeal, you are well advised to look even more carefully at the claims they are making.

A final psychological diversion or substitution is the appeal to peer pressure, which advertisers call the *bandwagon technique*. Here the essential appeal is that if everybody or even most people are doing it, it must be right. Climb on the bandwagon with the rest of the folks. Clothing styles that are "in," fads, and appeals to being "number one" all work because the pressure against being the exception or the oddball is very great.

As a listener you must realize that this is just another way of diverting your attention away from the essential issue—the quality of the claim and the data on which it is based.

Rationality As Transaction

Up to now we have been discussing reasonableness in a somewhat ideal sense. Consider this experience, however: One summer I had just finished some homemade ice cream and sent my son to dump the salt water behind the garage. He knew that we were having a drought and that the plants needed water. He further believed that wasting water was unfortunate. So he dumped the highly saline solution on a recently planted spruce tree. In the ideal sense it was a stupid thing to do, since the tree died, but he had drawn a perfectly reasonable conclusion from the data available to him! The foregoing discussion of rationality is designed to enable you to build your persuasive argument on the most reasonable foundation possible, as well as to evaluate the arguments of others. However, rationality, like all other communication variables, is a *transaction*. What seems reasonable to you may not seem reasonable to your listeners. You must not only find out *their* rationale, but attempt to determine what combination of data and claims cause their rationality to be different from yours. You will then know which data and claims to emphasize in order to help them share your rationality.

SHARING MOTIVATION

Perhaps you have had the experience of driving down the road—your eyelids drooping from boredom or lack of sleep—when a car swerves into your path. You swerve to miss it and narrowly escape a serious accident. Now you are really geared up: your heart is pounding, your palms are sweating, and you may even be cursing the other driver. In a less dramatic vein, you have probably attended a speech on a subject you either knew nothing about or could care less about. At the end of the speech you may have been excited, or at least concerned enough about the problem to take some immediate action. You were motivated. As we discuss sharing motivation with listeners we will examine the nature of motivation, some motivational appeals, and finally some methods for achieving motivation.

The Nature of Motivation

As the illustrations above suggest, *motivation* is the psychological state that prepares us to move, to act, or to decide. It is usually a level of excitation that involves us in the topic and makes us "spring-loaded" to do something about it. Motivation has to do with our needs, emotions, and values. Before we discuss these, however, let us look at some of the characteristics of these motives. We will discuss their variability, as well as the way they relate to rationality and behavior.

Variability. Motives vary in several ways. The first is in their *strength* within any individual at a particular time. At one point in your life you may be moved by a need to develop personal relationships. At another point, that motive diminishes and a need to achieve something significant in your work takes over. Sonia Johnson describes her motivation to work for passage of the E.R.A. as a conversion experience. At one moment she was unconcerned, and the next thing she knew she was ready to "lay down her life for the cause." Motives come and go as well as change in their strength and relative importance to us.

Motives also vary among *individuals*: everyone responds to somewhat different appeals. Some students want an education in order to make more money when they graduate, or for the power knowledge gives them. Others are simply thrilled by the learning process itself. You have probably known people who seemed driven by a desire to please others. And yet there are people who are equally driven by some internal force you don't quite understand. It is this wide difference in the motives to which people respond that makes your analysis of the audience so important.

Motives also vary over *time*. What motivates you today may bore you tomorrow and vice versa. You may donate a large amount of money to a heart association following a loved one's illness from heart disease, only to lose interest if he or she recovers. A caring person may be highly involved in world hunger one year and be demonstrating against the proliferation of nuclear weapons the next.

In any case, it is well to be aware of the way motives vary over time, both within an individual and among different individuals.

Rationality. Another characteristic of motives is that they are not necessarily irrational. A common misconception is that when people become "emotional" they lose their ability to reason. Earlier we described motivation as a level of excitation. The complete absence of motivation, however, would be sleep or, ultimately, death.

How reasonable can you be when you are asleep? Or even bored and sleepy? In my own case, I find I can read and write (that is, think) better in the morning when I'm alert (psyched up or motivated) than I can in the afternoon when my metabolism seems to drop and I get sleepy. How "rational" are you in those afternoon classes compared to those in mid-morning, especially if you are a "morning person"?

Not only can our thought processes function better when we are motivated, but motivational appeals themselves are not necessarily irrational. You can probably think of many situations in which an appeal to fear might have great survival value. An appeal to the value of hard work may reasonably result in greater productivity when that is needed.

Motivational appeals are not inherently rational either, however. How often have you seen a "workaholic" driven to "produce," resulting in stress-related illness or even death? We can see, then, that a certain amount of excitation or motivation is necessary to function rationally and that motivational appeals are neither inherently irrational nor inherently rational.

Relationships to behavior. Earlier we claimed that motivation prepares us to move, to act, or to decide. You might assume from this that you can therefore predict behavior from your analysis of people's motives. Unfortunately, this is not the case. Ideally it might be possible, if you could identify every motive of every person, quantify the strength, and run the quantities through a computer. In real life, however, there are simply too many different motives of too many varying strengths—many of which are contradictory—to accurately predict behavior. All we can realistically hope to do is raise our listeners' level of excitation with motive appeals that intuitively seem to move toward the desired response.

Motivational Appeals

Now that we have discussed the characteristics of motivation, let us turn to the types of motivational appeals that can be shared with listeners. We will discuss our shared needs, emotions, and values.

Needs. Psychologists have long been interested in identifying the basic desires that drive people to behave as they do. Early theorists focused on physiological needs such as food, reproduction, and shelter. More recently, social psychologists have demonstrated people's need for love, acceptance, and other forms of positive reinforcement which we sometimes refer to as *strokes*. One social psychologist, Abraham Maslow, combined these needs with some others into a hierarchical system that is useful in understanding not only the behavior of listeners, but one's own motivations as well.[6]

Maslow claims that our most basic needs are *physiological*. In a life sciences class you may have studied the characteristics of living animals. Most biologists would agree that the ability or need to ingest nutrients, eliminate waste, respond to sensory stimuli, grow, reproduce, and in most cases move about are basic to living organisms.[7] As human beings we experience these as hunger, thirst, boredom, need for sexual gratification, and so forth. These needs are met in different ways in different cultures. Public speakers usually refer not to the needs themselves, but to the socially approved ways of meeting these needs we call *motives*. In middle-class America we might be motivated to eat a hamburger, while in Mexico or Chicano neighborhoods in the U.S., tortillas and beans might be more motivating. Most audiences in this country are not physiologically deprived, but the diversity of motives by which basic physiological needs are met can be useful points of identification between speakers and listeners.

A second type of need which can motivate listeners is people's need for *safety*. The recent, rapid growth of survivalist groups underscores this basic human need. We all want to feel secure, not only in our person, but in our work and other segments of our lives as well. Inflation can pose a great threat to the future financial security of many people, especially those on fixed incomes. Note how many people purchase hand guns or a variety of safety devices for their homes in order to provide security against the threat of crime. Some people go to great lengths to provide for the financial security of their children. A casual glance at our national budget reveals that the vast majority of the expenditures are aimed at security against military threats from abroad or against the threat of poverty at home. So strong is our need for safety that Rheinhold Niebuhr even identifies it with original sin.[8]

Another basic human need is *love and belongingness*. Once considered nice but not basic, these needs are now being recognized as just as essential to human existence as food or safety. Small babies have been found to be less healthy if they are deprived of sufficient love and affection. Adult males seem to be physically healthier and live longer if they live in an intimate, supportive relationship (marriage) than when they live alone. Teenagers seem to be especially susceptible to the influence of their peer groups. Not to "belong" at this age can be perceived as a tragedy.

With more and more of our physiological and safety needs being met, people are becoming more preoccupied with needs of love and belongingness. The entire decade of the 1970s seemed to focus people's attention on their relationships with other people. Pop-psychological writings, workshops, and groups sprang up everywhere, assuring people that "I'm O.K. and you're O.K." This need to be loved by parents, children, spouses, and friends or to "belong" to a group, a cult, or a gang is a powerful mover indeed.

Still another social need people share is the need for *self-esteem*. This has to do with feeling good about ourselves and thinking that others do too. It is tied to our drive to achieve in our work or to earn an admirable reputation, status, or prestige.

Many people are motivated by what other people think of them. Some want to be admired—others feared. In any case, public speakers will do well to assess the degree to which their listeners are motivated by esteem needs and identify with them.

Perhaps the set of needs with which Maslow is most clearly identified is the need for *self-actualization*. This is the need to realize our full potential as human beings. Everyone has his or her unique set of gifts. Although some people seem more gifted than others, we all have abilities and talents which "need" to be developed. Self-actualization is not the degree to which we achieve, but the degree to which we develop the potential we have.

Perhaps you have had the opportunity to observe the Special Olympics for handicapped children. These are people whose level of achievement may not be great by absolute standards, but their thrill of achieving to the maximum of their potential meets a fundamental need, which seems to be shared by most of us.

Emotions. Earlier we described motivation as a level of excitement. Recall how excited or keyed up you get before an important examination or a heavy date. In addition to the needs discussed above, emotional stimuli can contribute to people's level of excitation. While some of these appeals may seem somewhat base, as speakers and listeners we need to be aware of their role in human influence. Therefore, we will discuss sharing fear, animosity, anger, sex, envy, and self-interest.

Perhaps the most powerful—and certainly the most studied—emotional response is *fear*. Threats to our person, our family, our property, and even our country can cause nearly hysterical responses. Although it is the opposite side of the safety coin, it occasionally goes beyond vague feelings of insecurity. Few of us have experieced the terror of looking down the barrel of a loaded gun, but who has not experienced a brush with death in a near automobile accident?

In public communication I have seen proposals for land-use planning, city-county consolidation, and E.R.A. defeated because of fear appeals that claimed "They will tell us what color to paint our house," "The cost of government will skyrocket," or "Men and women will be forced to use the same restrooms." In these cases, people preferred the status quo, however unsatisfactory, to the fear of the unknown.

Animosity is another strong motivator. Objective observers find it difficult to understand why family members refuse to speak to one another, or why Argentina and Great Britain would sacrifice 1,000 lives over the Falkland Islands, where there are fewer than 2,000 inhabitants. Even as I write these words, there are several wars being waged around the world—in El Salvador, in Lebanon, and on the Iranian-Iraqi border—all based on deep-seated animosities that date back hundreds of years. Contradictory as it may seem, people can be motivated by both love and belongingness on the one hand, and hatred on the other.

A third emotion that motivates people is *anger*. As individuals, we experience anger from an individual act or event. As groups, we more commonly become frustrated with some aspect of the "system" and become angry when we can find no way to deal with it. In the 1960s frustration over civil rights led to demonstrations. These in turn resulted in riots when the system was perceived to be unresponsive. Similarly, the "tax revolt" of the late '70s and early '80s was a reaction to people's frustration not only with rising taxes, but also with huge increases in the size of a seemingly unresponsive government.

Sex is yet another emotional motivator. Formerly euphemized as lust, we now call it by its more familiar name. Experienced persuaders know that sex sells. Advertisements for everything from diet drinks to mattresses picture beautiful young people who imply that you will be more attractive to the opposite sex if you just wear the right brand of panty hose and blue jeans, drink the right brand of soft drink, or eat the desired junk food. In perhaps the most successful advertising campaign in history, Marlboro cigarette sales skyrocketed following a blatantly sexist "he-man" appeal from the cowboys in "Marlboro country."

"Keeping up with the Joneses" is such a common phenomenon in the U.S. that it has become a cliché. Many of us seem to be motivated by a desire to have everything that everyone else has. I am not suggesting that this is a recent development, since the Tenth Commandment suggests that it was also a powerful motivator in Old Testament times. Appeals to *envy* have been with us for a long time and should continue to be effective motivators.

Finally, appeals to *self-interest* or greed have motivational appeal. "Looking out for number one" is a commonly encountered philosophy of life. Of course, I do not mean to imply that generosity and altruism do not exist. As we shall see in a moment, they can be powerful motivators for some people. However, you cannot follow the news without being aware of incredible instances of exploitation of people and the environment, from Love Canal to some nursing homes. While these cases may not be altogether typical, they do remind us of the appeal that self-interest has for all of us.

Values. *Values* are centrally held beliefs that serve as standards for behavior or as life's goals. As we confront the myriad of decisions we must make each day, we are guided by specific standards for behavior, such as "honesty is the best policy" or "cleanliness is next to Godliness." Our daily decisions may also be determined by our life's goals, such as "making a million" or "serving humanity."

Values seem to be learned from people close to us and are deeply rooted in our culture, subculture, or community. Hence people in some cultures or groups value cleanliness or hard work more than people from other cultures or groups. Although values vary from individual to individual, there are some similarities that many Americans share. In his pioneering research on values, Milton Rokeach attempted to identify some of those individual similarities.[9] More recently, Rieke and Sillars have attempted to combine these individual values into clusters or value systems.[10] I will discuss value systems and how they relate to the instrumental and terminal values identified by Rokeach. We will look at the personal success, Puritan, enlightenment, collectivist, progressive, and transcendental value systems, as well as security, which Rieke and Sillars do not mention.

Personal success has long been valued in our culture. "We're number one," chants the crowd at a college football game when their team makes a first down, and every little league team echos back, "We're number one." Ambition ranked number two among all instrumental values in Rokeach's studies.

Frequently our desire to demonstrate our success takes the form of seeking *status* in our work, club, or political party. People want to work up through the ranks until, as the Peter Principle states, they reach their highest level of mediocrity. Contrast this with the Japanese value of doing the best at whatever level you find yourself. Hence the president of a Japanese corporation may bow in respect to a dock loader out of recognition of the high quality of the (lower-status) person's work.

We also attempt to demonstrate our personal success through the acquisition of material goods. We push our credit to the limit and beyond to acquire more prestigious homes, automobiles, clothes, recreation equipment, and even investments. Contrast this with a Chicano value that "it is better to live 'richly' than to die rich."

Although this may be changing somewhat in recent years under the influence of counterculture groups, personal success through ambition, achievement, status, and material possessions is still highly valued in U.S. society.

A second value system is the traditional *Puritan-pioneer* ethic. This system has to do mainly with standards for behavior or *instrumental* values. Among the most consistent results I have seen in value research is the ranking of honesty as a premier American value. Also ranked high in Rokeach's studies is responsibility. Mentioned prominently by other writers are hard work, thrift, and duty. It seems that Americans want not only a stable environment in which to live, but they want dependable, productive people with whom to relate.

Another value system of Americans is what Rieke and Sillars call the *enlightenment* value system. This system is grounded in the belief that people are basically capable of solving their own problems, if given the opportunity to do so. It has to do with a trust of rationality, science, intelligence, and knowledge as well as freedom, individualism, and liberty.

Rieke and Sillars also identify a *progressive* value system which I think should be combined with the enlightenment value system. The progressive value system is predicated on the assumption that the foregoing rationality, science, and other values result in change that predominantly improves humankind's situation. It has to do with practicality, efficiency, progress, and modernization. And why shouldn't our citizens share these values? Since the founding of the Republic, American intelligence and ingenuity, combined with the freedom to exploit them, seem to have given us a living standard unparalleled in human history. Only recently has our consciousness been raised to the potential costs in both human and environmental terms. Even after several years of publicity on the energy problem, I have many students who have faith that scientists will discover some new source of energy before our fossil fuels run out. One even told me he had heard that engineers in Detroit had discovered a new engine that ran on almost no energy at all.

Of particular importance within these value systems is the high value we place on personal *freedom*. Of course, most Americans realize the necessity of relinquishing some personal freedom for the good of society. Most of us do, after all, stop at red lights, pay our taxes, and obey the law. However, our revolutionary and frontier heritage make it more difficult to get Americans to relinquish their freedom to purchase hand guns or develop their personal property than might be the case in Sweden or Japan. The antigovernment sentiment which was so strong in the late '70s and early '80s was in large part a revolt against what was perceived as the unwarranted encroachment of government on our personal freedoms.

Another value system in American culture is the *collectivist* value system. This value system is rooted in people's need to belong, which we discussed earlier. It has to do with cooperation, equality, unity, order, and "social good." Although groups and individuals certainly act in enlightened self-interest, there is a general respect paid to people who make personal sacrifices for the "good of the order." Most people generally recognize the value of the truism expressed by Benjamin Franklin: "We must all hang together or assuredly we shall hang separately." In the highest councils of government as well as every echelon of our society a good "team player" is highly valued in our culture.

Another value system related to the enlightenment is the *transcendental* value system. This system of values is based on the assumption that there is much more to human development and interaction than rationality and efficiency. This system emphasizes intuitive wisdom, feelings, and even mysticism. It has to do with humanitarianism, sensitivity, compassion, respect, common sense, and acceptance. You may hear criticisms of our "system" as impersonal and exploitative, but it is generally acknowledged by most Americans to be the least inhumane or insensitive system in history. Rooted in the idealism of Emerson and Thoreau, the human rights and peace movements of the 1960s seemed to be attempts to infuse more transcendental values into the "system." Transcendental values turned inward in the '70s, resulting in dramatic increases in meditation, being "in touch with one's feelings," and concern for the development and maintenance of personal relationships. One also must be impressed by the outpouring of public concern at personal crises and natural disasters. Evidence of the growing attraction of transcendental values, particularly among young people, is the dramatic growth of religious cults in recent decades.

Finally, I think that *security* constitutes a value system in U.S. culture. Although Rieke and Sillars do not identify it as such, the top two terminal values in Rokeach's research were "a world at peace" and "family security." Earlier we discussed our need for safety and people's response to fear appeals. Issues such as national defense, the draft, social security, and inflation, which threaten people's physical or economic security, should be handled with care by the public speaker. On the other hand, appeals to the high value people place on a stable and secure environment can be potent indeed.

Individual value systems. In addition to the foregoing value systems, which we have attempted to generalize to our whole culture, there are more specialized value systems that may be characteristic of a subculture or group. So-called counterculture groups seem to have repudiated traditional definitions of personal success, particularly the value placed on material possessions or status. There are groups that place much higher value on service to others than on personal gain.

Large ethnic, religious, or other minorities may dominate a community and, as we emphasized in Chapter 2, these group values must be seriously considered.

Conflicting values. The public communicator frequently encounters conflicting values. The same culture or subculture may value *both* individuality and conformity, ambition and selflessness, rationality and intuition, or security and risk. Again, your analysis of your audience will help you decide which of these conflicting values to emphasize or when to avoid the conflict altogether.

Another factor that underscores the need for audience analysis is that values vary not only from group to group, but seem to be in the process of rapid change in our society as a whole. After synthesizing numerous studies of public opinion over the past several decades, Daniel Yankelovich concludes:

> The rules of social behavior have expanded, moving us from a society with relatively homogeneous definitions of family, sex roles and working life toward an explosive pluralism on these and other fronts.[11]

Motivational Methods

Now that we have examined what motivates people, let us look at the methods a public speaker can use to incorporate these variables into public communication transactions.

Specific data. As we pointed out earlier, if listeners had had all of the experiences you have had with respect to your specific topic, they would probably already identify with your beliefs, attitudes, or behavior. However, since they have not, it is up to you to share with them the most persuasive data in such a way that they can identify with your specific purpose. This usually takes the form of concrete data, in general, and *specific examples*, in particular. These are the data that create vicarious experiences for your listeners and hence move them to belief or action. Recall that in our discussion of forms of support and the Matrixing Principle we emphasized that the more specific your data, the better.

Vivid description. Going hand in hand with the specificity of the data is the vividness with which it is described. In our discussion of imagery we pointed out that the more you can get your listeners to feel, see, touch, taste, and hear your data, the more likely they are to vicariously experience the same motives that caused you to believe or act as you want your audience to.

Emotionally loaded words. As we saw in Chapter 5, the words you use can create identification with listeners. Shared motivation is one dimension of that identification. There is a story of a person who gave a garden party at which exotic foods were served. The scene is right out of a movie—close-clipped lawn, iron-filigree furniture, elegantly set table. At the conclusion of the meal the host began quizzing the guests about the identity of the food they were eating. Many did not know. When they came to the large bowl of meat in the center of the table, guesses ranged from pheasant to pork. When the host said it was rattlesnake meat, one guest became ill and vomited—threw up in the grass! Now what caused the violent reaction—the food? Not at all; just a word that was extremely loaded for that individual. This is the same technique Churchill used when he said, "I have nothing to offer but blood, toil, tears, and sweat." Douglas McArthur used the same method with the cadets at West Point when he appealed to "duty, honor, country."

Showing your emotion. A final method of sharing motivations with listeners is to allow yourself to show, in your nonverbal delivery, the motivations you feel. You should never get so carried away that you lose control; however, to communicate the seriousness, sadness, or joy of your message, your posture, facial expression, and gestures can substantially enhance your motivational identification with listeners.

SHARING TRUST

In addition to sharing rationality and motivation with listeners, we also share influence in a personal way. Aristotle called this dimension of shared influence *ethos*, and claimed that it was the most important of all forms of influence. You know from your own experience that you are more easily persuaded by a person you respect and trust

Sharing trust is possible even with large, heterogeneous audiences

than one whom you don't know or, worse yet, one whom you either don't like or suspect of antagonistic motives.

Transactional Nature of Ethos

In recent years *ethos* has been referred to and extensively researched as *source credibility*. Speaking in these terms makes it sound like ethos is something that resides in a speaker and is transmitted to listeners who either "catch it" or not. Consider, however, a study that was recently conducted on doctor–patient communication. Shortly following an interview with their anesthesiologist prior to surgery, patients were asked two very indirect questions. First, "What ran through your mind when you were talking to the doctor?" Second, "What were you feeling as you talked to the doctor?" The questions were designed to produce data about shared rationality and shared motivation. Surprisingly, many of the responses dealt with *ethos*, for example, "I hoped he knew what he was doing," or "I feel confident with this one."[12] There were no objective data on the relative competence of the anesthesiologists, but the patient was creating perceptions and arguments that manifested a trust in the doctor.

This and other research clearly demonstrate that ethos or credibility is largely a matter of trust in the source *as perceived by the listener*.

Dimensions of Ethos

Aristotle claimed that ethos was derived from speakers showing good sense, good character, and good will. Contemporary research has strongly confirmed the first two of these as well as some secondary factors.

Probably the most consistent factor contributing to speaker–listener ethos is what Aristotle called *good character*. It is variously referred to by researchers today as integrity, safety, character, and other labels. It has to do with listener reliance on the honesty, dependability, and responsibility of the speaker.

The second major factor of ethos is what Aristotle called *good sense* or *sagacity*. It has emerged in contemporary research as listeners' perceptions of speakers' authoritativeness, qualifications, skill, or ability. I like to think of it as *perceived competence*. It is interesting to note that the study of communication between anesthesiologists and their patients was one of the few in which character did not emerge, but in which competence was the sole contributing factor in the doctors' ethos.

Other studies have identified such secondary factors as dynamism, personality, intention, and sociability.

Developing Trust

Having discussed the nature and factors contributing to ethos, let us now turn to ways of sharing it with your listeners. We will discuss extrinsic and intrinsic ethos.

Extrinsic ethos. *Extrinsic* ethos is the trust that is derived from the context within which your speech occurs. Of primary importance is the *reputation* that precedes you to the speaking event. This, of course, is developed over a lifetime.

Ethos can also be enhanced by the *setting*. Who is sitting on the speakers' stand and who introduces you? When presidential candidate Jimmy Carter delivered a key campaign speech at the Salt Palace in Salt Lake City, there were sitting behind him on the stage a U.S. Senator, a U.S. Representative, the Governor of Utah, and even an immensely popular former governor. Conspicuous by his absence was an incumbent U.S. Congressman who had recently been accused of being involved in a morals scandal. Carter was using the setting to communicate good character as well as support for his candidacy by people whom the audience perceived to be both competent and trustworthy. Finally, extrinsic ethos can be developed by the person who introduces the speaker, which we will discuss further in Chapter 9.

Intrinsic ethos. *Intrinsic* ethos is the trust that is developed during the speaking transaction itself. Earlier we spoke of the importance of creating identification or common ground with the audience in the introduction. Research has indicated that other message variables relate to ethos in interesting ways.[13]

First and most important is the use of *intrinsic references*. That is to say, if you point out in your speech that you or a respected third party have been personally involved with the question at issue it will tend to enhance both your credibility and effectiveness. Explicit references to your personal experience seem to be more effective than implied ones.

Long before Betty Ford courageously raised people's consciousness about the problem of breast cancer, I had a student who spoke on the same subject. She seemed involved but we were not sure to what extent. Later, in private, I learned that her mother had died of the disease. Without becoming maudlin, an explicit reference to that personal experience in her speech could have added to both her credibility and influence.

A second relationship between content and persuasiveness is your use of *evidence*, and this depends on your initial credibility with your audience. Using substantial amounts of evidence seems to enhance the influence of initially moderate- to low-credibility sources, but not for initially high-credibility sources. It stands to reason: initially high-credibility sources don't *need* the outside help, whereas moderate- to low-credibility sources need the additional reinforcement the evidence provides.

Your persuasiveness is also related to your use of *language*. Earlier we spoke of language varying according to its *intensity*. It can also vary by how opinionated or sure of yourself you sound. Your credibility and effectiveness can be enhanced with highly intense and opinionated language. I think these may be two of the variables that add to Ronald Reagan's persuasive appeal.

The use of *fear appeals* also relates to ethos or credibility. A highly credible source can use strong fear appeals more effectively than can an initially low-credibility source.

Finally, *obscenity* can increase dynamism, but decreases listeners' perception of your competence and integrity, and hence tends to diminish the trust bond.

Whether developed extrinsically or intrinsically, ethos is a balance between *similarity* and *dissimilarity* with listeners. You and your audience must share similar experiences, beliefs, values, and motivations to perceive yourselves as being members of the same "community."

At the same time, it is desirable that you, as the speaker, be perceived as being *dissimilar* from the audience in that you clearly have the competence and character to merit their trust. Simons calls such a speaker a *super-representative*.[14] As an accepted member of the black community and a Christian minister; exceptionally well educated, beautifully articulate, and nonviolent, Martin Luther King, Jr., was such a super-representative for the civil rights movement.

BUILDING RESISTANCE TO CHANGE

Until now we have been speaking of persuasion as a mutual transaction from the standpoint of influencing people to *change* their beliefs, values, or behavior. However, recall that we also said persuasion is important in contexts in which people strengthen their beliefs and values, on the one hand, or resolve to continue their present behavior, on the other. In these cases persuasive speaking results not in change but in resistance to change.

You can, of course, utilize any of the principles and techniques discussed in this chapter to induce resistance to change, but there are some additional ones that are particularly applicable to this kind of speaking. We will discuss anxiety, hostility, commitment, linking, cognitive consistency, and inoculation.

Anxiety

Earlier we discussed fear as a human motivator. Actually, the relationship between fear and change is more complex than this; it is curvilinear. If you want people to change, arousal of an intermediate level of fear is optimal—either extreme tends to induce resistance to change. Recall that we defined emotion in general and fear in particular as a level of excitation. If you have no fear or anxiety at all, you tend not to change. At the other extreme, if you are petrified with fear, you tend to adopt a defensive posture, and not change in this case either. You are well advised to consider this relationship between fear and change in light of your purpose to effect change or to induce resistance to change.

Hostility

We have already discussed mild animosity or hatred as a motivator. Extreme hostility, however, tends to cause people to resist suggestions for changing their beliefs, values, or behavior. Thus if you wish to persuade your audience not to buy a product, political candidate, or idea, creating hostility toward the object, person, or idea, tends to induce the resistance you desire. There is an important exception to this: If the idea or behavior itself involves violence, then frustration and hostility may facilitate change. It is easier to get an angry mob to loot and burn than to persuade a happy group to do so.

Linking

Another way to influence people to resist change of beliefs, values, or behaviors is to link or combine them with others, or with valued individuals or groups. If you have ever cooked spaghetti, you know how easy it is to break a single dry piece before you put it in the water to boil. But if you try a whole package at once, it is almost impossible to break. By linking beliefs, values, and behaviors together, they support each other so that it becomes more difficult to change any of them.

There is one danger in linking, however. If one belief, value, or behavior is changed, the rest of them may change as well.

Commitment

One of the most effective ways of inducing resistance to change is by strengthening the commitment of listeners. This can be done in a number of ways. The most common is to change a belief to an opinion by getting the listener to verbalize or state the belief in public. Sometimes a speaker will ask for *overt feedback* from an audience. In other public contexts, testimonials are offered by members of the group, strengthening the beliefs of the speaker as well as the listeners.

Other common ways of making a belief public are asking for the signing of written *pledges* for time or money, and stating that a third party believes in the commitment of the audience; both can further induce resistance to change.

The key to commitment is active involvement. The more public the belief is made and the more actively the listeners are involved in articulating the belief and behaving on it, the more resistance there will be to subsequent change.

Cognitive Consistency

Earlier we pointed out that people are more likely to be persuaded if their emotions, values, and behaviors are out of balance. It follows, then, that the creation of balance or a feeling *cognitive consistency* will help listeners be more resistant to change. Incumbent politicians often attempt to convince voters that the status quo is a good one, or that they are well-off and not likely to improve the situation with a change of leadership. People don't go shopping for cars, washing machines, or churches if they are content with the ones they have.

Inoculation

One of the most fascinating methods for inducing resistance to change is called *inoculation*. Like its medical metaphor, inoculation involves giving the listener a weak dose of the opposing arguments so that they will develop an immunity to them.

In most instances, a persuasive speaker should be well aware of opposing arguments. Indeed, counterarguments usually constitute the other side of the issues you address. You can inoculate your listeners by recognizing the opposing arguments they are likely to hear, and then helping them develop answers by presenting arguments and data in direct response to them.

ORGANIZING PERSUASIVE SPEECHES

In Chapter 4 we discussed the organization of speeches in general. Here we discuss the organizational issues unique to persuasive transactions.

Organizational Patterns

Your first consideration is what organizational pattern to use. This depends entirely on how the audience perceives the specific purpose and central idea. If you are focusing the transaction on a particular problem, you might use Dewey's approach, described in Chapter 2. If you want to focus primarily on *need*, you might organize the speech around the scope, effects, causes, or so on. If the audience is already cognizant of the need, you may want to remotivate them in the introduction and focus on *comparing solutions* in the body. If the audience is aware of the details of the solutions, you might focus only on the *comparative advantages* of each.

One pattern of organization which has proven popular over the years is called the *motivated sequence*.[15] It goes as follows:

Motivated Sequence	Parts of Speech
Attention	Introduction
Need	Body
Satisfaction	Body
Visualization	Conclusion
Action	Conclusion

Please note that these patterns of organization do not constitute a formula, but options to be selected and adopted to fit the needs of the transaction, in general, and the audience, in particular.

One-Sided Messages

Another organizational issue which is important in persuasive situations is whether to offer a one-sided or balanced approach to the issue or problem inherent in your central idea. Most people's first reaction is that it would be foolish not to load the arguments as much in your favor as possible. This is not always the case, however. It depends greatly on where the audience is on the spectrum of initial agreement or disagreement with your central idea. If the majority of the audience is generally in agreement with your central idea and you simply wish to strengthen their beliefs or move them to action, then a one-sided case can be the most effective.

If, on the other hand, the audience is initially negative or even antagonistic toward your central idea, then it is more effective to balance your arguments. Because a negative audience will be more critical of your arguments, by acknowledging counter-arguments (without supporting them strongly) you establish more common ground with your listeners, enhance your own ethos, and hopefully receive a more open-minded hearing for your side of the issue. Balanced arguments also serve to inoculate listeners against subsequent exposure to those opposing arguments.

Revealing Your Purpose

As in the case of one-sided messages, the method of revealing your purpose is dependent on your audience. In the case of favorably disposed listeners, I recommend the *direct* approach (discussed in Chapter 7) of stating your purpose and/or central idea in the introduction so that the audience does not feel you are attempting to deceive them.

In the case of antagonistic audiences, however, you may want to be more *indirect*. This does not mean that you deceive your audience. It only means that you reveal as much of your purpose as the audience is ready to accept. In the introduction, the orientation may be to a more general topic like money management rather than mutual funds; or family planning rather than abortion. After you have outlined the problem, you can then be more direct about your specific proposal.

The indirect approach also involves proceeding from data to claim instead of the reverse. In the direct approach, with favorable audiences you may state an idea and then prove it. With antagonistic audiences, it is more difficult for them to quarrel with a statistic or a concrete example than with the generalization or claim that follows. So you begin with the data and, hopefully, the listeners will have arrived at the claim before you need to state it. Again, this is not a deception, but only a method of obtaining an open-minded hearing for the data that should reasonably support your claim.

SUMMARY

In this chapter we have described persuasive speaking transactionally as responsible communication leading to shared beliefs, values, or actions between speaker and listeners.

Sharing reasonableness is primarily a matter of drawing claims from substantial data. Data can be tested by the speaker for its consistency, recency, and specificity. Examples and statistics should be representative and sufficient in number, with exceptional cases accounted for.

Authoritative data should be tested for qualifications, ability to observe, and bias. Comparisons should be alike in all relevant variables.

Claims can also be faulty from hasty generalization and faulty causal reasoning, as well as diversions and substitutions.

Sharing motivation is primarily a matter of getting listeners to share your level of excitement about your topic. Motivation varies within and among individuals. Emotion is not necessarily irrational, nor is it a perfect predictor of behavior. People's needs can be categorized as the following types: physiological, safety, belongingness, self-esteem, and self-actualization. We can share emotions like fear, animosity, anger, sex, and self-interest.

Values are powerful motivators. Values in the U.S. can be clustered into systems of personal success, the Puritan-pioneer ethic, enlightenment, progressive, collectivist, transcendental, and security.

Methods of sharing motivation are using specific data, vivid description, emotionally loaded words, and showing your own motivation nonverbally.

Ethos is shared trust derived primarily from perceived competence and integrity. It can be developed extrinsically from reputation, the setting, and the introduction of a speech. What the speaker says can of course also enhance ethos. The speaker should be a super-representative—similar to the audience in most beliefs, values, and behaviors, but dissimilar in qualifications and leadership.

Resistance to change can be developed or enhanced through use of anxiety, hostility, linking, commitment, cognitive consistency, and inoculation.

Persuasive speeches can be organized in a variety of patterns, depending on the situation. Balanced arguments and an indirect approach to revealing your purpose should be practiced with antagonistic audiences.

"Stay the Course"

Ronald Reagan

Following is a transcript of the address by the President to the nation from Washington last night, as recorded by The New York Times *on Thursday, October 14, 1982:*

My fellow Americans, in recent days all of us have been swamped by a sea of economic statistics, some good, some bad, and some just plain confusing. There

From *The New York Times*, October 14, 1982. © 1982 by The New York Times Company. Reprinted by permission.

are times when I think that the paper traffic that crosses my desk in a week could fill a big city phone book, and then some.

The value of the dollar is up around the world. Interest rates are down by 40 percent. The stock and bond markets surge upward. Inflation is down 59 percent. Buying power is going up. Some economic indicators are down. Others are up. But the dark cloud of unemployment hangs over the lives of 11 million of our friends, neighbors and family.

At times, the sheer weight of all these facts and figures makes them hard for anyone to understand. What do they really mean, and what can we do to make them better?

Well, the first step is to understand what they mean in human terms, how they're affecting the everyday lives of our people. Because behind every one of those numbers are millions of individual lives: young couples struggling to make ends meet, teenagers looking for work, older Americans threatened by inflation, small-business men fighting for survival, and parents working for a better future for their children.

'WANT TO MAKE IT A BETTER PLACE'

All of them have one thing in common. They're Americans who love this country of ours and want to make it a better place. They're brave, hardworking people who know that America today faces serious problems that were long years in the making. And they're desperately trying to make sense out of all the statistics, slogans and political jargon filling the airwaves in this election year. Above all, they're concerned citizens who are looking for guideposts on the road to recovery, for ways to help see our country through to better times.

I know because I hear from hundreds of them every day, in meetings here at the White House, on visits to schools, meeting halls, factories and fairgrounds across the country, and in thousands of phone calls and letters. I only wish I could share with you tonight all that they have to say—their hopes, their fears, their concerns and, most of all, their quiet, patient courage.

LETTER FROM SELMA, ALA.

But let me just give you one example that speaks for so many of you, a letter from a wife and mother named Judith, who lives in Selma, Ala.

"Dear Mr. President," she writes.

It's 3:45 A.M., and for over an hour I've been unable to sleep . . . this morning I need very much to believe in something . . . I'm not writing so much as an individual, but as a representative of so many. We need to talk with you—to believe that you hear us. . . .

After years of training and experience, we can't find jobs. National unemployment figures sound almost healthy next to the almost 19 percent we're enduring in Selma.

The costs for basic survival are nearly beyond belief . . . there may never be a house—home of our own—that dream we've worked for for so many years . . . We have said 'no' to so many things . . . we're afraid and confused. We've worked hard—we conserved—we planned—we were frugal—careful. We feel so out of control. We don't want a handout—we just want to help make the system well again.

We must know that in the tons of bureaucracy . . . we've not been lost . . . we want to help. We want a better life, and we're willing to work for it. We believe. We must—it's all we have.

THE AMERICAN DREAM

Well, Judith, I hear you. And millions of other men and women like you stand for the values of hard work, thrift, commitment to family and love of God that made this country so great, and will make us great again. And you deserve to know what we're doing in these difficult times to bring your dream—the American dream—back to life again after so many years of mistakes and neglect.

Tonight, in homes across this country, unemployment is the problem uppermost on many people's minds. Getting Americans back to work is an urgent priority for all of us—and especially for this Administration.

But remember, you can't solve unemployment without solving the things that caused it—the out-of-control inflation and interest rates that led to unemployment in the first place. Unless you get at the root causes of the problem—which is exactly what our economic program is doing—you may be able to temporarily relieve the symptoms, but you'll never cure the disease. You may even make it worse.

I have a special reason for wanting to solve this problem in a lasting way. I was 21 and looking for work in 1932, one of the worst years of the Great Depression, and I can remember one bleak night in the Thirties when my father learned on Christmas Eve that he'd lost his job. To be young in my generation was to feel that your future had been mortgaged out from under you—and that's a tragic mistake we must never allow our leaders to make again. Today's young people must never be held hostage to the mistakes of the past.

RONALD REAGAN: STAY THE COURSE

The only way to avoid making those mistakes again is to learn from them.

The pounding economic hangover America's suffering from didn't come about overnight and there's no single, instant cure. In recent weeks, a lot of people have been playing what I call the "blame game." The accusing finger has been pointed in every direction of the compass and a lot of time and hot air have been spent looking for scapegoats.

Well, there's plenty of blame to go around. The problems we face are bigger than any one party or group of people. They're the result not of weeks or months, but of years—even decades—of past mistakes. The problem isn't who to blame—it's what to blame. So tonight let's forget about party politics and take a look at how our country got into this fix and what we can do to get her out of it.

When I said this problem was years in the making, I wasn't just using a figure of speech. This chart shows you what I mean.

You see that red line. It represents the rate of unemployment from 1963 through the present and it tells us two important things. First of all, it's a jagged line, representing rises and dips in unemployment as our economy passed through boom periods and bust periods over the past decade. This reminds us that the current recession hasn't stopped because, in the past, when the crunch came, too many in government resorted to quick fixes instead of getting to the root cause.

Each time they applied the quick fixes, unemployment dipped for awhile, only to take off again. In that sense, you could say that we've been on a decade-long roller coaster ride.

The only difference is that, on a roller coaster, you end up on solid ground once the ride is over. As you can see from the chart, while unemployment zigzagged from year to year, its long-term direction kept notching upward. Notice that each so-called recovery left unemployment higher than before the recession.

In 1968, unemployment stood at 3.6 percent. In 1971, it shot up to 5.9 percent. Then it started coming down again, but instead of going all the way back to 3.6 percent, it bottomed out at 4.9 percent. In 1974, it started shooting up again, and the same thing happened. It bottomed out at a higher level than before. In other words, for all its short-term ups and downs, the unemployment roller coaster was really an escalator, edging its way up the charts throughout the last decade. Unless we reverse that trend, it can only get worse, not just for us, but for our children and grandchildren.

Now let's look at what's behind this bad trend in unemployment. What's been causing it for over a decade?

A second chart tells much of the story, but before we look at it, I'll bet many of you've already come up with the answer.

It's a phenomenon that, last year, a majority of Americans correctly identified as our single most pressing long-term problem—inflation.

Inflation, and the high interest rates it leads to, are the real culprits. They create the economic climate that leads to unemployment.

This blue line represents inflation. Like unemployment, inflation has zig-zagged over the last decade, but you can see that, up to now, the long-term trend has been upwards. Again, as with unemployment, the old quick fixes simply did not work. Each time they were applied, they gave a little temporary relief to the patient, but left him weaker than he was before.

It's a consistent pattern. Each time inflation has shot up since 1969 there has been a deadly, delayed reaction of rising unemployment. Inflation is like a virus in the economic bloodstream, sometimes dormant and sometimes active, but leaving the patient weaker after every new attack.

My fellow Americans, we've got to stop these trendlines to disaster. To do that we have to understand what causes them. Well, for starters, our Federal Government has been living beyond its means for more than a generation. One of the wisest of our founding fathers, Thomas Jefferson, warned that the public debt is "the greatest of dangers to be feared." He believed that it was wrong for one generation to forever burden the generations yet to come, and, for the first 150 years of our history, our leaders heeded Jefferson's warning.

But not lately. In our lifetimes we've seen Government spending rage out of control. We've only had one balanced budget in the last 22 years.

So now, we're staggering under a trillion dollar debt. This year, before Government can spend one dime to feed the hungry, care for the sick or protect our freedom, it must plan to spend $110 billion just to pay interest on that debt. And still the big spenders wonder why the American people want what a stubborn minority in the House of Representatives denied them just 12 days ago, a Constitutional amendment to balance the budget.

All of this Government spending and red ink can only spawn higher taxes and whopping deficits which, for nearly two decades, led to inflationary increases in the money supply. Inflation and massive Government borrowing drive up interest rates. That makes it difficult or impossible for families to get the credit they need to buy homes, cars and appliances, or for businesses to invest in greater productivity. And, ultimately, inflation leads to recession and unemployment. We've had eight recessions since World War II.

IMPACT OF INFLATION

At the bottom of it all is inflation—Government-caused inflation. Over the years, our leaders adopted something called the "new economics" based on a belief that a little inflation each year created prosperity. But, each time the economic disruption caused by inflation triggered another round of recession and high unemployment, the Government reacted, not like your family would—by putting its own house in order—but by spending, borrowing and printing more money.

Unemployment would dip for a time, but the same quick fix that temporarily eased unemployment was sending inflation back through the ceiling.

It was a vicious cycle. Too many people played politics with the economy for too long, and those twin disaster lines kept inching ominously upward, bringing our society closer and closer to catastrophe.

In a way, I guess I can understand why so many of our political leaders fell into this trap. I'm sure they did it with the best of intentions. It's easy to lose touch with reality when it's other people's money that you're spending and there are so many things you want to do for those or this or that special-interest group—so many programs, many of them quite attractive and well-meaning, that can only be subsidized by more Government taxing, spending and borrowing. I can understand how it happened. Indeed, like many others, for a time I accepted Government's claim that it was sound economics, but there came a day when I, and millions of other Americans, began to realize the terrible consequences of all those years of playing politics as usual while the economic disaster lines crept higher and higher.

Well, at my age, I didn't come to Washington to play politics as usual. I didn't come here to reward pressure groups by spending other people's money. And, most of all, I didn't come here to further mortgage the future of the American people just to buy a little short-term political popularity. I came to Washington to try to solve problems—not to sweep them under the rug and leave them for those who will come later.

WORST ENEMY IS ECONOMIC

A President's greatest responsibility is to protect all our people from enemies, foreign and domestic. Here at home, the worst enemy we face is economic—the creeping erosion of the American way of life and the American dream that has resulted in today's tragedy of economic stagnation and unemployment.

Now I don't pretend for a moment that, in 21 months, we've been able to undo all the damage to our economy that has built up over more than 20 years. The first part of our program has been on the books only one year and 13 days. Much of the legislation we need has still not been enacted. We've still got a long way to go before we restore our prosperity. But what I can report to you tonight, my fellow Americans, is that, at long last, your Government has a program in place that faces our problems and has already started solving them.

Twenty-one months ago, we faced five critical problems: high taxes, runaway Government spending, inflation, high interest rates and unemployment.

Getting to the roots of unemployment meant fighting inflation and high interest rates caused by runaway Government spending and taxing because we know that, when inflation shoots up, it triggers a delayed-action rise in unemployment; now inflation is being driven back down, and lower unemployment will follow.

So we started by winning the first real tax cut for the American people in nearly two decades. Our program brings down income tax rates 25 percent. At the same time, we've been cutting costly, wasteful Government regulations and the rate of increase in Government spending. We've reduced the rate of Government spending growth by nearly two-thirds.

CITES DECLINE IN INTEREST

Inflation which registered 12.4 percent in 1980, is down to just 5.1 percent so far this year.

Interest rates, which had climbed as high as 21½ percent before we took office, have this week fallen to 12 percent, not low enough, but certainly heading in the right direction.

Unemployment, always a lagging indicator in times of recession[,] has not yet stopped its upward drift.

But in 21 months, we've already brought tax rates down by a quarter with the third installment coming next July, and brought down the rate of increase in Government spending by nearly two-thirds. That's helped us to bring down the rate of inflation by more than half, and that's helped us to bring down interest rates by 40 percent.

So, on four out of five problems that faced us in 1980, we've made important progress. We haven't solved them all, but we're making headway. Just last week, the Federal Reserve Bank decided to lower its discount rate to 9.5 percent, the first time this key interest rate has gone below two digits since 1979, and the fifth reduction in just four months. This demonstrates the Fed's confidence that inflation and market rates will continue coming down, and its confidence that we can work together for a healthy, noninflationary recovery. All of this lays the ground work for a recovery that will mean more jobs and more opportunity for all our people, but it's a delayed reaction.

'REMEMBER THE TRENDLINES'

Remember the trendlines. Just as surely as skyrocketing inflation created a negative reaction that drove up unemployment, bringing down inflation and interest rates is creating a positive reaction that will boost employment. I wish there were a quicker, easier way, some magic short cut, but unemployment is always one of the last things to turn around as an economy heads into recovery.

And make no mistake, America is recovery-bound and the world knows it. The American dollar, beaten down and distrusted in the late 1970's, is showing new strength. Recently, we've been seeing a surge of investment in our stock and bond markets. This is no flash in the pan. Markets will go up and they will come down, but the trend in the United States is up.

What's more, this investment is coming from all over, from home, from abroad, from small investors on Main Street, to those who manage billions of dollars, including our workers' pension funds.

'THIS ONE IS BUILT TO LAST'

Why aren't these people heeding the drumbeat of doom and gloom coming from Washington? Because they've been watching this country's inflation and interest rates dropping for months. They realize this Administration means business in the battle against inflation. Their decision to put cash on the line is a strong vote of confidence in the foundation being laid for America's recovery. Healthy, stable growth that will bring new jobs and opportunity for our people without returning us to runaway inflation and interest rates.

That's the one big difference between the recovery America is headed for today, and the shaky, temporary recoveries of the recent past—this one is built to last.

With your support we can show the world that we've learned our lesson and that this time we're going to get the job done and get it done right. This time we're going to keep inflation, interest rates and government spending, taxing and borrowing down, and get Americans back on the job.

Much of the work that remains to be done requires Congressional cooperation. As you know, Congress adjourned Oct. 2 for the election campaign, but it left behind a lot of unfinished business. For this reason, I urged the Congress to reconvene, after the elections, so it can do its part, as quickly as possible, to continue the work of recovery. We simply can't afford to wait until next year when something as vital as the economic health of America is at stake.

The Congress will return on November 29. It will face five top economic priorities—priorities that must be addressed.

HE LISTS THE PRIORITIES

First, the Congress must do its part to control Government spending. Before adjourning, it sent me only two appropriation bills. Eleven more remain to be passed, and I will use the veto if necessary to keep them within the budget. When the Congress passed the tax package this summer, it pledged to save $3 in outlays for every $1 in new revenues. I intend to hold the Congress to its word.

Second, I urge the Congress to reconsider the Constitutional Amendment to balance the budget. This crucial measure was passed by the Senate and supported by a clear majority in the House of Representatives. It was only defeated because of the hard core opposition of a minority of Representatives who prefer continued big spending.

Third, the Congress should act on regulatory reform to help make Government more economical and efficient, and the private sector more productive. Regulatory reform legislation was passed unanimously by the Senate, but was bottled up in committee in the House.

Fourth, the time has come for passage of the Enterprise Zones initiative to revive declining inner city and rural communities by providing new incentives to develop business and jobs. This program was approved by Senate Finance Committee but still awaits action on the Senate floor and in the House.

And, fifth, we need to pass the Clean Air Bill which, while protecting the environment, will make it possible for industry to rebuild its productive base and create more jobs.

'IT IS NOT AN EASY JOB'

But it isn't an easy job, this challenge to rebuild America and renew the American dream. And I know it can be tempting, listening to some who would go back to the old ways and the quick fix. But consider the choice. A return to the big spending and big taxing that left us with 21½ percent interest rates is no real alternative. A return to double-digit inflation is no alternative. A return to taxing and taxing the American people—that's no alternative. That's what destroyed millions of American jobs. Together we've chosen a new road for America. It's a far better road. We need only the courage to see it through. I know we can. Throughout our history, we Americans have proven again and again that no challenge is too big for a free, united people.

Together we can do it again. We can do it by slowly but surely working our way back to prosperity that will mean jobs for all who are willing to work, and fulfillment for all who still cherish the American dream.

> We can do it, my fellow Americans, by staying the course. Thank you, good night and God bless you.

ENDNOTES

1. Herbert W. Simons, *Persuasion: Understanding, Practice, and Analysis* (Reading, Mass.: Addison-Wesley, 1976), p. 21.
2. Mary John Smith, *Persuasion and Human Action: A Review and Critique of Social Influence Theories* (Belmont, Cal.: Wadsworth, 1982), p. 7.
3. David Jabusch and Stephen Littlejohn, *Elements of Speech Communication* (Boston: Houghton Mifflin, 1981), p. 6.
4. For a more detailed discussion, see Wallace Fotheringham, *Perspectives on Persuasion* (Boston: Allyn and Bacon, 1966).
5. Richard Rieke and Malcolm Sillars, *Argument and the Decision Making Process* (New York: John Wiley and Sons, 1975), pp. 76–80.
6. Abraham Maslow, *Motivation and Personality* (New York: Harper & Row, 1970).
7. M.W. de Laubenfels, *Life Science* (New York: Prentice-Hall, 1949), pp. 31–32.
8. Reinhold Niebuhr, *The Nature and Destiny of Man*, vol. I "Human Nature" (New York: Charles Scribner's Sons, 1961).
9. Milton Rokeach, *The Nature of Human Values* (New York: Free Press, 1973).
10. Rieke and Sillars, pp. 124–131.
11. Daniel Yankelovich, *New Rules: Searching for Self Fulfillment in a World Turned Upside Down* (New York: Random House, 1981), p. 87.
12. David M. Jabusch, Victoria Smith, and K.C. Wong, "Patient Image of the Anesthesiologist," paper delivered at The American Association of Anesthesiologists, St. Louis, Mo., 1980.
13. Velma Lashbrook, "Source Credibility: A Summary of Experimental Research," paper presented at Speech Communication Association Convention, San Francisco, December, 1971.
14. Simons, pp. 161–162.
15. Douglas Ehninger, Bruce Gronbeck, Ray McKerrow, and Alan H. Monroe, *Principles and Types of Speech*, 9th ed. (Glenview, Ill.: Scott, Foresman, 1982), pp. 151–166.

9

Specialized Transactions

In this chapter:
Transactions that entertain
Transactions that pay tribute
Transactions of courtesy
Combative transactions
Summary
Abraham Lincoln, Gettysburg Address

In the summer of 1863, the Civil War was not going particularly well for the North. Divisiveness among northern factions and the indecision among its generals had resulted in lost opportunities and had cost dearly in time and resources. General Robert E. Lee's army had penetrated deep into northern territory. Finally, the two great armies inevitably met on the rolling hills outside the little town of Gettysburg, Pennsylvania. For three days the battle, and probably the preservation of the Union, hung in the balance. By the narrowest of margins, the North prevailed, but not without cost. Forty thousand casualties, from both armies, were suffered at Gettysburg. Preparations began immediately for the dedication of a national cemetery. The great orator and president of Harvard University, Edward Everett, was chosen to deliver the keynote address. Almost as an afterthought, President Lincoln was invited to "say a few appropriate remarks." Contrary to popular belief, Lincoln prepared carefully. As he rose to speak at Gettysburg, the crowd was restless and noisy. They had hardly settled down to listen before his beautifully brief commemoration was finished. With no public address system, it is doubtful that more than a small fraction of the audience heard the speech. And yet this was the speech that rhetorical critics would acclaim as the most eloquent commemorative address ever spoken.

As we have seen in earlier chapters, most speeches have as their general purpose either to inform or to persuade listeners, in common contexts such as classroom lectures, political rallies, and sermons. However, some important types of occasions call for more specialized transactions, and occur with enough regularity that they deserve special attention here. Furthermore, there are many common misconceptions about these transactions which lead to repeated mistakes that substantially reduce the effectiveness of many speakers on these special occasions. We will discuss transactions that (1) entertain, (2) pay tribute, (3) extend courtesy; and (4) combative transactions.[1]

TRANSACTIONS THAT ENTERTAIN

Speeches to entertain occur during events that have as their transactional purpose to get listeners to share enjoyment about a particular topic. Since entertaining content is frequently found in informative and persuasive transactions, entertaining transactions are here distinguished by entertainment or enjoyment constituting their primary purpose. Although speeches to entertain may be called for in a variety of situations, they most frequently occur in after-dinner or other celebrative situations.

Before we discuss the recommended approach to speeches to entertain, let us dispel a common misconception that anything entertaining is a speech to entertain. First, speeches to entertain are not a string of jokes, however funny. When comedians such as Bob Hope or Johnny Carson perform their routines, they may be immensely entertaining, but this does not constitute a speech to entertain. Similarly, a speech to entertain is not a stunt. I once observed a student hold a class in stitches by doing a "bandana trick" while substituting a *banana* for the bandana. He flattened out the bandana (i.e., squashed it), put it on top of his head, and the like. It was one of the most hilarious and entertaining stunts I have ever seen, but unfortunately it did not meet the minimum requirements of the assignment since it was not a *speech* to entertain.

We prepare for entertaining transactions the same way we prepare for any other public communication event. We consider organizational pattern, ideas, content, and so forth. All of these are simply focused on the enjoyment transaction. Let us look at how a speech can be made entertaining. We will discuss (1) topics, (2) ideas, (3) content, and (4) delivery.

Topics

As is the case with other kinds of classroom speeches, students wonder, "What can I talk about in a speech to entertain, of all things?" Just look around you. Humor abounds in nearly every aspect of life. People, in particular, are entertaining. New students,

TRANSACTIONS THAT ENTERTAIN

professors, salespersons—there is no class of people who do not have entertaining foibles. Events can also be entertaining. Unusual experiences like sky diving or running the Colorado River through the Grand Canyon can be spellbinding. Even common experiences such as leaving home for college or preparing for a blind date can be fun. One of the funniest speeches I ever heard was about drinking fountains. Even seemingly serious events can have their humorous side. I have seen divorced people have each other in stitches over some of the humorous things that happened to them as they attempted to cope with their single status. In other words, topics for speeches to entertain are everywhere. Someday I may even share one about my ongoing war with the weeds and pests in my lawn (if it weren't so serious)!

Ideas

Ideas in a speech to entertain differ from those to inform and persuade, in that they should be simple and easily assimilated. Throughout this book I have emphasized that topics and the ideas to support them should be significant to your listeners and

A teacher entertains students while discussing a serious subject

challenge their intellect. Speeches to entertain are the exception. In entertaining transactions, listeners don't want to work at listening. They want (and you want them) to sit back and enjoy themselves. Hence, you must keep the topic and ideas easy to understand.

The organizational format, which is dictated by the topic, should be kept simple. Ideas can be arranged in any of the patterns we discussed under informative or persuasive speaking. Most common, perhaps, is the topical or *characteristic* approach. I have heard highly entertaining speeches on the humorous characteristics of everything from drinking fountains to college professors. The humorous process of preparing to leave home for college was of course developed chronologically.

Content

Perhaps the distinguishing characteristic of entertaining transactions is their content. Content is distinguished by either novelty or humor.

Novelty. Nonhumorous speeches to entertain usually have novel content. Recall that novelty and contrast are among the prime factors of attention and interest. Earlier we spoke of choosing topics dealing with novel or unusual events, experiences, or processes.

When developing even an ordinary idea, however, novel or extraordinary events and experiences can add entertaining content. If you do not consider yourself a humorist, perhaps you should share some unusual experience such as "my day in a Buddhist monastery," or "campaigning for candidate X." Most people may experience an airplane ride as routine, but not my friend who had to escape a minor crash through an emergency exit over the wing!

Humor. One of the most delightful aspects of many speeches to entertain is the use of humor. As we pointed out earlier, humor is also used effectively in other types of speeches, but is used with more frequency in entertaining transactions. Here we will discuss the use of humorous content from the standpoint of its characteristics and sources.

How can I be funny, especially if I *have to*? These are the characteristics that make otherwise ordinary content humorous: the unusual turn, exaggeration, pun, incongruity, irony or sarcasm, and burlesque.

One characteristic of humorous content is the *unusual turn*. This is where you seem to begin to say one thing, and then give it the opposite twist at the end, catching the listeners by surprise. Our earlier example of "We always knew he was a successful politician—he just never got caught at it" is a case of unusual turn.

Another characteristic of humorous content, somewhat like the unusual turn, is the use of *incongruity*. People tend to be amused with things out of context. A demure looking and apparently feeble little old lady (not in tennis shoes) once approached my son with the question "Where the hell can you go fishing around here?"

I recall a television extravaganza in which the old "pea picker," Ernie Ford, was to crown a beauty queen. The setting was regal, the women beautiful and formally dressed. In this elegant setting Ford walked up to the queen and asked in a slightly Ozark accent, "How does it feel to be the pick o' the litter?"

Exaggeration is an effective characteristic of humorous content. Most of us are familiar with the overused exaggerations that "the mosquitos were so large they could carry you away" or "the beef was so rare it was still kicking." As many times as you've heard them, they still elicit good humor, and the first time most people find them very humorous. Exaggeration, of course, involves distortion, but in entertaining contexts people accept the enjoyment transaction and suspend their need for literal accuracy. One of the humorous types of drinking fountains was the one that runs all the time—appropriately labeled by the speaker "Old Faithful."

Puns, or playing on the multiple meanings of words, are yet another characteristic of humor. Because of the multiplicity of meanings that can be attributed to most words, people who are skillful with words and know the language well enjoy a good *double entendre*, or play on words. Punning, of course, requires considerable linguistic sophistication on the part of both speaker and listeners. In order for the transaction to be enjoyable, all parties need to share the multiplicity of meanings alluded to. In the drinking fountain speech, one category was the drinking fountain whose handle you just barely touch and it shoots five feet in the air—punningly labeled by the speaker "old face-full."

Irony and *sarcasm* can also add to the humor of a speech to entertain. Similar to incongruity and the unusual turn, these techniques involve either the unexpected, or saying the opposite of what you mean. It is irony when a minister's child "raises hell." President Reagan used irony effectively when he poked fun at the Russians for having had a "crop failure" so frequently under the communist system.

An example of sarcasm is for someone to say, "I guess I can gag it down," when offered seconds at an unquestionably delicious meal. Irony and sarcasm should be used with care, however. Since you are saying the opposite of what you mean, it is easy to be misunderstood or to offend your listeners. Hence, you need to know your audience extremely well to be sure they will enjoy your irony and sarcasm.

A final characteristic of humorous content is *burlesque*. Burlesque is doing a "take off" on an idea, event, or person. By dramatizing, in an exaggerated way, the foibles of a person or characteristics of an event, you can get people to laugh—even at themselves. One of the most humorous after-dinner speeches I ever heard was given at a retirement party. The speaker (a skilled actor) traced the history of the retiree's career, doing brief, exaggerated characterizations of some of the people in the audience who had worked with the man. One need not pick on people. Humorous events can be recreated, or serious ones redone, in order to bring out the humor in them. As in the case of punning and language play, burlesque requires considerable skill on the part of the speaker and should be handled with care.

Supports. Let us now take a look at some sources of humorous content for speeches to entertain.

Your main sources of humorous content are the three forms of support we discussed in Chapter 3. Humorous examples, anecdotes, comparisons, or even ironic statistics may be sources of enjoyment for you and your listeners.

We can all recall *examples* we have found humorous—stories with which we can share enjoyment with others—but perhaps the most obvious humorous content is *anecdotes* or jokes. Earlier I cautioned that a speech to entertain is not a string of jokes, but a few jokes, appropriately placed to develop ideas in a speech to entertain, can work well. You may want to keep a file of them, classified by subject or order, to have them handy.

Comparisons are also sources of humorous content. They can be used effectively with exaggeration and unusual turn, but especially with incongruity. The fabled "bull in a china shop" has been used so often that its humorous image has become a cliché, but how about the person who said, "It was colder than a brass toilet seat in the Klondike"?

Statistics, stories, and even reiteration can also be sources of humorous content. We need only see the humor in them, and communicate it appropriately.

Transactional nature of humor. As we conclude our discussion of humorous content, let us look at two words of caution, based on its transactional nature. First, humor, like nonverbal communication, is very *culturally based*. The connotations of words, on which puns are based, are shared only by members of a culture or those who understand the culture. And in order to enjoy the humor in examples, comparisons, or anecdotes, your audience must be familiar enough with the culture to be able to picture the situation in their minds. Hence, you must analyze your audience carefully in order to be sure they will appreciate your wit. Such was the case of a Japanese student who visited Salt Lake City. He knew the local culture well enough to be familiar with the label *Jack-Mormon*, which refers to a nonpracticing Mormon. When asked what his religion was, he brought down the house (and communicated his agnosticism) when he said, "I'm a Jack-Buddhist."

The second caution is about off-color or ethnic jokes or allusions. Ethnic or off-color humor has the high potential of offending people in your audience. Humor that may be funny in one context or with one group of listeners may be entirely inappropriate in another. Because of the heterogeneity of audiences in most public communication contexts, I would caution against either profane or ethnic humor, as a general rule. Rare exceptions exist, but they must be approached with great caution.

Delivery

A final aspect of speeches to entertain is the way in which they are delivered. As a general rule, you should try to maintain an attitude of light-heartedness and good humor in your delivery. If you appear to be enjoying yourself, your audience is more likely to do so also.

A particular problem is how to handle audience laughter—or the lack of it. First of all, don't anticipate it. Listeners laugh when you least expect it and may not laugh when you want them to. Some of the most enjoyable humor is that which we just chuckle to ourselves about. If the audience is not laughing, just assume they are enjoying the speech and are chuckling to themselves.

When they do respond with laughter, it is fine for you to join in. Just remember to start laughing after they do, and to stop before they do.

Whether the audience laughs or not, you can be sure that when you have chosen a novel or humorous topic, devised some meaningful but light-hearted ideas, developed novel or humorous content, and communicated with good-humored delivery, your listeners will be sharing your enjoyment.

TRANSACTIONS THAT PAY TRIBUTE

Among the most common occasions for commemorative transactions are those on which we pay tribute to events, places, or people. Here we will discuss commemorations and dedications, as well as eulogies and commendations.

Commemorations and Dedications

During our nation's Bicentennial many speeches were delivered to commemorate the founding of the Republic. It is common on the anniversary of events which are significant to groups, communities, or countries to celebrate those events with speeches of commemoration. Similarly, the founding of an organization or the completion of a significant structure such as a public building, bridge, or monument calls for some appropriate words of dedication. Such was the task of Lincoln at Gettysburg.

Speeches of commemoration and dedication usually have as their purpose not to change attitudes, nor create new beliefs, nor even exhort people to action, but rather to induce resistance to change by strengthening the audience's beliefs, attitudes, and especially values. One of the most productive ways of studying the history of American values is to study some of the great commemorative speeches of the period. Speeches commemorating an event will usually reinforce the group values that the event either established or helped to preserve. On the Fourth of July it is not uncommon for speakers to extol what they consider to be the most important human values expressed in the Declaration of Independence—life, liberty, and the pursuit of happiness. More creative speakers may use any one of these as a springboard to discuss similar values, as Franklin Roosevelt did when he expressed the "four freedoms"—freedom of speech, freedom of religion, freedom from want, and freedom from fear.

Speeches of commemoration and dedication can be organized in any of the ways we discussed earlier, but a discussion of values is particularly amenable to a topical structure, as in Value I, Value II, Value III, and so on.

The content of speeches of commemoration and dedication could include any one of the forms of support discussed in Chapter 3. However, the forms of support used with the most frequency and greatest effect seem to be specific examples, historical and literary quotations, stories, and reiteration. Since audiences at commemorations and dedications are usually well disposed toward the speaker and the event, content can effectively contain emotional appeals to loyalty, patriotism, or pride.

Delivery of commemorative or dedicatory speeches is not particularly distinctive, but as always should be appropriate to the purpose, content, and context of the transaction.

In his survey of the greatest public speeches delivered in the United States prior to 1900, Glenn Capp includes five commemorative speeches: Washington's Farewell Address, Lincoln's Gettysburg Address, Emerson's "The American Scholar," Grady's "New South," and Booker T. Washington's Atlanta Exposition Address.[2] In each of these cases the speaker was careful not to contradict the values of his listeners. As the first black to appear on the public platform with whites in the South, Booker T. Washington even circulated drafts of his speech to people representing differing points of view in his audience for criticism prior to final delivery of the speech.

In some cases, however, significant special occasions are used by speakers to shock their audience into attention, and to attempt to raise consciousness on a heretofore obscure issue or point of view. Such was the case of Frederick Douglass in his Fourth of July oration in 1852. In that speech he spoke on the familiar theme of citizenship, but developed the unexpected thesis that blacks were really not citizens and their loyalty could not be taken for granted because they did not enjoy their constitutional citizenship rights.

Whether you decide to reinforce existing values or attempt a more radical specific response depends, of course, on your analysis of your audience and what, in your judgment, they are ready for. As always, it is better to attempt and accomplish a modest attitude shift than to try to accomplish too much and achieve nothing—or worse, a "boomerang effect." On the other hand, this special occasion may be your one and only chance at this particular audience, and you don't want to waste it.

Eulogies and Commendations

Eulogies and commendations are speeches of tribute to one or more people. *Eulogies* are given at funerals or on the anniversary of the birth or death of a deceased person. *Commendations* are similar, but given on the occasion of an award, retirement, promotion, or other recognition of a living person.

Tributes to people occur in situations that place some of the most severe constraints on the speaker. They usually have as their primary purpose to make all participants feel good about the life of the person to whom the tribute is being paid. Further, they usually focus on either the commendable characteristics or the major accomplishments of the person or both. As in the case of other speeches of tribute, the values of the people assembled are usually stressed. American values of honesty, hard work, responsibility, or achievement in vocation or family are frequently emphasized. It is well to remember that no one exemplifies all cultural values but that everyone exemplifies some.

An issue that pervades a tribute to a deceased person or eulogy is that of immortality. Immortality can be achieved either religiously or temporally. In cultures that believe in life after death, that comforting thought is usually mentioned with appropriate scriptural support. In the case of people or cultures who do not believe in life after death, immortality can be achieved by accomplishments on earth which have impacted peoples' lives or the environment in enduring ways. For instance, the creation of a work of art, a significant invention or discovery, or the relationship of the deceased to others all allow people's influence to endure beyond their life on earth. Obvious examples are people like Shakespeare, Mother Teresa, and Jonas Salk. But consider also the man who repeatedly handed the rescue line to other survivors after an airliner crashed in the Potomac River, only to sink beneath its murky surface before the helicopter could return to rescue him. He gained a measure of immortality in the lives he died to save.

Another issue frequently raised by people who are preparing a eulogy, especially a funeral talk, is whether to emphasize the person's death and immortality, or the person's life. While all funerals must acknowledge the mourning after the person's death, I personally find it more uplifting when the eulogy is more a celebration of the person's life. For the best adaptation to this specialized transaction, however, the eulogizer should be sensitive to the beliefs and conventions of the audience, just as you would for other types of speeches, and perhaps consult with the deceased's family before deciding on the tone of a eulogy.

Regardless of the "tone" of the event, eulogies and commendations usually make extensive use of specific instances, in the form of remembrances from the life of the person to whom the tribute is being paid. Literary and scriptural quotations are also effective supports for the ideas developed in eulogies and commendations. Don't be afraid to help people smile or even laugh at a funeral. Wit in the form of a humorous remembrance can relieve tension, but should be subdued, subtle, and handled with great care.

Delivery of eulogies should be mellow but not maudlin. Dress should conform to the standards of the culture. In middle-class America black is no longer required, but semiformal attire is usually expected. Various subcultures may be less formal.

Note how Robert G. Ingersoll incorporates all the above principles in the following tribute to his brother:

ORATION AT HIS BROTHER'S GRAVE

Friends, I am going to do that which the dead oft promised he would do for me.

The loved and loving brother, husband, father, friend died, where manhood's morning almost touches noon, and while the shadows still were falling toward the West.

* * *

SPECIALIZED TRANSACTIONS

This brave and tender man in every storm of life was oak and rock, but in the sunshine he was vine and flower. He was the friend of all heroic souls. He climbed the heights and left all superstitions far below, while on his forehead fell the golden dawning of the grander day.

He loved the beautiful, and was with color, form, and music touched to tears. He sided with the weak, the poor, and wronged, and lovingly gave alms. With loyal heart, and with the purest hands, he faithfully discharged all public trusts.

He was a worshiper of liberty, a friend of the oppressed. A thousand times I have heard him quote these words: "For justice all place a temple, and all season, summer." He believed that happiness was the only good, reason the only torch, justice the only worship, humanity the only religion, and love the only priest. He added to the sum of human joy; and were every one to whom he did some loving service to bring a blossom to his grave, he would sleep tonight beneath a wilderness of flowers.

Life is a narrow vale between the cold and barren peaks of two eternities. We strive in vain to look beyond the heights. We cry aloud, and the only answer is the echo of our wailing cry. From the voiceless lips of the unreplying dead, there comes no word; but in the night of death hope sees a star, and listening love can hear the rustle of the wing.

He who sleeps here, when dying, mistaking the approach of death for the return of health, whispered with his latest breath: "I am better now." Let us believe, in spite of doubts and dogmas, of fears and tears, that these dear words are true of all the countless dead.

And now to you who have been chosen, from among the many men he loved, to do the last sad office for the dead, we give his sacred dust.[3]

TRANSACTIONS OF COURTESY

In addition to speeches of tribute to people or events, there are numerous occasions where people in responsible positions are obligated to make short speeches of introduction or nomination, presentation, welcome, and farewell.

Introductions and Nominations

Although speeches of introduction and nomination occur in somewhat different settings and have slightly different purposes, I will discuss them together because of their great similarities. In both cases, your purpose is to "sell" the person you are introducing with the object of getting the audience to either listen intently to what he or she is going to say or, in the latter case, to vote for the person you are nominating.

Before we discuss how you should prepare yourself for transactions of introduction and nomination, let us look at the two practices that most commonly ruin their effectiveness.

210

First, they are frequently much too long. In their desire to present the introducee in the best light, inexperienced introducers transform a brief speech of introduction into a lengthy speech of tribute. This is not your purpose. In speeches of introduction, present the person in the best light possible in two to four minutes and sit down. Speeches of nomination may be somewhat longer, but even then you should not give every detail of the person's life—only the most salient ones.

A second error frequently observed in speeches of introduction is for the introducer to steal the speaker's message by talking at length on the same topic before introducing the speaker. With one minor exception we will discuss later, I would *never* make comments of my own on the topic of the speaker I am introducing.

Well then, what do you do? First recall that your overriding purpose is to create *identification* between the audience and the person you are introducing or nominating, by focusing on the person's *qualifications*. These qualifications are usually evidenced by major biographical milestones, vocational experience, or other major accomplishments. The trick is to select only those which will have major impact on audience identification. Take, for example, educational qualifications. In introducing someone, I would give only their final degree along with any diploma or degree that bore directly on the topic or was shared by the audience.

The same is true of vocational experience. Most of it will be irrelevant to the occasion. Point out the current status of the speaker as well as other experiences that may be relevant. If, for instance, you were introducing a realtor to a P.T.A. meeting, it would be appropriate to point out not only the speaker's business expertise, but also his or her twenty years as a former teacher and school administrator. Military service as well as a plethora of part-time jobs should be ignored on this occasion.

Another way of heightening identification between the audience and the speaker is to *briefly* underscore the timeliness of the topic. This can be done with a quick reference to a relevant current event, local custom, or point of interest. Recall my injunction against stealing a person's speech, however. Any such references should be to things which you know are familiar to the listeners. If they require development or description, let the speaker do it. As a further precaution, I usually ask the speaker if he or she is planning to use a particular reference, and if so, I use one that is original or none at all.

It should be clear that in a speech of introduction or nomination you are merely a link in the identification between the audience and the speaker or nominee. This realization will give you the screen through which to decide what you want to say, and thereby make your remarks useful rather than detrimental to your efforts.

Presentations

Perhaps none of us will ever be prominent enough to be asked to present a Nobel Prize or Congressional Medal of Honor. Numerous presentations of lesser acclaim are made every day, however. Presentations of gifts, awards, and even merit badges are made by the thousands.

The purpose of presentations is to recognize some meritorious achievement ranging from years of service to an organization, on the one hand, to a significant single achievement, such as the conquering of Mount Everest, on the other.

As in the case of other speeches of tribute and courtesy, presentations should be brief and to the point. They should focus only on the recipients' most significant achievements, especially the one for which the award is being given.

Welcomes

At most conventions, conferences, and other meetings where visitors are present, it is a matter of courtesy for a representative of the host institution to offer a few words of welcome. The purpose, of course, is to make the visitors feel as comfortable as possible in their unfamiliar surroundings. It is important not only to help visitors feel welcome, but also to launch the event on a positive note. The significance of the purpose of the meeting can be stressed without going into great detail. And the common purpose and background of the participants can begin to establish identification among conferees.

Farewells

Speeches of farewell constitute some of the most interesting of all special transactions. They occur on the occasion of the departure of a leader from office or a member of longstanding leaving an organization or group. Presidents Washington, Lincoln, Eisenhower, and Nixon all gave farewell messages that make interesting reading. Why? Because of the unique characteristics of the situation.

First, the speaker is usually a person of great wisdom, which has been gained through years of experience in the office or organization. Secondly, since the speaker is *leaving*, he or she has few of the usual personal or political constraints of a continuing member or officer. The speaker can therefore address the question "Out of all of my experience and expertise what can I say to this audience that they most *need* to hear?" Washington chose to warn against "entangling alliances," while Eisenhower (the former general and probusiness president) warned against the power and influence of the "military–industrial complex."

Farewell messages can be devoted to any informative or persuasive purpose but, perhaps more than any other special occasion, they offer a unique opportunity for transacting with an audience you care about in a significant way.

COMBATIVE TRANSACTIONS

So far, we have discussed specialized speaking transactions that are generally cooperative and almost ritualistic in nature. There are special occasions, however, where either you or your ideas need defending, or opposing ideas need to be refuted. These occasions imply that, in addition to two opposing views, there is either a large middle-of-the-road group in your audience or a disinterested third party or judge who will decide the outcome. You would certainly not want to use attack and defense techniques *against* the people you were trying to persuade! We will discuss speeches of justification and refutation.

Justification

It is not uncommon for people in leadership positions to justify their actions or decisions before their organization or constituency. We are all familiar with the elaborate justifications of incumbent politicians as they seek re-election. Business and professional leaders, however, are also called upon to defend a particular position, an unpopular decision, or an antisocial behavior. This is to justify themselves.

The need for justification generally arises from two situations: either you have been misunderstood or misrepresented in some way, or you have been accused of violating the beliefs, values, or normative behaviors of the group.

In the case of misunderstanding or misrepresentation, the content of your message should be mostly concrete, accurate, and well-documented data. Your object is to clarify your position and rebuild trust. In this case, there is no substitute for factual data that are credible to your listeners. If you have been misquoted or quoted out of context, give the accurate statement in its complete context. If you have been wrongly accused of something, document your actual belief or behavior for your listeners.

In the case of an accurate accusation that your ideas or behaviors have violated the accepted norms of the group you represent, your problem is more serious and complex. In Chapter 8 we pointed out that people's behavior is influenced by a variety of beliefs, values, and motives, many of which are conflicting. We further stated that there is a hierarchy of these motives for every individual and most groups. In justifying yourself with a group whose norms you or your ideas have violated, you need to show where you were in conformity with other beliefs, values, and motives that the group accepts. Then you need to convince your audience that in this particular case the beliefs, values, or motives that guided you took precedence over those you violated.

In the 1924 Olympics, popularized in the movie "Chariots of Fire," Eric Liddell put his religious values above his country when he refused to compete on Sunday and thereby disqualified himself. This was a classic case, not of good versus evil, but of one accepted value taking precedence over another.

During his long and stormy political career, Richard Nixon was called upon to justify himself on numerous occasions. Two of these occasions became classics: his "Checkers Speech" justifying his campaign financing in 1952, and his speech of resignation following the Watergate scandal. The Checkers Speech is well worth reading, but his resignation speech is an example of Nixon's consummate skill at self-justification:

PRESIDENTIAL RESIGNATION
LET HE WHO IS WITHOUT SIN CAST THE FIRST STONE

Good evening. This is the 37th time I have spoken to you from this office in which so many decisions have been made that shape the history of this nation.

Each time I have done so to discuss with you some matters that I believe affected the national interest. And all the decisions I have made in my public life I have always tried to do what was best for the nation.

Throughout the long and difficult period of Watergate, I have felt it was my duty to persevere; to make every possible effort to complete the term of office to which you elected me.

In the past few days, however, it has become evident to me that I no longer have a strong enough political base in the Congress to justify continuing that effort.

As long as there was such a base, I felt strongly that it was necessary to see the constitutional process through to its conclusion; that to do otherwise would be unfaithful to the spirit of that deliberately difficult process, and a dangerously destabilizing precedent for the future.

But with the disappearance of that base, I now believe that the constitutional purpose has been served. And there is no longer a need for the process to be prolonged.

I would have preferred to carry through to the finish whatever the personal agony it would have involved, and my family unanimously urged me to do so.

But the interests of the nation must always come before any personal considerations. From the discussions I have had with Congressional and other leaders I have concluded that because of the Watergate matter I might not have the support of the Congress that I would consider necessary to back the very difficult decisions and carry out the duties of this office in the way the interests of the nation will require.

I have never been a quitter.

To leave office before my term is completed is opposed to every instinct in my body. But as President I must put the interests of America first.

America needs a full-time President and a full-time Congress, particularly at this time with problems we face at home and abroad.

To continue to fight through the months ahead for my personal vindication would almost totally absorb the time and attention of both the President and the Congress in a period when our entire focus should be on the great issues of peace abroad and prosperity without inflation at home.

Therefore, I shall resign the Presidency effective at noon tomorrow.

Vice President Ford will be sworn in as President at that hour in this office.

As I recall the high hopes for America with which we began this second term, I feel a great sadness that I will not be here in this office working on your behalf to achieve those hopes in the next two and a half years.

But in turning over direction of the Government to Vice President Ford I know, as I told the nation when I nominated him for that office 10 months ago, that the leadership of America will be in good hands.

In passing this office to the Vice President I also do so with the profound sense of the weight of responsibility that will fall on his shoulders tomorrow, and therefore of the understanding, the patience, the cooperation he will need from all Americans.

As he assumes that responsibility he will deserve the help and the support of all of us. As we look to the future, the first essential is to begin healing the wounds of this nation.

To put the bitterness and the divisions of the recent past behind us and to rediscover those shared ideals that lie in the heart of our strength and unity as a great and as a free people.

By taking this action, I hope that I will have hastened the start of that process of healing which is so desperately needed in America.

I regret deeply any injuries that may have been done in the course of the events that led to this decision. I would say only that if some of my judgments were wrong—and some were wrong—they were made in what I believed at the time to be the best interests of the nation.

To those who have stood with me during these past difficult months, to my family, my friends, the many others who've joined in supporting my cause because they believed it was right, I will be eternally grateful for your support.

And to those who have not felt able to give me your support, let me say I leave with no bitterness toward those who have opposed me, because all of us in the final analysis have been concerned with the good of the country however our judgments might differ.

So let us all now join together in affirming that common commitment and in helping our new President succeed for the benefit of all Americans.

I shall leave this office with regret at not completing my term but with gratitude for the privilege of serving as your President for the past five and a half years.

These years have been a momentous time in the history of our nation and the world. They have been a time of achievement in which we can all be proud—achievements that represent the shared efforts of the administration, the Congress and the people. But the challenges ahead are equally great.

And they, too, will require the support and the efforts of a Congress and the people, working in cooperation with the new Administration.

We have ended America's longest war. But in the work of securing a lasting peace in the world, the goals ahead are even more far-reaching and more difficult. We must complete a structure of peace, so that it will be said of this generation—our generation of Americans—by the people of all nations, not only that we ended one war but that we prevented future wars.

We have unlocked the doors that for a quarter of a century stood between the United States and the People's Republic of China. We must now insure that the one-quarter of the world's people who live in the People's Republic of China will be and remain, not our enemies, but our friends.

In the Middle East, 100 million people in the Arab countries, many of whom have considered us their enemies for nearly 20 years, now look on us as their friends. We must continue to build on that friendship so that peace can settle at last over the Middle East and so that the cradle of civilization will not become its grave.

Together with the Soviet Union we have made the crucial breakthroughs that have begun the process of limiting nuclear arms. But, we must set as our goal, not just limiting, but reducing and finally destroying these terrible weapons so that they cannot destroy civilization.

And so that the threat of nuclear war will no longer hang over the world and the people, we have opened a new relation with the Soviet Union. We must continue to develop and expand that new relationship so that the two strongest nations of the world will live together in cooperation rather than confrontation.

Around the world—in Asia, in Africa, in Latin America, in the Middle East—there are millions of people who live in terrible poverty, even starvation. We must keep as our goal turning away from production for war and expanding production for peace so that people everywhere on this earth can at last look forward, in their children's time if not in our time, to having the necessities for a decent life.

Here in America we are fortunate that most of our people have not only the blessings of liberty but also the means to live full and good, and by the world's standards even abundant lives.

We must press on, however, toward a goal not only of more and better jobs but of full opportunity for every man, and of what we are striving so hard right now to achieve—prosperity without inflation.

For more than a quarter of a century in public life, I have shared in the turbulent history of this evening.

I have fought for what I believe in. I have tried, to the best of my ability, to discharge those duties and meet those responsibilities that were entrusted to me.

Sometimes I have succeeded. And sometimes I have failed. But always I have taken heart from what Theodore Roosevelt said about the man in the arena whose face is marred by dust and sweat and blood, who strives valiantly, who errs and comes short again and again because there is not effort without error and shortcoming, but who does actually strive to do the deed, who knows the great devotion, who spends himself in a worthy cause, who at the best knows in the end the triumphs of high achievements and with the worst if he fails, at least fails while daring greatly.

I pledge to you tonight that as long as I have a breath of life in my body I shall continue in that spirit. I shall continue to work for the great causes to which I have been dedicated throughout my years as a Congressman, a Senator, Vice President and President, the cause of peace—not just for America but among all nations—prosperity, justice and opportunity for all of our people.

There is one cause above all to which I have been devoted and to which I shall always be devoted for as long as I live.

When I first took the oath of office as President five and a half years ago, I made this sacred commitment: to consecrate my office, my energies and all the wisdom I can summons to the cause of peace among nations.

As a result of these efforts, I am confident that the world is a safer place today, not only for the people of America but for the people of all nations, and that all of our children have a better chance than before of living in peace rather than dying in war.

This, more than anything, is what I hoped to achieve when I sought the Presidency. This, more than anything, is what I hope will be my legacy to you, to our country, as I leave the Presidency.

To have served in this office is to have felt a very personal sense of kinship with each and every American. In leaving it, I do so with this prayer: May God's grace be with you in the days ahead.[4]

Refutation

It is common for you to be misunderstood or attacked, but it is even more common for your ideas to be challenged. In a meeting or other public context a person speaking on the opposite side of the issue may make such a persuasive appeal for an opposing point of view as to cry out for someone to answer those arguments. This situation calls for a speech of refutation.

The general purpose of a speech of refutation is attack and defense. That is to say, you either tear down the opposing arguments or build up your own—or both. Refutation is organized around a series of individual points at issue. In order to attack each single opposing point you address the following steps:

1. State the opposing point clearly and fairly.
2. Point out any faulty data or claims in the opposing point.
3. State your answer to the point, or counterclaim.
4. Support your counterclaim with data.
5. Tie the counterclaim back into the point at issue.

Content for a speech of refutation should include any of the rational, motivational, or personal identifications discussed in Chapter 8. However, since you are dealing with the possibility of being counterattacked by an opposing speaker, particular care should be taken to see that the *basic rationality* of your speech will make sense to your listeners.

Finally, it is necessary to rank the importance of your arguments carefully. No doubt there will be numerous small and large points you could attack, but with a limited amount of time you should focus on those ideas that will be the most important to the particular audience transaction in which you are participating.

SUMMARY

In this chapter we have discussed specialized informative and persuasive transactions that occur with sufficient frequency to merit special attention.

Entertaining transactions have enjoyment as their primary purpose. Topics as well as content can be novel or humorous. Humor can be developed by exaggeration, incongruity, pun, irony or sarcasm, and burlesque. Any of these can be developed with the use of novel or humorous examples, anecdotes, or comparisons.

Ideas in a speech to entertain should be relatively simple. Delivery should be good-natured and light-hearted.

Occasions of tribute include commemorations and dedications as well as eulogies and commendations. The former pay tribute to events and places, while the latter tribute people. Speeches of tribute focus on the significant contributions made by the people or events. The content emphasizes the shared beliefs, behaviors, and especially values of the group or culture addressed.

Speeches of courtesy include introductions and nominations, presentations, and speeches of welcome and farewell. Introductions, nominations, and presentations attempt to present a person in the best, most relevant light to the audience. They focus on major accomplishments and personal attributes. They should be brief and to the point.

Speeches of welcome are designed to help listeners feel comfortable and positive in new surroundings. Speeches of farewell offer a unique opportunity for an experienced, objective look at the future.

Combative speeches include justification and refutation. They are directed at undecided groups or objective judges. Justification focuses on changing the hierarchy of norms and values. Refutation involves either attacking opponents' arguments or reinforcing your own.

Gettysburg Address

Abraham Lincoln

Four score and seven years ago our fathers brought forth on this continent, a new nation, conceived in Liberty, and dedicated to the proposition that all men are created equal.

Now we are engaged in a great civil war, testing whether that nation or any nation so conceived and so dedicated, can long endure. We are met on a great battle-field of that war. We have come to dedicate a portion of that field, as a final resting place for those who here gave their lives that that nation might live. It is altogether fitting and proper that we should do this.

But, in a larger sense, we can not dedicate—we can not consecrate—we can not hallow—this ground. The brave men, living and dead, who struggled here, have consecrated it, far above our poor power to add or detract. The world will little note, nor long remember what we say here, but it can never forget what they did here. It is for us the living, rather, to be dedicated here to the unfinished work which they who fought here have thus far so nobly advanced. It is rather for us to be here dedicated to the great task remaining before us—that from these honored dead we take increased devotion to that cause for which they gave the first full measure of devotion—that we here highly resolve that these dead shall not have died in vain—and that government of the people, by the people, for the people, shall not perish from the earth.

From John G. Nicolay and John Hay, eds., *Complete Works of Abraham Lincoln*, vol. 9 (New York: Appleton-Century-Crofts, 1905), pp. 209–210.

ENDNOTES

1. This approach to special occasions is adapted from Charles Mudd and Malcom Sillars, *Speech: Content and Communication*, 4th ed. (New York: Harper & Row, 1979), pp. 343–364.
2. Glenn R. Capp, *Famous Speeches in American History* (New York: Bobbs-Merrill, 1963).
3. David J. Brewer, *The World's Best Orations* vol. VII (Chicago: Ferd. P. Kaiser Publishing, 1923), pp. 128–129.
4. Delivered from the White House, Washington, D.C., August 8, 1974. Reprinted by permission of *Vital Speeches of the Day*, August 15, 1974, pp. 643–644.

Index

A

Accreditation, 76–77
Activity, bodily, 126–130
Aids, multisensory, 57–62
   coordination of, 62
   principles of, 60–61
   types, 58–60
Allusion, 107
Analogy, figurative, 55
Analysis, transactional:
   of central idea, 35–36
   continuing, 23
   culmination of, 35–36
   of specific purpose, 35
Anecdotes, 56
Anger, appeals to, 178
Animosity, appeals to, 178
Antithesis, 108
Anxiety, 186
Appeals, motivational, 176
Appearance, 126–127
Approach, organizational, 70–71
   deductive, 70–71
   general, 70–71
   inductive, 70
Appropriateness, of language, 104, 132–133
Articulation and pronunciation, 130
Attention, 76, 122
Attitudes and beliefs, 48
Audience, analysis of, 16–17
   demographic variables, 18
      age, 18
      education, 19
      geographic location, 20
      life style, 10
      occupation, 19
      marital status, 20
      religion, 19
      sex, 19
   fundamental variables, 18
   group characteristics of audiences:
      analysis of, 21–22
      homogeneity, 21–22
      involvement, 22
      position, 22
      self-selection, 21
Audience, 9
Audience orientation, 7
Audio-visual aids, 57–58

B

Behavior, overt, 48
Behavior, relationship of motivation to, 176
Beliefs and attitudes, 48
Bodily activity, 126–130
Bodily movement, 127
Bryan, William Jennings, "Cross of Gold":
    scene, 121–122
    text, 138–144

C

Causation testing, 171
Chalkboard, 56
Change:
    adaptability to, 3
    building resistance to, 186
Characteristics of delivery, traditional, 124–135
Claims testing, 171
Clarity, of language, 47, 102
Commemorations and dedications, 207
Commendations and eulogies, 208–209
Commitment, 187
Communication, 6–7
Comparisons, 55
    tests of, 171
Competence, professional, 4
Concepts, abstract, 148
Conclusions, transactional functions, 78–80
Consistency, cognitive, 187
Content, 204–206
Continuing analysis, 23
Contrast, 104
Coordination, of multisensory aids, 62
Correctness, of language, 103
Credibility, 123–124
Criteria, in questions of value, 52
Cumulation, 102

D

Data-claim relationship, 48–50
Data from authority, testing of, 170
Dedications and commemorations, 207
Delivery, 206–207
    modes, transactional, 134–135
    preparation for, 134–137
    transactional functions of, 122–129
Demonstration, 60 (*see also* Aids, multisensory)
Description, vivid, 182
Dewey, John, 50
Diversity, of language, 101–102
Diversions and substitutions, 172–173
Dyad, 7

E

Emotions, 177
Emphasis:
    in delivery, 131
    in organization, 73
Environmental sensitivity, 3
Envy, appeals to, 178
Ethos:
    dimensions of, 184
    extrinsic, 185
    intrinsic, 185
    transactional nature, 183
Examples, hypothetical, 53
    and statistics testing, 169
Explanation, 57
Expression, facial, 128–129
Extempore speaking, 135
Eulogies and commendations, 208–209
Eye contact, 129

F

Facial expression, 128–129
Fact, questions of, 51
Farewells, 212
Fear, appeals to, 178
Feedback, 7

G

General education, 2–4
Generalizations testing, 171

INDEX

Gestures, 127–128
Gibb, John Douglas, 56
Grady, Henry W., "The New South":
    scene, 95–96
    text, 111–118
Graphics, 59 (*see also* Aids, multisensory)

H

History, in informative transactions, 149
Hostility, 186
Humor, 203–204 (*see also* Transactions, entertaining)
    transactional nature of, 206

I

Iceberg Principle, 74
Ideas, 203
    audiovisual aids to the development of, 57–58
    developing, 49–51
    information-oriented, 49
    problem-oriented, 49–50
Identification, 124
Informative transactions:
    analyzing, 147–149
    body, 154
    categories, 150–151
    common misconceptions about, 150
    comparisons, 152
    conclusions, 154–155
    content, 151–153
    distinguishing characteristics, 149
    examples, 151
    functions, 150
    introductions, 153
    language in, 155
    organizing, 153–155
    perspectives, 150
    reiterations, 152
Imagery, 107
Immediacy, of language, 101
Impressiveness, of language, 106–107
Impromptu speaking, 134
Inoculation, 187

Intelligibility, 60–61, 122–123
Intensity, of language, 100, 132
Interaction, between speaker and listener, 7
Intercultural awareness, 3
Interestingness, of language, 104
Interpreting supporting material, 57
Introductions, transactional functions, 75–78
Introductions and nominations, 210–211

J

Johnson, Sonia, 21
Jordan, Barbara, Democratic Keynote Address:
    scene, 1–2
    text, 11–14
Judgment, standards of, 52
Justification, speeches of, 213–214

K

King, Martin Luther, Jr., "I Have a Dream":
    scene, 45–46
    text, 63–66

L

Language:
    emotional, 173
    transactional nature of, 96–98
Language variables, transactional, 98–102
Lasso Principle, 74–75
Leadership, 4–5
Liberal education, 2–4
Lincoln, Abraham:
    First Inaugural Address:
        scene, 15–16
        text, 37–43
    Gettysburg Address:
        scene, 201–202
        text, 218
Linking, 186
Littlejohn, Stephen, 14
Love and belongingness, 177

M

Manuscript, written, 135
Material, supporting, generation of, 53–57
Matrixing Principle, 75
Meaning:
  connotative, 98
  denotative, 98
Medium, of communication, 98
Memorability, of language, 47–48
Messages, 7
  one-sided, 188
Metaphor, 55
Models, as aids, 60
Motivation, 76
  nature of, 174–175
  sharing, 174–176
Motivational appeals, 176
Motivational methods, 181
Movement, bodily, 127
Multisensory aids, 57–62
  principles of, 60–61
  types, 58–60

N

Needs, appeals to, 176
Nominations and introductions, 210–211
Novelty, of language, 204

O

Openmindedness, 3
Oral style, development of, 109–110
Organization, 71–85
  general principles, 71–76
  techniques, 80–85
Orientation, as purpose of introduction, 77–78
Outline, 80
Outlining, 80–84
  mechanics, 81–82
  principles, 82–85
  symbols, 81

P

Parables, 56
Parallelism, 109
Personal integration, 4
Personal success, 179
Perspective, 8–10
  interactional, 9
  transactional, 9–10
  transmissional, 8
Persuasion:
  defined, 164
  Toulmin model, 166
  traditional model, 165–166
Persuasive transactions:
  organizing, 188
  testing data in, 168
Peterson, Chase, Post-Operation News Conferences:
  scene, 145–146
  text, 157–162
Pictures, 59 (*see also* Aids, multisensory)
Pitch, of voice, 125
Policy, propositions of, 51
Preparation, techniques of, 136–137
Presentations, 211
Problem solving, 3
Processes, as topic, 148
Pronunciation, 130
Psychological appeals, 173
Psychological climate, 28–29
  current events, 29
  images, 29
  traditions, 28
Public, defined, 7
Public speaking, defined, 6–10
Public speaking, study of:
  critical evaluation, 6
  how, 5–6
  practice, 5
  principles, 5
  why, 2–4
Purpose, revealing, 189
Purpose, transactional formulation of, 33–36

Q

Quotes, 107–108

INDEX

R

Rate, of speaking, 125
Rationality, 175
    sharing, 165
    as a transaction, 174
Reagan, Ronald, "Stay the Course":
    scene, 163–164
    text, 190–199
Recordings, 60 (see also Aids, multisensory)
Refutation, 216
Reiteration, 56–57
Relevance, of aids, 62
Remotivation, 78–79
Reorientation, 78
Repetition, 56
Resistance to change, 186
Response, to message, 7
Restatement, 56

S

Scheidel, Thomas, 7
Self-actualization, 177
Self-analysis, 24
    desire to communicate, 24
    speaker apprehension, 24–26
Self-esteem, 177
Self-interest, appeals to, 178
Sentences:
    length, 108
    structure, 108–109
Setting, physical, 26–28
    arrangement, 27
    decor, 28
    equipment, 27
    location, 26
Simile, 55
Simplicity, of language, 61–62
Sincerity, 132
Social situation, analysis of, 26–29
Space relations, in informative transactions, 149
Specific data, 182
Specificity, 99
Specimen, as aid, 60

Stage fright, 24
State apprehension, 24
Statistics, 54
Stereotypes, 96
Stories, 55–56
Style, characteristics of, 102–110
Supporting materials:
    forms, 53
    selection, 74–75
    use, 74–75

T

Termination, 79–80
Testimony, 55
Testing claims, 171
    from authority, 170
    comparisons, 171
    examples, 169
    generalizations, 171
    in persuasive transactions, 168
    statistics, 169
Thinking, critical, 3
Topic:
    analysis of, 29–33
    choosing of, 30
    focusing of, 30–31
    researching of, 31–33
        government and private agencies, 32
        interviews, 33
        library, 32
Topic-specific analysis, 22–23
Topics, 202
Toulmin, Stephen, 48
Trait apprehension, 24
Transactional characteristics, of delivery, 131–134
Transactional situation, analysis of, 16
Transactions of courtesy, 210–211
Transactions, combative, 212–213
Transactions, entertaining, 202
Transactions, tributary, 207
Trust:
    developing, 194
    sharing, 182

INDEX

U

Understanding, shared, 46–47
Unity, of ideas, 72

V

Values, 179
   conflicting, 181
Value system, individual, 181
Variability, of motives, 175
Variety, in delivery, 131
Visual aids, 58–60

Voice, 125–126
   pitch, 125
   quality, 126
   rate, 125
   volume, 125–126

W

Ward, Barbara, "Only One Earth":
   scene, 69–70
   text, 88–93
Welcomes, 212
Words, 102–106
   emotionally loaded, 182